A Fork and Spoon Field Guide™

Feeding the Kids

The Flexible, No-Battles, Healthy Eating System for the Whole Family

Pamela Gould and **Eleanor P. Taylor,** RN, CDE

With **Dr. Katherine Cason,** RD

MANCALA PRESS

Feeding the Kids:
The Flexible, No-Battles Healthy Eating System for the Whole Family
Book One of A Fork and Spoon Field Guide Series

Published by
Mancala Publishing, LLC
PO Box 247
Clemson, South Carolina 29633
www.feedingthekids.com

All rights reserved. No part of this book may be reproduced or transmitted in any form or by any means, electronic or mechanical, including photocopying and recording, or by any information storage and retrieval system, without written permission from the authors.

Publisher's Cataloging-in-Publication
(Provided by Quality Books, Inc.)
Gould, Pamela.
     Feeding the kids : the flexible, no-battles, healthy eating system for the whole family / Pamela Gould, Eleanor P. Taylor ; with Katherine Cason.
        p. cm. -- (A fork and spoon field guide ; bk. 1)
     Includes index.
     ISBN-13: 978-0-9789385-4-3
     ISBN-10: 0-9789385-4-2

        1. Children--Nutrition. 2. Nutrition. 3. Cookery.
     I. Taylor, Eleanor P. (Eleanor Perry) II. Cason,
     Katherine L. III. Title. IV. Series.

RJ206.G68 2007   649'.3
                                QBI07-600009

AUTHORS Pamela Gould, Eleanor P. Taylor, RN, CDE
CONSULTING DIETITIAN & FOREWORD: Dr. Katherine Cason, RD
EDITOR: Mary Anne Maier
COPY EDITOR: Dianne Nelson
COVER & INTERIOR DESIGN: F + P Graphic Design, Inc., Fort Collins, CO
COVER PHOTOGRAPHY: Samual Trojanovich

ISBN 978-0-9789385-4-3

To Sue Patchen Taylor,
who inspired me with her lifelong dedication
to eating well. The beloved mother, grandmother,
or great-grandmother to everyone in our family,
she taught us to love whole grains, vegetables, fruits and
healthy oils before research verified the value of these foods.

— E P T

To my kids, who are my inspiration and my joy.
As you grow, I hope you always eat with pleasure
and excitement, continue making messes in the kitchen . . .
and never stop laughing with loved ones
around the table each day.

— P T G

Thanks...

We have discovered that books don't magically appear. They are written with the help of friends, relatives and colleagues who offer steady support every step of the way. It is with gratitude and humility that we say "thank you" to the many people who have generously shared their time, patience, wisdom and expertise with us over the past two years.

What would we have achieved without our loving families? Our husbands, Carl Gould and Ted Taylor, not only tolerated our endless hours on the phone and non-stop enthusiastic talking about every detail of this book, but also accepted the job of proofreading the manuscript. Stephen Taylor served as a creative consultant throughout the entire process and came up with many of the ideas that make this book unique. Scott and Susan Taylor gave generously of their insightful feedback.

Friends stepped up to help in incredible ways. Thanks to Jenny Oldfield not only for testing recipes, but also for providing insights into parenting with love and respect and for sharing her innovative approach to enjoying a selective eater. Thanks to Lauren Alley for ongoing support and recipe testing. And thanks to Angie Lorraine for testing every recipe that didn't involve seafood, for reading and re-reading the text, for offering perspective as a nurse and mother... and for always being willing to listen, sympathize and give honest opinions. Tricia Lightweiss, owner of The Booksmith, shared her vast wisdom and experience about books and the world of publishing. Sylvia Titus joyfully edited our first writings and offered sage advice that put us on the right track. Thanks also to: Vasilka Markoff, Kristie Brice-Schwartz, the Scott family, Matt and Yoko Burde, Greg Arguello, Holley Ulbrich and all the other friends who offered support, ideas and help along the way.

Of course, this book couldn't have been created without the kids! First, thanks to all our past students and clients who inspired this book in the first place. Next, we have to acknowledge our young, enthusiastic taste-testers who gave us delightfully honest reactions to many different recipes: Margaret Jane, Tess, Sam, Hope, Max, Trinity, Meredith, Julia, Alex, Luna, Zoë, Helen, Phillip, Aidan, Emma and all 60 of my recipe tasters in Miss Sheela and Miss Samantha's classes at Free Horizon Montessori. Also, thank you to all the good-looking, incredibly cooperative models on our cover. You know who you are!

Many colleagues shared their time and professional insights. Katherine Cason, our consulting registered dietitian, inspired us with her personal dedication to nutrition as well as her vast experience in making nutrition relevant to parents. She spent many hours editing our book for technical content and accuracy. Liz Halpin shared her incredible storehouse of information on recipe construction. Linda Crew McNamara offered continuous encouragement and help with the manuscript. Elizabeth Yarnell, author of *Glorious One-Pot Meals,* generously shared her insights, advice and experience in publishing and marketing books. The other members of CIPA provided information about the world of publishing and ongoing support.

Finally, we have not only immense appreciation, but also admiration, for the professionals who helped us put this book together. Sam Trojanovich was willing to go on location, to a grocery store at night no less, to take the awesome photograph on the cover. We wish to especially thank our editor, Mary Anne Maier, who blessed us with kindness, enthusiasm, encouragement, brilliant suggestions and some seriously picky editing. Another huge thank-you to Rebecca Finkel, our interior and cover designer, who patiently listened and advised, created an innovative design out of our vague notions, was willing to give our crazy cover idea a shot and, finally, turned our manuscript into a real book. Thanks also to Dianne Nelson for her sharp-eyed line-editing of the manuscript.

Table of Contents

Foreword

By Dr. Katherine Cason, Registered Dietitian

Throughout my career as a professor, educator and researcher in food, nutrition and eating behaviors, it has been my privilege to work directly with parents. One thing is clear—parents (myself included) care passionately about the health of their children. We do everything we can to protect them.

Among the top health and safety concerns for parents is what to feed their kids. Parents are well aware that a healthy diet is extremely important, and they want to make certain that their children eat "correctly" according to the latest recommendations. Nevertheless, most parents find their biggest challenge is to understand current dietary guidelines in a way that they can actually use in day-to-day life.

To put it simply, there is confusion about what to eat. Parents are confronted daily with often-conflicting information about nutrition provided through television, radio, magazines, the Internet and popular diet books. This causes great concern for parents who want to do the right thing and make sure that the newest nutrition ideas are actually okay for their growing kids.

Food shopping and eating environments are also problematic for parents. Stores and restaurants present parents with endless decisions about what to buy. Modern grocery stores offer staggering numbers of food choices with new products being introduced weekly—many catering to our desire for "healthy," "natural" or "vitamin-packed" choices for our children.

Much of our food supply today is designed with marketing and selling as a priority—not health promotion. Many of the most popular foods for children are high in calories from sugars and unhealthy fats, yet are very low in fiber and nutrients. As a result, parents and others who feed children often unwittingly buy foods that are deficient in the nutrition needed by growing children.

Just as difficult, many parents have limited time to focus on food preparation and family meals. Many of us eat in a grab-and-go style that creates lingering feelings that maybe the family should be eating better. Yet, eating out or buying store-prepared foods often feel like the only options—and sometimes, they are!

So, despite this amazing food abundance and our best parenting efforts, I know only too well that many children are eating a poor diet. A study by the USDA Economic Research Service showed that only 12 percent of American children ages two to four, regardless of family income, had "good diets"—the rest were "poor" or "in need of improvement." The data were similar for older children except that more of these children had "poor diets," probably because they started choosing more of their own food away from home.

Our current diet has contributed to the growing prevalence of overweight and obesity among both children and adults. The number of kids who are overweight in America has doubled since the 1970s for both preschoolers (ages two to five) and teens (ages 12 to 19). At the same time, it has tripled for school-aged children (ages six to 11). Both boys and girls are equally at risk. Further, what used to be diseases of "old age" are now popping up in young children. Children are becoming diabetic at an alarming rate, and more are showing signs of high blood pressure and high cholesterol. Research shows that these consequences can persist right into adulthood as chronic diseases such as obesity, type 2 diabetes, high blood pressure, heart disease, osteoporosis, liver and gall bladder diseases, stroke and heart attack. Other costs of a poor diet are not as obvious or dramatic but are nonetheless serious, such as tooth decay.

Governmental agencies and schools know the seriousness of our children's current poor dietary practices and have rallied around improving nutrition for children and even their adult employees. They know that just telling people what to do is a small part of making actual healthy choices. Vending machines and cafeteria foods are now being held to new standards, serving more nutrient-dense foods such as fruits and vegetables. Soda is being replaced with water and nonfat milk. White bread is being replaced with whole wheat.

Still, the family plays the key role. The family can exert a strong influence on children's diet and food-related behaviors. Home is where children learn about food and eat the majority of their meals. For kids to adopt a healthier lifestyle as a way of life, they need to see adults in a variety of settings reinforce the same concepts. They need to experience eating healthier foods and learn to enjoy them. It is at home where this foundation is laid and where parents serve as important role models.

We have now learned the significance of eating meals together as a family. Research shows that the family meal has a significant impact upon the nutritional quality of children's diets. A higher frequency of family meals is associated with a greater intake of fruits, vegetables and milk and a lower intake of fried foods and soft drinks. Family meals also can impact the development of language and literacy skills and can generate a decrease in risk-taking behaviors.

A healthy diet in childhood establishes lifelong protective habits. Knowing how to eat well helps kids have more energy, resist illnesses such as the common cold, reduce risk for chronic disease and maintain a healthy weight. Good nutrition has even been linked to brain and eye wellness. In addition, teaching children skills to maintain healthy dietary habits and active lifestyles helps prevent obesity not only in youth, but also in adult life.

While research about healthy eating continues to evolve and we can expect legitimate changes in dietary guidelines in this century, the basic advice about what to eat has not changed much in the past two decades. Fortunately, kids and adults need the same foods for a healthy diet.

I believe what parents need to help them through the confusing maze of food and nutrition messages are three things: 1) practical daily routines for incorporating current dietary guidelines into a busy life, 2) simple methods for identifying the healthiest versions of recommended foods and 3) realistic and achievable ideas for helping their family both eat and enjoy a healthier diet.

In my opinion, Pamela and Ellie have written a book that I wholeheartedly can say does these three things exceptionally well. They have succeeded in writing about a complicated subject with humor and practicality. Written as an adventure through the "wild, wonderful (and sometimes frightening) world of food," the field guide style provides a friendly backdrop for a usually intimidating subject.

In fact, Part 1 of this book offers sage advice about exploring the world of great nutrition in a relaxed way, allowing kids to naturally refuse certain foods or even get involved in picking out their favorites in a healthier version at the store. The book features "Food Adventures," too—stories about families who are finding their way through the "jungle" to bring healthy food routines to life.

I am thrilled that instead of removing family favorites, this book offers a weekly schedule for adding in healthy foods. In my opinion, this approach can work for many people who, like me, resist the idea that eating a healthy diet requires sacrifice or that eating well means "no fun" because of the required daily doses of nasty-tasting "health foods." The authors help parents set up a daily routine that is tailored to their unique schedule and family preferences. And the book also explores background information on serious issues in segments called "A Closer Look."

If this book ends up in your kitchen, your family will reap the benefits for years to come. After all, knowing about nutrition will not by itself result in better health—but taking action to eat healthy foods can have a major impact on the current and future well-being of everyone in the family. Every aspect of this book is about just that—"doing" healthy food in a fast-paced world filled with confusing choices.

Enjoy the journey—but more importantly, I hope you will find enormous pleasure in watching your kids grow up loving healthy foods and passing on that value to your grandchildren. However, don't forget yourself: Eating well can contribute greatly toward your own healthy aging. If there was ever a family win-win, this book is it!

How to Use This Book

Feeding a family can seem incredibly complicated. To start with, the typical supermarket carries more than 30,000 items. Add to that the restaurants, fast-food places and quick-stops that line the streets. Plus, our children are the targets of cool advertising campaigns for foods we wish they'd never heard of. Meanwhile, most parents have no extra time for menu planning and fancy cooking. And even when you get healthy food on the table, you still have to convince the kids to eat it. It's not simple.

Enter this *Fork and Spoon Field Guide*. People often turn to field guides to help them simplify or clarify a subject of interest such as birds, hiking in the Rockies, flowering trees or amphibians. Like other field guides, *Feeding the Kids* organizes a lot of information into a simple, easy-to-use format. And like other field guides, it is specific in detail and meant to be used for both study and quick reference. Unlike other field guides, this one won't help you in the wilds of nature—but it **will** help you in the wilds of the grocery store!

You Decide

There are two ways to use *Feeding the Kids*. One way is as a six-week, step-by-step eating "makeover" program. Your other option is to use this book as a quick reference guide for solving common challenges in feeding a family. It's up to you.

Following the Six-Week Journey to "Smarter" Eating

This program explores one category of healthy food each week. You will gradually add these healthy foods to your regular meals and snacks, but without taking away favorites. Then, at the end of the six weeks, you will have created a simple pattern for eating well most of the time. To follow this program:

- First, read through **Part 1** for strategies that will make change a whole lot easier and success more likely.

- Then, move on to **Part 2.** This part contains the step-by-step instructions for making healthy changes. During this process, consult **Part 4** for easy recipes that work with the program.

- After completing the six weeks, decide whether you want to read **Part 3** now, or just glance through. You may want to come back to this part later if you hit a snag in maintaining your new eating habits.

Chart Your Own Path Using This Guide as a Reference

If you just want information on specific topics, use *Feeding the Kids* as a reference. Simply look up what you need to know.

- In **Part 1,** you'll find strategies for deciding which foods to eat, helping kids eat the right amount for their bodies and getting them to taste new foods without fights.

- Consult **Part 2** for how-to tips on feeding your kids specific foods. There are chapters on fruits, vegetables, dairy, grains and protein foods. Additionally, the last section in Part 2 has information on cutting back on "Empty" junk foods.

- Look through **Part 3** for strategies and suggestions for handling common problems and pitfalls. This section deals with everything from Halloween to birthday parties to boredom with healthy foods.

- Find recipe ideas for healthy kid-friendly food in **Part 4.**

Other Important Resources

A Closer Look at Important Topics
If you want more information on the "whys" behind the recommendations, look for these Closer Look boxes with a binocular icon. Each one contains more in-depth information such as research and scientific explanations covering a variety of food topics.

Stories about Kids, Parents and Their Eating Adventures
Throughout this book, you will find true stories that offer valuable ideas for changes you can make for your own family. Even more importantly, they will help you see that you are definitely not alone in your food dilemmas. (Of course, names and details have been changed to protect privacy.)

A Field Guide for the Whole Family

Unlike some field guides that limit information to a specific state, species or outdoor adventure, this *Fork and Spoon Field Guide* provides information that can be used to feed every healthy member of your family over age two (see caution below). Preschoolers, teens and adults can sit down to the same food prepared the same way.

All the advice in this book can be adapted for use with children, teens and adults. However, kids over 12 may need more flexibility and independence.

Caution: This Book Is Not Recommended for Babies, Children Under Age Two or Any Person with Special Health Problems or Dietary Needs
The information in this book is for healthy families with children age two or older. Babies and children under age two have special dietary needs related to rapid growth and development. You should consult your pediatrician if you have a child under age two.

In addition, the nutrition recommendations in this book may need to be adapted for some people who need special diets, such as family members with diabetes, obesity or risk factors for illness. If your family has health problems or other special needs, be sure to talk with your doctor or a registered dietitian for help.

For example, teens often eat away from home and make their own eating decisions. On the other hand, teens are also old enough to understand the benefits of eating healthier food. So, as with every other aspect of family life from allowances to using the family car, I recommend you adapt and modify the guidance offered in this book to meet the unique personalities, ages and needs of your maturing children.

However you use it, I truly hope *Feeding the Kids* makes feeding your family easier . . . and that it helps your whole family eat well—while *enjoying* eating!

The Wild, Wonderful (and Sometimes Frightening) World of Food

Remember when your child was a baby, keeping you up all night drinking milk and spitting up in the midst of each meal? Did anyone take you aside then and tell you that feeding your offspring was only going to get *harder*?

The moment kids learn to talk, they seem to begin telling you that the food you serve them is "yucky," "gross" or just plain "uuuugh." At the same time, you're trying to make family food choices based on changing food pyramids, media reports that offer contradictory messages, supposedly healthy diet trends such as low-carb and low-fat eating and crazy claims on the food packages themselves. Add to that the occasional attempt to serve the "right" portion size, an opinionated spouse and a busy schedule, and feeding the family can feel more complicated than any trek through the jungle or foray into the desert. And you have to do it three times a day!

It's tempting to retreat and just eat whatever you can grab quickly and serve without listening to too many complaints. Often that can mean greasy fast food or less-than-healthy pre-packaged foods. These options are quick, get the family fed and usually raise few objections, at least from the kids. But parents are then stuck having to swallow their own food between stabs of parental guilt.

Even worse than guilt is the fear fueled by almost daily news reports about the increase in chronic diseases caused in part by eating too much of the wrong foods and too little of the right ones. Sad to say, most of those reports are true. Researchers have found repeatedly that obesity, cancer, heart disease, type 2 diabetes, stroke, osteoporosis and many other serious health problems can often be linked to daily food choices. Simply put, eating a really bad diet can be dangerous.

The time has come to get rid of all this confusion, guilt and fear and chart a sensible path through the wilds of the food world. That is what this field guide is all about: helping your family *enjoy* eating a (mostly) healthy diet, while making the buying and preparing of food easier and more fun for you.

CHAPTER 1

The Smart Food Identification System

Picture stepping into your local grocery store: You are immediately surrounded by literally thousands of things to eat. Most of the food has dramatic packaging that seems to scream at you from the shelves. A voice suggests various food products amid songs from somewhere in your past. A nice lady leans toward you offering a bit of deep-fried sausage speared on a toothpick. Kids (possibly your own) run up and down the cereal aisle trying to out-shout each other in hopes of getting their parents to buy Sugar-Frosted Double-Choco-Monsters or Frooty-Tooty Sugar Looties … Let's face it—it's a jungle out there!

As a shopper, you have to know how to hunt down and capture the best foods for your family. This is where identification comes into play. The easiest way to pick your way through the wilds of modern grocery shopping is to categorize foods. I've chosen to group all foods into three very simple categories: very healthy foods, junk foods that contain almost no nutrition at all and foods that are somewhere in between those two extremes. I refer to these categories as Smart, Empty and In-Between.

Smart Foods

Of course, "Smart" foods are the best, healthiest choices. They contain healthy fats, carbohydrates or proteins, or a combination of these. They also have lots of vitamins, minerals and fiber. In other words, Smart foods are packed with good nutrition. Some examples of Smart foods are carrots, apples, grapes, bananas, skim milk, whole-wheat bread, potatoes, oatmeal, fish, extra-lean beef, nuts and beans.

On the other hand, Smart foods *don't* contain large amounts of added sugar, refined flour (also called white or wheat flour) or unhealthy types of fats.

Obviously, not all Smart foods are the same. Some contain more of one nutrient than another. Some have lots of protein, while others have none. They have different amounts of fiber. Luckily, you really don't have to carefully track the exact nutrients in everything you eat. Instead, you just have to be sure to get in a variety of healthy foods each week. That's good news because it makes feeding your family much simpler.

More good news is that most people—even kids—can tell when they are full from eating these Smart foods. This natural ability to listen to inner hunger cues is called "self-regulation." When their children are eating Smart foods, parents do not have to measure out correct portion sizes. Nor do parents need to make kids eat "a few more bites." Instead, you simply have to coach your children to stop when they are full—while you role model noticing your own body's cues.

Serving Smart foods solves many problems for parents who worry that their child eats too much or too little. First, with Smart foods, kids will have a harder time overeating because Smart foods tend to fill people up before they get too many calories. Also, when kids are allowed to self-regulate and decide for themselves how much to eat, they learn to eat for enjoyment and satisfaction. Parents, meanwhile, can relax knowing that the food their child is eating is healthy.

Empty Foods

"Empties" are the opposite of Smart foods. They are junk foods that contain lots of calories—but almost nothing else your body needs.

Empties contain mostly sugar or other sweeteners, or unhealthy or excess fat. They are designed to taste good but contain almost no nutrition that helps your body stay healthy. As all parents know, Empties are absolutely everywhere. A few examples of Empties are soda, candy bars, potato chips, doughnuts and sausage.

Empty foods have become a serious problem for both adults and kids. Why? Because each person only needs a certain number of calories each day, and eating too many Empties usually results in one of these problems:

- You get too full to eat healthy foods.
- You gain weight from eating too many calories.
- Or both! You are too full to eat healthy food *and* you gain weight.

On the other hand, nobody should have to give up *all* Empties! They taste great and are lots of fun. If you want to maintain a mostly healthy diet, you can still enjoy Empties to enhance Smart foods or for occasional treats.

> **A Closer Look at How Empties Are Linked to Overweight**
> Researchers have long known that energy "imbalance" is the reason people gain weight. Individuals need a certain number of calories each day to meet the energy needs of their body. Energy needs vary depending on many things, including body size and level of physical activity. When people consume more calories than they need, the extra calories end up stored as body fat for later use—and this shows up on the scale as weight gain.
>
> Major reasons that both children and adults become overweight are lack of physical activity and drinking or eating too many high-calorie Empty foods such as convenience foods and sodas. Empties are most often served in large portions, are loaded with calories and can be eaten quickly, often without much chewing. The easiest way to get the right number of calories each day is to increase Smart foods and decrease Empties. Smart foods usually take longer to eat, are more filling and provide nutrients needed for optimal wellness.

In-Betweens: Combining Smart with Empty

"In-Betweens" are combinations of Smart foods and Empties. In-Betweens occur naturally (such as sirloin steaks that contain some saturated fat), in the kitchen (such as sugar on oatmeal) or in the factory (such as sugar in nonfat yogurt).

In-Betweens are always better choices than Empties, and they can often be used to painlessly replace Empties your family enjoys now. For the most part, it's a good idea to limit In-Betweens to just one for most meals and snacks.

Starting to think in terms of which foods are which—Smart, Empty or In-Between—is a great way for you and your family to begin your journey toward enjoying mostly healthy eating. Just remember, and be sure your kids know, that there's no such thing as a bad food. There are just some foods that should be eaten a lot more often than others.

CHAPTER 2

Head for Health, Not Weight Loss

Weight is such a big issue in our society!

I'm sure you have seen the nonstop media coverage of the childhood obesity epidemic and all the problems that go along with it, such as the increase in childhood diabetes. And being overweight can be really hard emotionally, especially for a child. Other kids—and thoughtless adults— can be quite cruel. Many overweight kids are pretty hard on themselves, too.

Putting your child on a diet may seem like the obvious solution. Don't do it! Restricted-calorie diets are not healthy for most growing children. Just as important, imposing a diet is hard on your relationship with your child as well as on the child's relationship with food. And dieting implies that there is some-thing wrong with the child's body, which can negatively affect her body image.

So instead of trying to help your child lose weight, teach your family to love their bodies by taking good care of them. That means eating healthier food. And in the long run, eating well is the best way to maintain a healthy weight and to prevent future weight gain for both adults and kids.

Also, dieting is about not getting the food you want. That's no fun! Your kids should be allowed to love food—and learn to love healthy food. By feeding them healthy food, you can feel good about letting your children eat until they feel full. You don't have to fight with them over portion sizes; they will learn to self-regulate the amount of food that is right for them. Learning these two things—to love healthy food and self-regulate portions—will help your kids be among those "lucky" people who have a healthy weight without even trying.

A Closer Look at Why Weight-Loss Programs Are Not for Kids

Weight loss is usually not recommended for growing kids. Although following the advice in this book can help your family maintain healthy body weights and possibly prevent obesity, it is not intended to be a weight-loss program.

Popular weight-loss programs and diet books can cause children to miss out on vital nutrients needed for growth by limiting the amounts they eat. Most diets are based on restricting calories, either through careful calorie counting or by restricting food choices. This is often accomplished by the unhealthy practice of eliminating a whole food category such as carbohydrates or fat. But regardless of the system, parents should never place their children on a weight-loss plan without medical help.

In the rare case when a child is put on a "lower-calorie diet," it must be under the direct and ongoing supervision of a qualified healthcare provider such as a physician or nurse practitioner. Or, work with a registered dietitian, often referred to as an "R.D." Registered dietitians are licensed professionals with a degree in nutrition science. You can usually locate one through your local hospital, health department or university.

Often your healthcare team will suggest an approach to a child's excessive weight that focuses on having the child slow down weight gain and gradually grow into an ideal weight by getting taller. This is done by planning a diet rich in healthy foods to be eaten by everyone in the family. It is not fair to single out one family member (adult or child) for a change in diet while everyone else continues eating the "old way." Overweight children will always benefit far more from eating healthy foods along with the rest of the family.

Physical Activity

Being active is wonderful for both physical and mental health. I definitely recommend finding some form of physical activity that you really enjoy. It can go a long way toward helping you maintain a healthy weight. In fact, it's been shown that kids who have fun experiences with physical activity at a young age are more likely to continue being active when they grow up.

However, this field guide does not include recommendations for exercise. Why? Because I believe that most parents, like me, appreciate making changes one at a time. Changing your diet will probably be enough of a challenge without being told to add in daily stretching, jogging and free weights!

Actually, once your diet is improved, you may find that being physically active is easier for the family because everyone feels better. If you decide to add in some extra activity, the most important thing to remember is that most children just naturally like to play and move. They don't need to go to a health club or gym. Your kids would probably be happy to have a water balloon fight, play tag, play catch, go for a swim or walk to the park. Make a list of fun things that involve movement—then use the "need to exercise" as your excuse to have some fun!

In the same way that loving healthy food is the best way to eat right for a lifetime, being active for fun is more likely to become a lasting habit.

CHAPTER 3

Battles, Boundaries and Behaviors:

Moving from "Picky" to Pleasant

Eating should be fun. Ideally, this means kids and parents should actually enjoy eating together—and feel good about what they're eating. Of course, that is easier said than done! Mealtimes can be especially stressful if you have a so-called "picky eater" at the table. However, you can cut down on battles by changing *how* you manage food issues before you tackle changing *what* foods you eat.

Battles

As every parent knows, many battles can be prevented with the right set of easily enforceable rules. Here are my favorites:

The "Just Look at It" Rule

Whenever you give your child food, be polite—just offer it! The word "offer" means that you are going to expose your children to various foods and allow them to decide whether or not they choose to eat them.

"Offer" also means that you go one step further than just asking if your children want something. You should actually put the food on their plate or in their cup, hand it to them or pass them the serving bowl. If you are worried about wasting food, just dish up a tiny amount of the food. The children can always ask for more.

Having a questionable food in front of them lets kids get used to its look and smell. Plus, if the kids get curious after seeing other people enjoying the food, they can easily sample it without drawing attention to themselves. That is why, at my house, the kids must have a little of each food on their plate—I call this the "Just look at it" rule.

The "Notice When Your Own Stomach Is Full" Rule

Realistically, there is no way for you to know exactly how much each child needs to eat on a given day. Sometimes kids will eat what looks like huge quantities of one food. On another day, they might eat very little. That is fine. Just like adults, kids have varying appetites. When given a choice of mostly Smart foods, children are able to feel how much their body needs and more easily eat the right amount.

If you've been regulating or restricting your child's food intake, try allowing self-regulation of healthy foods for at least one month. At first, your child might stuff himself, but you should let him eat what he wants and resist the impulse to interfere. Tell him that you are going to let him feel for himself when his stomach is full. Alternatively, he might seem to eat very little of certain foods. That is also fine. You might remind him that the food is available and even comment on how much you are enjoying it. Then leave him alone to try the food or reject it.

Some parents have trouble allowing children to self-regulate, especially if they're worried about a child weighing too much or too little or are just concerned about healthy eating in general. However, healthy children will

> **A Closer Look at Parents' Concern about Children's Eating Habits**
> It is natural for parents to worry if a child overeats or is a "picky eater." Current research has shown, however, that parents should avoid labeling their child. The best strategy is to make healthy foods available, role model enjoying these healthier foods and have confidence that children can learn to regulate their own food intake. If a parent is worried about a child's overly selective eating behaviors or weight, it is best to speak to a registered dietitian (at a hospital, university or health department) or another qualified healthcare provider who can offer guidance, reassurance and appropriate care if needed.

eat the amount they need when allowed to simply enjoy their food and stop when they feel full.

The "Nobody Has to Eat Anything They Don't Want to Eat" Rule

It's easy to get into the trap of negotiating with a child about eating, but using pressure, coercion or restriction usually ends up just making the situation worse. Children rarely learn to enjoy the food you make them eat because they'll associate it with the unpleasant feeling of being pressured to eat it.

And making children eat for reward, to please you, to escape punishment or to be excused from the table overrides their normal self-regulation impulses to eat the right amount of food for their body.

As a child, Lexi had to eat a certain number of lima beans before she could leave the table. Everyone who knew her then agrees that Lexi was a very stubborn kid. But she had a stubborn mom, too, and ended up eating several hundred lima beans over the course of her childhood. Unfortunately, her well-meaning mom's tactics backfired. To this day, Lexi despises lima beans and never, ever eats them.

As I'm sure we've all experienced, trying to make kids eat—or even just taste—food they don't want is miserable for the kid, for the "enforcer" and for everyone else at the table. Imagine if you went to a friend's house and she made you take a "bunny bite" before you could go home! That experience would probably *not* help you learn to like that food.

Eating healthy food needs to be associated with a pleasant experience. So remember that while *eating* healthy food is important, *loving* healthy food is far more important than any individual serving of broccoli or peas. When kids love healthy food, they'll eat it whether you're around or not.

So instead of focusing attention on what your child is *not* eating, focus on really enjoying what *you* are eating. Continuous exposure to a food has been proven to be the most effective method for expanding kids' tastes.

The "No Bad-Mouthing the Food" Rule

If you have a child at your table who is often critical of the food, consider a "No bad-mouthing the food!" rule. By criticizing a food out loud, the child will usually further convince himself that he dislikes a given food. Few people, even adults, like to admit that something they just decided is proven wrong! Even worse, other children at the table may have trouble even tasting a food, much less enjoying it, once they've been warned by another child that it's "yucky."

And if that is not enough, bad-mouthing the food is a very rude habit! If you are going to the effort of preparing a meal, you deserve to enjoy your meal with polite, considerate diners.

While testing out some recipes at a local school, I served hummus to six suspicious children. The oldest kid in the group announced he happened to know that hummus tasted "really terrible" so he definitely would not try it. Instantly, the eyes of the younger children widened and their jaws clenched. Only half the children finally tasted it, but none of them would admit to liking the hummus. When the next (equally suspicious) group came over, I told them they were doing secret taste tests and asked them not to let anyone know what they thought until everyone had a chance to taste. All but one child tried it, and they all loved it! Nothing ruins a food like hearing it is awful before you even taste it.

Boundaries

Set yourself up for peace at the table by establishing some boundaries around what you will and won't do.

React as Little as Possible to Rejection of Food

Don't make the mistake of being terrified by the idea of your children being hungry or malnourished when they don't want a food. Kids can decide not to eat a particular food or even an entire meal once in a while and survive very well. You've done your part by serving them a healthy, reasonably kid-friendly meal.

If a child says, "No, thank you," respond with a relaxed, "You can choose to eat it or not. It's up to you." That's all. Sometimes (though by no means always!) just ignoring the situation is all it takes to get a kid to taste something, especially if other people at the table obviously enjoy it. Studies show that many kids need to "just look at" a food 10 to 20 times before they'll try it.

On the other hand, sometimes a child just has a natural dislike of a particular food. Most adults have a few foods they won't eat, either. That really is okay! Don't worry about it.

Meanwhile, remember that a diet of mostly Smart foods is very protective. The foods that they're eating are packed with nutrition that will generally compensate for what they're refusing to eat at the moment.

> **A Closer Look at Exposing Your Kids to New Food Experiences**
> Research is clear: It takes 10 or more exposures to a new food before many kids take a sample bite. The recommended strategy is to casually invite the child to try the new food. Using this approach has been shown to increase the likelihood that your child will develop greater food flexibility. If a food is declined, it does not mean that the child will never eat it. It has been shown that if a parent keeps serving a food to the rest of the family, offers it to the child again and emphasizes how good it tastes by eating it, the child is more likely to try it. However, the child may or may not learn to like a new food because of developing taste preferences, and that is okay.

Don't Make Separate Meals for the Kids

If someone doesn't like a particular food, she can choose not to eat it. But, whatever you do, don't cook or serve her something else! Eating a variety of foods is a skill that your child will only learn after lots of practice.

Eating studies show that continued exposure to a food will often entice doubters to sample a food. If you like the rejected food, continue to serve and eat it yourself. Without your saying a word, you may notice that your child eventually takes a taste. You can note kids' expanding "taste bud maturity" when they do start liking it!

When you limit children's meals to ones you know they love, you deprive them of the chance to learn about new foods they might also enjoy.

Limit Munching by Scheduling Meals and Snacks

Make life easier by limiting eating times to three regularly scheduled meals a day, plus snacks. Snacks should be spaced between meals, but each family must decide for themselves how many snacks they need.

For younger kids, consider having three snacks: one at mid-morning, one in the afternoon and possibly a bedtime snack. For older kids, you should definitely plan on a large after-school snack. They will probably want an evening snack as well. Or, for children who have homework after dinner, try delaying dessert to have as a homework break later in the evening.

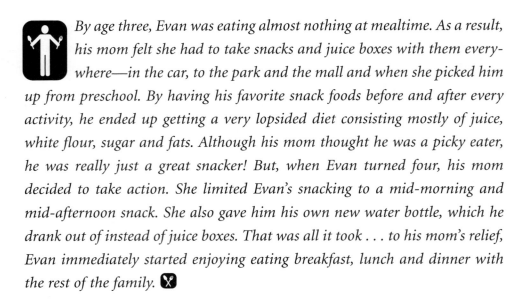

By age three, Evan was eating almost nothing at mealtime. As a result, his mom felt she had to take snacks and juice boxes with them everywhere—in the car, to the park and the mall and when she picked him up from preschool. By having his favorite snack foods before and after every activity, he ended up getting a very lopsided diet consisting mostly of juice, white flour, sugar and fats. Although his mom thought he was a picky eater, he was really just a great snacker! But, when Evan turned four, his mom decided to take action. She limited Evan's snacking to a mid-morning and mid-afternoon snack. She also gave him his own new water bottle, which he drank out of instead of juice boxes. That was all it took . . . to his mom's relief, Evan immediately started enjoying eating breakfast, lunch and dinner with the rest of the family. ✖

Whatever your snack schedule, stick to it! Don't let your kids (or yourself) munch whenever they wish. If you limit munching, everyone approaches meals and snacks feeling hungry. They are much more likely to actually eat and enjoy whatever is being offered. In addition, "munching people" who snack all day are not usually picking healthy options! So by limiting snacking, you may automatically cut back on some Empties. Also, when selective eaters are allowed to snack too much, they lose an important incentive to eat well at mealtimes: hunger.

As you cut back on munching, teach your children that short-term hunger is not dangerous. It's just a sign that they will really enjoy their next meal. You'll be surprised and delighted at the difference limiting snacking makes to your kids' appreciation for your cooking, so give it a try.

Of course, all rules get broken sometimes, and you may end up having your kids snack "off schedule" occasionally. If a meal is late and your kids are starving, or you need an emergency snack to distract them (and thereby keep your own sanity!), offer them raw vegetables or fruit. However, when your meal and snack times are reasonably well spaced throughout the day, you will rarely have kids feeling very hungry at other times.

Behaviors

As parents, we have all been told that actions speak louder than words. Well, here are a few actions that can help your family eat well.

Role Model Loving Healthy Foods

If you really want your kids to enjoy eating well, show them how it is done! Eat healthy foods you honestly like in front of them. For greater impact, you might even beg them for some of the healthy food on their plate.

If you enjoy cooking, baking, gardening, berry picking or tasting new exotic foods, make sure your children witness your enthusiasm. Even if they roll their eyes, they will absorb the idea that healthy food can be fun.

Of course, children can learn to be negative about foods as well from overly "selective" adults. If you or other adults your kids spend time with tend to dislike healthy foods or often reject foods without trying them, see if you can reserve the negative commentary for later when the kids aren't around. On the other hand, if kids ask for an opinion, adults should be honest and role model how to "not love" a food and say, "No, thank you," in a polite way.

A Closer Look at Orienting Kids toward Smart Foods

Research studies show again and again that parents are the primary reason behind attitudes children adopt toward various foods. If parents enjoy Smart foods, their children are more likely to eat them, too. One research study demonstrated that small children get equal enjoyment from "healthy" and "unhealthy" foods—a good reminder to parents that it is not depriving a child to offer a Smart snack (such as fruit) instead of an Empty one (such as cookies). Another study showed that children who ate the most fruits and vegetables had parents who ate the most fruits and vegetables. Research also indicates that putting pressure on kids to eat healthy foods (an "eat as I say, not as I do" approach) backfires and often results in kids rejecting the Smart foods. The conclusion: Kids are more likely to eat a healthy diet when they see parents enjoying Smart foods (an "eat as I eat" approach).

Eat Meals Together When You Can

It's not easy for most of us to do these days, but try carving out the time to let your family eat dinner together most nights. During family meals, the children can start associating healthy food with happy times. (OK, there's no guarantee that family dinners will always be happy—but we can do our best!) Eating together in groups is normal human behavior, and it just feels good to most people. It encourages everyone to eat more slowly, talk to each other and learn to enjoy being together. And it also gives you a chance to role model enjoying healthy foods.

Studies show that children benefit emotionally, physically and mentally from regular meals with the family. In fact, the benefits from regular family meals far exceed the benefits from the very after-school activities, sports, clubs or lessons that often interrupt dinner.

A Closer Look at Eating Together

Several research studies have shown that eating meals together as a family encourages children and teens to eat a healthier diet. A major study involving children ages nine to 14 showed that family members who ate together at home on a regular basis ate more Smart foods, including fruits and vegetables. They also ate healthier foods throughout the day, resulting in higher intakes of important nutrients such as calcium, vitamins and fiber. Many studies show that children benefit in other ways from eating meals with parents: higher grades at school, lower use of drugs, enhanced social skills and lower rates of eating disorders, especially in girls. The bottom line: Family meals can make an important contribution to your child's development, socialization and health.

Tips for Dealing with the Really Cautious Eater

Throughout the following chapters, you will find lots of advice on convincing doubtful kids to eat specific types of healthy foods. However, one situation deserves a special mention.

Some children are born with extremely sensitive palates. To these kids, tasting disliked foods seems to cause something akin to physical pain. This situation is hard on kids—and very hard on parents. Although the guidelines already discussed may help your picky eater gradually expand her tastes, no parenting tactic is going to suddenly transform a very selective eater into a child who eats everything. But, over the course of years, gentle exposure to a variety of foods will result in expanded tastes. Meanwhile, here are extra ideas to make feeding (and eating with) a highly cautious eater more pleasant:

- Try to avoid labeling him negatively. If the word "picky" has become a put-down in your house, look for a more positive word such as "selective," "sensitive" or "cautious."

- Do not allow a cautious eater to stop you from making needed improvements in your family food choices! Go ahead and make the changes, and have confidence that your fussy eater will catch up with the rest of the family over time.

- Teach your selective child to be polite. Talk about polite ways to move unwanted food to the side of the plate. Practice saying a simple "no, thank you" when offered a disliked food. Discuss how to subtly inspect food to decide whether she wants to try it. You may also want to teach her how to spit food out into her napkin discreetly and quietly.

When Jake was a child, he was exquisitely sensitive to tastes, smells, textures and colors. Food was no exception, and the variety of foods he would eat was very limited. His mom tried to just accept his strong food preferences by serving at least one thing that Jake liked at each meal but never fixing him separate foods. Still, his limited diet worried her. Finally, she decided to write down everything he ate one week and was pleasantly surprised at the variety of foods he actually did eat. It let her know that he would survive and thrive—and he did! Being fairly relaxed about his selective habits worked well. By the time he went to college, Jake had matured into a healthy adult with a very flexible—even adventuresome—appetite. **X**

- Decide when you can compromise. You might be willing to compromise on texture, for instance, and blend his smoothies well or grind up nuts for baked goods. Or you might be willing to let him sit near a window or run the kitchen fan to help him avoid smelling objectionable food odors. Or pack only favorites in his lunch box for school.

- Attempt to understand what she dislikes about foods. Often, selective eaters are sensitive to bitterness, textures or strong odors. Once you understand the problem, you might be able to find better compromises. Note, however, that these conversations should take place away from the dinner table and away from siblings. (Remember the "No bad-mouthing the food!" rule.)

- Try to have one food at each meal that your cautious eater does like. Having something easy to eat will make other disliked food seem less overwhelming.

- Don't lose faith in the child's ability to eat a variety of foods. Keep encouraging him. In fact, as adults, many formerly "picky" eaters turn out to have finely tuned palates that allow them to truly appreciate gourmet foods.

Perfection Is Impossible

We live in a world where there are many barriers to eating well, including busy schedules, eating out more often, both parents working, after-school activities and television. Adults often feel rushed and out of control about feeding their children. This field guide is designed to make this process easier and more fun for the whole family—including the moms and dads responsible for putting the food on the table.

It's important to realize that sometimes an eating situation, such as a school cafeteria, is entirely out of your control. A useful rule of thumb is to decide not to let yourself stress over a situation if you know you can't influence a change. To compensate for this type of situation, make sure you feed your kids healthy food when you're able to make the decision. If you feed your family well when they're with you, they will be just fine!

Above all, take your time and work gradually through the steps in this book. Always remember: *Perfection is not possible.* It's far better to keep your goals realistic by making the most important changes gradually and finding ways to enjoy them.

Major Points of Interest:
What to Keep in Mind about the Wild World of Food

- All foods can be categorized as Smart, In-Between or Empty. During the next six weeks, your family is going to gradually add in lots of Smart foods, learn to use In-Between foods to replace less-healthy foods and get rid of some of the Empties you usually eat.

- While adding food to your family diet, allow each person to self-regulate the amount of healthy foods desired without being bribed or forced to eat anything.

- Try to increase your family's enthusiasm at mealtime by cutting back on nonstop snacking. Instead, have meals and snacks at somewhat regular times, and try to have some meals as a family so you can role model eating well.

- Most important, remember that loving food—healthy food—is your family's biggest goal.

- As you head into this adventure with your family, let Smart foods crowd out the unhealthier foods. Don't try to change everything at once—just add in the healthier foods recommended each week. Keep in mind that every Smart food your children eat will help their bodies fight diseases, feel energetic and grow up healthy!

A 6-Week Journey to Smarter Eating

Hopefully, the previous section has given you some helpful general strategies for coping with the daily task of feeding your favorite natives.

This section is your guide to gradually improving what your family eats by adding in extra servings of one type of Smart food at a time, starting with fruit. These healthy Smart foods will either be additions to your usual foods, or they will naturally replace some of the foods you already eat. Your family shouldn't focus on giving things up, but the Smart food additions will probably make you less hungry for some of the Empties you normally eat. Only in the sixth week, after adding lots of fun and healthy foods that your family enjoys, will you actually take anything out of your diet.

While making these changes, your family will need to explore options and choose a path that works best for all of you. There's no one perfect way to eat healthy because every family has its own preferences, interests, traditions and schedules. As you chart your way into new eating territory, don't try to be someone you aren't—find a way to make changes that feel right to your family.

You're bound to take some wrong turns, of course, maybe trying a new food you all end up hating, making changes too fast or just getting stopped in the process by a bout of the flu. That's all part of the journey. It doesn't mean you have to pack up and head back to the way you were eating before. It just means you need to figure out a solution. Each section of this guide has lots of ideas to get you back on track.

Make a Plan

Each time you add in another healthy kind of food, it will help to think about when your family is most likely to enjoy that sort of food. Making an itinerary to follow each day is the easiest way to make sure your family eats all the things they need.

Although following the same plan each day might seem uptight at first, parents who've tried this approach find that it's really much easier in the long run. By having a regular routine of when to eat certain types of healthy foods each day, you don't have to spend as much time pondering what to eat. Even more important, following a schedule helps you make sure that your family gets the right foods most days. And you'll discover that your family won't get bored, because you won't be eating the same foods every day—just the same categories.

The Daily Itinerary chart is one way of planning your daily food itinerary. It doesn't include everything your family will eat! You will want to add extra servings of the foods listed, plus other items such as treats, toppings, condiments, beverages and oils used in cooking.

DAILY ITINERARY (after completing the 6-week journey)					
	Fruits	**Veggies**	**Dairy Foods**	**Grains**	**Proteins**
Breakfast	✔		✔	✔	
Lunch	✔	✔	✔	✔	✔
Dinner		✔✔		✔	✔
Snacks/Desserts	✔		✔		
Pick mostly Smart choices. Try to limit In-Betweens to one per meal or snack.					

Of course, the suggested times are only guideposts to lead you into this new territory. You can use the plan as it's mapped out here or create your own—whichever works best for *your* family. For example, I suggest having two vegetables with dinner, but one mom decided to give her children vegetables as an after-school snack and offer just one vegetable with dinner, because that was easier for her. You'll find that following the same general plan every day will serve as one of your most important survival tools in your family's adventures in healthy eating.

Over the next six weeks, you will gradually build up to a plan that contains enough Smart foods to meet current dietary recommendations—and to help you all feel great. To add some flexibility and fun to your plan, you will want to replace some of the Smart foods with In-Betweens. You'll still be eating a really healthy diet if you limit In-Betweens to about one per meal or snack.

Take This Trip at Your Own Speed

The following six sections are arranged by weeks. However, you might decide to take a longer amount of time to accomplish changes that represent a big shift for your family. That's fine! The changes you make are meant to become habits—and habits take time and practice to establish. Make changes at a pace that works for your family.

While you're exploring each step of the program, remember that every Smart food your family eats will make them healthier! Even if your family takes months before they're ready to move on to the next "week" of the program, you're doing something great for the health of everyone at your table.

Or, Chart Your Own Course

Although the following sections are laid out as a six-week process, you might prefer to use them as a reference guide instead. If you are most concerned with figuring out what to do if your child won't drink milk, or need new ideas for eating whole grains, by all means head straight to those sections and get the information you need. In fact, even families who do the six-week plan might eventually want to refer back to these chapters for new ideas or review.

Starting the Adventure with Fruit

For the first step of this journey, you don't need to stop eating anything that's part of your routine now. Instead, you need to add in enough extra fruit so that your family has three opportunities to enjoy it (nearly) every day. Of course, your children may turn down some servings or just eat a small amount. That's fine!

Adding in fruit works well as a great first step for most people. It tastes good, and it's easy to buy and quick to pack. Most of us already eat at least some fruit, and most kids like it already. The two key points to focus on this week will be making sure your family eats *enough* fruit and eats mostly Smart fruits.

A Daily Itinerary: Planning When You'll Eat Fruit

To figure out how to fit enough fruit into your busy routine day after day, you need a plan of action! First, pick three times during the day when your family will have fruit. For most people, the easiest way to fit in fruit is to offer it for breakfast, lunch and as either dessert, an afternoon snack or an evening snack. Then, see how your plan works. Your family may need to experiment with having fruit at different times to see what's most convenient and, of course, enjoyable. Whatever fruit-eating schedule you decide on, be sure to follow it each day to make fruit eating an automatic habit.

DAILY ITINERARY 3 Fruits a Day

Breakfast	✔	Eat with breakfast and/or as mid-morning snack.
Lunch	✔	Pack in lunch box, as dessert and/or eat your fruit on your way to a restaurant.
Dinner		
Snacks/Desserts	✔	Pick one (or more): After school, an afternoon pick-me-up, in the car on the way home, dessert and/or an evening snack.

Let your family self-regulate. Some kids may turn down all or part of some servings.

Why Eat Fruit?

Adding fruits to your family diet is one of the best and easiest ways to assure better short-term and long-term health. Here are just a few good things eating fruit can do:

- Provide a sweet-tasting snack full of great nutrition that is lower in calories than Empty high-calorie desserts and snacks (such as cookies or chips).
- Give quick energy.
- Supply vitamins, minerals, fiber and other nutrients that work together to create better absorption and utilization by the body than a vitamin pill (called "food synergy").
- Support the immune system with nutrients, such as vitamin C, that promote healing and help prevent acute illnesses, including colds and flu.
- Provide fiber that helps prevent constipation, lower bad cholesterol, keep the colon healthy and make people feel full, which often prevents overeating.

How to Identify Smart Fruits– And Avoid Empty Ones

Finding Smart fruit is easy. Any plain fruit, if it has no added sweetener or fat, is a Smart choice. Most grocery stores carry lots of great fruit; the trick is to buy enough fruit so you don't run out.

Spotting Smart Fruits

- **Identifying features:** All fruits qualify as Smart unless they have added sweetener or fat.
- **Best aspects:** Sweet tasting, lots of variety, often popular with kids.
- **Number of servings to offer:** Three each day—or more!
- **Varieties:**
  - Fresh
  - Frozen without added sweetener
  - Canned in 100% fruit juice and no added sweetener
  - Dried without added sweetener

Sweetener Makes Smart Fruit into an In-Between or Empty

Sugar, honey and other sweeteners turn Smart fruits into In-Betweens or Empties. You can find out if fruit has added sweeteners by reading the Ingredients list on the package.

WORDS USED FOR ADDED SWEETENER

Brown Rice Syrup	Dextrose	Maple Syrup
Brown Sugar	Evaporated Cane Juice	Mannitol
Concentrated Apple Juice	Fructose	Powdered Sugar
	Glucose	Raw Sugar
Concentrated Pear Juice	High Fructose Corn Syrup	Rice Syrup
		Sorbitol
Corn Sweetener	Honey	Sucrose
Corn Syrup	Lactose	Sugar
Corn Syrup Solids	Malt Syrup	Turbinado
Crystalline Fructose	Maltose	Xylitol

But, look out for any of the words shown on the sweetener chart, not just the words "sugar" or "corn syrup." All non-artificial sweeteners, including sugar, honey, concentrated fruit juice, maple syrup, raw sugar, brown rice syrup and corn syrup, contain about 800 calories per cup. And *none* of the sweeteners have significant nutritional value. Natural sweeteners are, however, sometimes less processed.

If the Ingredients list contains any type of sweetener, look for a different product—or just serve fresh fruit.

When checking fruit products for sweetener, don't rely on the Nutrition Facts label on the package. The problem is that all fruit contains natural fruit sugar known as "*fructose*." That is what makes it sweet! This means the Nutrition Facts label will always show that the fruit contains some number of grams of "sugar" even if no sweetener was added.

When buying fruit, use the simple Field Test below to decide if it is Smart, In-Between or Empty.

Field Test for Fruit

1. Look for fresh, plain fruit and unsweetened frozen, canned or dried fruit.
   - If the fruit **has nothing added to it,** it is a **Smart fruit.**
2. Read the Ingredients list. Check for added sweeteners. For drinks, skip to step 3.
   - If the fruit contains **fruit plus fruit juice,** but **no added sweetener,** it is S**mart.**
   - If **fruit is first on the Ingredients list,** but the fruit contains **added sweetener,** it is an **In-Between fruit.**
   - However, if **fruit is not first on the Ingredients list and it contains sweetener,** it is an **Empty.**
3. For a drink, read the Ingredients list.
   - If the drink is **100% fruit juice,** without added sweeteners, it is an **In-Between fruit.**
   - If a drink's Ingredients list includes added **sweetener,** it is an **Empty.**

A Closer Look at Artificial Sweeteners

The U.S. Food and Drug Administration (www.fda.gov) has approved five artificial no-calorie sweeteners for general use, including aspartame (NutraSweet and Equal), saccharin, acesulfame-K, neotame and sucralose (Splenda). These sweeteners appear in a variety of foods, such as yogurts and beverages, as a way to lower the calories. Most dietitians and health professionals currently see occasional use of artificial sweeteners as safe for children and teens.

Three other sweeteners, xylitol, mannitol and sorbitol, are lower-calorie sugar alcohol sweeteners used in a variety of products. Though they sometimes cause gas or diarrhea, they are also approved by the FDA.

However, some experts suggest limiting artificial sweeteners because regular use can accustom kids to eating very sweet foods and drinks. Other experts (and many parents) choose not to give artificial sweeteners to children routinely because they are not certain that they can be completely trusted in a child's growing body.

Using the Field Test for Fruit

You don't need to use the Field Test for Fruit when buying plain, fresh fruit. It is always Smart! But, if you want to buy packaged, canned, frozen or dried fruits, the field test can simplify your fruit-gathering expeditions. This label is from a package of fruit chews. Here is how to use the steps from the field test to decide if this food is a healthy choice:

1. Look at the package. Clearly the box does not contain just plain fruit. Words like chews, roll-ups, jams, jellies and bars usually mean the food is an Empty.

2. Check the Ingredients list for added sweeteners. This one contains corn syrup as the first ingredient. Down the list are more sweeteners: sugar, apple juice concentrate and pear juice concentrate. There is no actual fruit. This food is an Empty.

NOTE: These chews also contain partially hydrogenated soybean oil. Partially hydrogenated oils contain unhealthy trans fat and make any food an Empty.

NOTE: This candy does contain 25 percent of the Daily Value of vitamin C from the "ascorbic acid" listed on the Ingredients list. However, you do not need to feed your family candy to get vitamin C.

The conclusion? Like most individually packaged fruit gummies, rolls and chews, these chews are not fruit at all! They are fruit-flavored candy and should be served only as treats, if at all. Dried fruit or raisins would be a much Smarter choice. (For more examples showing how to use the field test for fruit, see the Appendix.)

Try to Buy a Variety of Fruits

The wider variety of fruit you have for your family to enjoy, the better. However, don't let the idea of needing variety stop you from buying lots of the fruits your family likes most. Eating any fruit, even the same fruits over and over, is *much* better than skipping it!

Fake Fruit Is Not Smart

The vast majority of fruit drinks, chews, snacks, bursts and roll-ups are mostly corn syrup or other sweeteners and contain almost no fruit. These foods are Empties unless they are made from 100 percent real fruit. Read the label to be sure.

Any drink that contains corn syrup or other sweeteners is an Empty, no matter what the packaging says! Those little boxes of fruit-flavored sugar water (including those containing 10 percent juice or with labels that say "Made with fruit juice") are never a good choice for your kids because they contain roughly 100 calories while providing almost no nutrition.

A lot of fake fruit foods contain added vitamin C. It's important to remember that this does not make them healthy! These drinks and foods are just sugar, corn syrup or another sweetener mixed with a tiny bit of inexpensive vitamin C powder. Even a food whose package promises "100% of your day's supply of vitamin C" (or any other nutrient) can be an Empty.

> **A Closer Look at Juice-Drinking Precautions**
>
> Juice drinking is known to be a major reason that kids are not hungry at mealtime. Juice contains the same number of calories as soda (about 12 calories per ounce) and can be drunk just as quickly as a soda by a thirsty child. Even though official government food guidelines say that half of daily fruit servings can be from juice, the American Academy of Pediatrics recommends limiting juice intake. They say that one- to six-year-olds should drink no more than four to six ounces of juice in a day, which is the size of a small sippy cup. Children ages seven to 18 should get no more than eight to 12 ounces of juice, which is a small drinking glass. They also recommend that, given a choice, parents should opt for regular fruit; it is a much better deal than juice because it includes fiber and takes longer to eat. Serving real fruit instead of juice also establishes a healthy fruit-eating habit that can last a lifetime and may help your kids avoid many chronic diseases.

Your kids will easily get enough vitamin C by eating real fruits and vegetables or, if their doctor recommends it, taking a multivitamin. They don't need all that sugar or corn syrup just to get some vitamin C.

100% Fruit Juice Is NOT a Smart Fruit

Kids love juice, but it really isn't as healthy as the fruit itself. The problem is that fruit juice doesn't contain the fiber, so it doesn't make you feel full for long. Since juice doesn't need to be chewed, kids can easily drink too much and get too many calories. They will also not feel like drinking milk or water, both of which are important for kids' health.

If you decide to serve juice, use only 100% fruit juice and count it as that meal's In-Between choice. Read more about cutting back on juice under "Fruit Survival Tips" on page 38 and "A Closer Look at Juice-Drinking Precautions" above on this page.

Should You Buy Organic Fruit?

The most important fact to know about all organic foods, including fruits, is that the word "organic" does not mean "healthy." There is no evidence that organic foods consistently contain more nutrition than conventionally produced foods. Organic foods that contain lots of sugar or unhealthy fats are

FRUIT IDENTIFICATION CHART

Next time you go on a grocery store expedition, keep on the lookout for sugar camouflaged to seem like fruit. This chart will help you hunt down fruits that are Smart or In-Between and avoid Empties.

SMART	**Fresh fruit** such as bananas, apples, kiwi, peaches, watermelon and strawberries. **Frozen fruit** packaged without added sweetener. **Canned fruit** packed in 100% juice or water with no sweetener. **Dried fruit** made without added sweetener. **Fruit leather** that contains fruit only.
IN-BETWEEN	**100% fruit juice** **Fruit, canned or frozen with light or heavy syrup** (preferably drained). **Dried fruit** with added sweetener. **Fruit desserts** made out of mostly Smart ingredients and small amounts of sweetener.
EMPTY	**"Fruit drinks" and "fruit punch"** containing sweetener. **Lemonade, limeade and powdered flavored drink mixes,** even if fortified with vitamin C. **Fruit roll-ups, chews, candies, jams, jellies or bars,** even if fortified with vitamin C. **Anything "fruit flavored" or "containing real fruit juice"** but listing sweetener as the first ingredient (examples include many popsicles, sorbets and sodas). **Pie fillings, fruit topping and fruit syrups** **Fruit desserts** including most pies, cakes, breads, some flavored yogurts or smoothies, sauces or cookies.

A Closer Look at Selecting Organic Foods

Organic foods are becoming more widely popular. If you decide to buy organic food, make certain you know what the label means:

- "100% Organic, USDA Organic": Government organic standards have been met, the food contains no synthetic ingredients and there has been independent approval of food production methods.
- "Organic": 95 percent of ingredients used are organic.
- "Made with Organic": 70 to 94 percent of ingredients used are organic.
- "Natural" or "Naturally Made": Not regulated—a meaningless term.

Parents can also stay informed about which foods are more important to buy organic. For example, you can read about the "dirty dozen" fruits and vegetables at the website for the Environmental Working Group: www.foodnews.org.

definitely still Empties. Another fact to know is that organic foods will taste the same as regular foods.

"Organic" simply means that the food was raised without pesticides, herbicides, antibiotics or hormones. As for safety, there is evidence that pesticides and herbicides do show up in the bodies of adults and children. Since I like to expose my family to as little of these chemicals as possible, I personally buy organic when it is available, fresh looking and not too expensive. (Also, see a "Closer Look at Selecting Organic Foods" on page 34).

Eating In-Between Fruit

Try to use mostly Smart choices for your fruit servings. You might decide to serve some In-Between fruits now and then as fruit servings, too. However, over the next six weeks you'll be limiting your In-Between foods to just one per meal or snack, so you might not want to use up your In-Between choice on something as naturally sweet as fruit!

How to Get There: Actually Eating the Fruit

It's one thing to know which fruits to buy and plan when you're going to eat them. But actually doing it day in and day out can be a challenge. Here are some strategies:

Try Not to Run Out of Fruit

Learn to buy lots of fruit. Buy plenty of your favorite fresh fruits, but also buy frozen fruit and keep a supply of canned, dried or bottled fruit. For example, you might buy a few bags of frozen berries, some cans of pineapple or peaches and a big jar of applesauce. That way, if you run out of fresh fruit before you get back to the store, your family can still have fruit three times a day.

While shopping, do a quick calculation to be sure you buy enough fruit. Multiply the number of people in your family times three fruits per day.

Then, pick out that amount of fruit for each day until you plan to shop again. For example, if you have four people in your family, you will go through twelve servings each day. This calculation will probably make you realize that you need to get more fruit than you're used to buying.

Keep Fruit Out in the Open

Most fruit can be kept in a bowl on the counter or table where everyone can see it and, hopefully, be tempted to eat it. Or consider buying one of those three-layer hanging wire baskets to keep fruit visible but out of the way.

Offer Fruit at Snack Time as a Finger Food

Many kids love still-frozen fruit for quick snacks—raspberries, blueberries, pineapple, mango chunks and cherries. Fresh fruit is great, too. Less-enthusiastic kids might be more inspired if you cut the fruit into smaller chunks served on toothpicks, or serve it with some flavored nonfat yogurt for dipping.

Combine Fruits with Other Smart Foods

The ideas for combining fruit with other Smart foods are endless: Put sliced bananas on a peanut butter sandwich, add chopped apples or mandarin oranges to a tossed salad or put blueberries in cooked oatmeal. Not all kids will like every idea, but experiment to see what you can get away with, and ask your kids for their ideas. A favorite fruit combination is a smoothie. You'll find smoothies and other fruit ideas in the recipe section.

Fruits Are Great On-the-Go Foods

If you need to pack fruit for school lunches or other outings, here are a few quick ideas:

- Some of the easiest fruits to pack are bananas, clementines (tiny oranges) and apples.
- Wash and dry, then wrap pears, plums and peaches in a paper towel so they won't bruise—and so kids can clean up drips.
- Use small plastic containers for packing berries, grapes and melon chunks.

- Freeze batches of smoothies in plastic, lidded bottles. They will thaw by lunchtime and help keep other foods in a lunch bag cold.
- Use prepackaged fruits: individual containers of unsweetened applesauce, mini-cans of fruit packed in 100% juice and small boxes of raisins.

Serve Fruits for Dessert

If you decide that having fruit for a snack is too complicated, try serving it for dessert most nights. Besides adding the fruit, you will also have an excuse for eliminating the usual Empty dessert.

Consider serving dessert a bit later in the evening, after the dishes are done or as a homework break. The fruit will taste even better when everyone has had a chance to get a little hungry, and it may help eliminate some of the typical evening snacking.

Provisions:
Ideas for Fruit to Serve

Need some ideas for what to serve? Here are some of my favorites. The ones with an asterisk (*) are located in the recipe section of the book.

Breakfast

- Fresh fruits such as bananas, apples, oranges, plums and pears
- Strawberries, blueberries, raspberries or blackberries
- Super Smoothie *
- Fruit-n-Oats *
- Tropical Yogurt*
- Warm Fruit Sundae made from any frozen fruit*
- Fruit on cold cereal
- Melon slices
- Applesauce
- Canned-in-juice fruits such as peaches, pears, pineapple

Lunch

- Grapes, bananas, apples, clementines, peaches, plums or other fresh fruits
- Fruit slices dipped in nonfat yogurt
- Pack-n-Go Berry Dessert*
- Mandarin Orange Salad*
- Box of raisins
- Dried apricots, apples or bananas
- Individual containers of unsweetened applesauce
- Mini pop-top cans of fruit in 100% juice

Snacks or Desserts

- Sorbet*
- Fruit slices with flavored nonfat yogurt for dipping
- Almost Instant Pudding* mixed with berries or cherries
- Fruity Yogurt*
- Banana Milkshakes*
- Popsicles*
- Still-frozen fruits such as cherries, blueberries and raspberries

*In recipe section

Fruit Survival Tips

As you work on adding fruit into your family's diet, you may hit a few snags. Here are some tips that should help:

Dislike of Fruits

It can be so frustrating when one member of the family freaks out over certain foods you serve. Believe me, I've been there! But remember, everyone doesn't always have to be delighted with every food you serve.

If someone in your family is occasionally fruit resistant, look for the one or two fruits he likes most and serve those often. Then, if you decide to serve a less favored fruit at a meal or snack and one child refuses to eat it, don't worry about it. Kids don't have to eat anything they don't want to eat, but you don't have to be a short-order cook either! (See "Don't Make Separate Meals for the Kids," on page 16.)

On the other hand, if you have a child who *never* wants fruit, consider keeping a supply of baby carrots, cucumbers or whatever other raw vegetables he prefers. When the other family members have fruit, he can go to the refrigerator and get his veggies to munch on instead. This is a great alternative as long as you don't end up having to debate what he can or cannot eat each time it happens.

Meanwhile, serve a variety of fruits to the whole family. When done in a relaxed way, this exposure may eventually lead the resistant person to start sampling. (Or, it may not!) Keep trying new and different fruits. Limiting the types of fruit the family eats just to satisfy one person's tastes ensures that the selective person will never learn to eat other foods, and the rest of the family will miss out on lots of great fruits.

Rushed Mornings

If your mornings are super-rushed, here are a few ideas for getting your morning fruit:

- Put frozen fruit in bowls the night before and put them in the refrigerator. In the morning, the fruit will be ready to eat.

- Use applesauce or mini-cans of fruit.

- Feed the kids whole pieces of fruit (bananas, apples, plums) in the car or at the bus stop.

Angie's kids wake up with tons of energy—and they always wake up hungry. Angie, on the other hand, wakes up slowly, thinking only of coffee. So she has started leaving containers full of cut-up fruit, frozen berries or even applesauce in the fridge each night. The kids wake up each morning, run to the fridge and scarf down an entire serving of fruit, leaving Angie free to stretch, yawn and make her coffee. ⊗

- If their school allows a mid-morning snack, pack fruit.
- If you have time for a mid-morning snack, take fruit to work.
- Teach your oldest (or most responsible) kid to be the smoothie master and make smoothies while you're in the shower.

Fruits in Restaurants

Fruit is hard to find in restaurants. Sometimes it's available on salad bars or as a fruit salad or fruit cup, but many restaurants just don't serve fruit at all.

One solution is to eat an apple, banana or box of raisins on the way to the restaurant. That way everyone has some good nutrition in case the meal is not healthy. And overeating Empties at the restaurant isn't as tempting. The fruit snack also makes it easier for kids to wait for the food to be served. This works well for adults, too.

Or, instead of eating fruit at a restaurant, have some fruit as dessert when you get back to your home, your car or your office. If you don't want to pack fresh fruit each morning for these situations, keep a stash of dried fruit or raisins in your office, car or bag. That way, you'll have a ready supply of fruit snacks with you for many different situations.

Big Juice Drinkers

A lot of "poor eaters" are really just great juice drinkers. They can easily fill up on juice at or before every meal and during every car ride.

But if your child is really in the habit of drinking juice, you'll need to "wean" her off it gradually. If she's old enough, try giving her a budget of one juice a day to be enjoyed whenever she likes. Having this type of control makes change easier on most kids. If your child is too young for the budget approach, she's probably young enough that you can get away with diluting her juice with more and more water until she's getting mostly water.

As you get your family to drink less juice, it will be important to replace that liquid with *water*. Your child might be more enthusiastic if you allow him to buy his own water bottle and let him fill it with water and ice. Also, try adding a twist of lemon or lime, or just a dash of cranberry juice for extra flavor or a change of pace. Your family might also enjoy unsweetened sparkling water (sometimes referred to as seltzer or bubble water) or herbal tea.

Major Points of Interest
What to Keep in Mind about Fruit

Your journey to eating better has begun! Here are a few guideposts highlighting what you've seen and done so far:

• Offer your family fruit at least three times a day, at the same times each day, to create a fruit-eating habit. Most people prefer having fruit for:

   • Breakfast
   • Lunch
   • Either for dessert or as a snack

• Choose mostly Smart fruit without added sweeteners or fats. Quality fruit is naturally sweet.

• Juice is an In-Between and should be limited.

• "Juice drinks," pies, cookies and "fruit chews" are Empties.

• Never force, bribe or beg your children to eat fruit. Instead, role model enjoying fruits by offering fruits you love, and experiment with finding fruits your children will actually enjoy.

Exploring Vegetables

This week, you'll be tracking down ways to eat lots of vegetables each day—three, four or even more servings. For some families, eating that many vegetables may seem like an overwhelming feat! But most families can learn to do it fairly painlessly using some of the tricks and techniques in this chapter. A healthy dose of determination to keep exploring options until you find the ones you like really helps! If you keep at it, you'll eventually find a plan that works for your family. During this vegetable week, of course, you should continue to offer everyone fruit three times each day, too. And just like Week 1, the focus of this week is still on *adding* healthy food to your regular diet.

A Daily Itinerary: Planning When You'll Eat Vegetables

Almost everyone knows that they should eat lots of vegetables. The problem is actually doing it! It is especially overwhelming if you try to cram all three

Why Eat Vegetables?

Vegetables are great for you and have even more health benefits than fruit. In fact, they are so packed with nutrition that current guidelines encourage exposing kids and adults to as many servings as they will eat each day. Here are some facts about vegetables to motivate you to eat more:

- They supply nutrients that promote high-level functioning of the immune system as well as cell repair and growth. Darker colors such as orange, red, green or purple yield amazing amounts of vitamins and minerals.
- Veggies contain the perfect combination of nutrients that result in full absorption by the body (called "food synergy") and do it better than a vitamin pill.
- Three or more servings each day can help lower the risk of chronic diseases such as diabetes, heart disease, high blood pressure, obesity and even certain cancers.
- Vegetables have superior nutrition for few calories. They can replace Empty high-calorie snacks such as crackers, cheese, chips and fries.
- There is no such thing as overeating vegetables because they are low in calories, especially compared to other foods.
- Veggies provide a lot of fiber that creates a feeling of fullness, helps control appetite and reduces cravings.
- Vegetables provide a great opportunity for adding in Smart, unsaturated fats as toppings.

vegetable servings into one meal—dinner. That just doesn't work. Nobody— or at least no one I know—wants to eat three servings of vegetables with their dinner every single day.

So the challenge is to find a pattern that works for your family, and then make that pattern a habit by repeating it each day. The easiest pattern for most people is to eat one serving for lunch, have raw vegetables (perhaps a salad or veggies and dip) just before dinner and then eat one vegetable with dinner. If you can't fit in the vegetables for lunch, consider having an extra serving of vegetables as an after-school snack or as an evening snack. The main thing is to create a pattern and stick to it most days in addition to your three servings of fruit!

DAILY ITINERARY	3 (or More) Vegetables a Day	
Breakfast		Optional, but fun change of pace.
Lunch	✔ or more	Pack in lunch box, order when eating out or include in lunch at home.
Dinner	✔✔ or more	One serving before the main meal (salad, soup, veggies and dip). Plus one or more vegetables with the main course.
Snacks/Desserts		Optional as a great afternoon snack
Plus, encourage extra servings of vegetables any time of the day. Let your family self-regulate. Some kids may turn down all or part of some servings.		

How to Identify Smart Vegetables— And Avoid Empty Ones

Like fruits, any plain vegetable, if it has no added fat or sweetener, is a Smart choice. Contrary to popular belief, tasty vegetables are *not* an endangered species! There are many great vegetables to be found in any expedition to the grocery store. The trick is to buy enough so you never run out and find ways your family enjoys eating them.

Spotting Smart Vegetables
- **Identifying features:** All vegetables, if they are low in added fat (especially partially hydrogenated vegetable oil [which contains trans fat], butter, lard and cheese).
- **Best aspects:** Variety of colors that are loaded with nutrients, many flavors and textures, lots of ways to prepare and eat.
- **Number of servings to offer:** Three or more. Try to include at least one brightly colored vegetable if possible (orange, green or red).
- **Varieties:**
  - Fresh
  - Frozen with little or no fat
  - Canned with little or no fat
  - Deli salads or trays without added fat or sweetener

Why search out vegetables without added fat? Because manufacturers who add fat to vegetables usually add bad-tasting and/or unhealthy fats. In general, you're better off adding your own dressings and toppings made with healthier fats. When your family adds their own fats to food, such as salad dressings or slivered nuts, they will enjoy the fat more because it is very noticeable on top of the food. Also, letting them add their own toppings allows each person to self-regulate how much they want and need.

Many packaged vegetables contain partially hydrogenated vegetable oil, sometimes called shortening. Partially hydrogenated oils contain trans fats that raise "bad" cholesterol levels. If the food contains more than half a gram of trans fat, the Nutrition Facts label will show a number, in grams (g), after the words "Trans fat." However, foods that show "0 g" for trans fat still contain a small amount of trans fat if the Ingredients list includes "partially hydrogenated oil." Because there are plenty of fat-free vegetable choices, I don't buy any foods with Ingredients lists that include partially hydrogenated vegetable oil,

---

Field Test for Vegetables

1. Read the Ingredients list. Look for added fats and oils.
   - If a vegetable has **no added fat,** it is a **Smart vegetable.** All fresh, plain, unpackaged vegetables are Smart.

2. Check the Nutrition Facts label for trans fat and/or check the Ingredients list for "partially hydrogenated" oil (which contains trans fat).
   - If the vegetable **contains trans fat,** it is an **Empty.**

3. Double the calories from fat** listed on the Nutrition Facts label. Compare that number to total calories per serving.
   - If the **total calories are MORE than two times the fat calories,** it is **at least an In-Between vegetable.** But, it could be Smart . . . so, do step 4.

   - If the **total calories are LESS than two times the fat calories,** it is an **Empty.**

4. Multiply the number of calories from fat by 3.** Compare the number to the total calories.
   - If the **total calories are MORE than three times the fat calories,** it is a **Smart vegetable.**

If you prefer, round all numbers to the nearest 10 for easier math.

even when there is so little that the label reads "0 g" for trans fat. (Read more in "A Closer Look at Types of Fats," on page 51.)

At restaurants, plain steamed and boiled vegetables are almost always Smart. Salads are also Smart if you have the dressings served on the side so you can self-regulate how much you are putting on. Vegetables that look or feel greasy, or are covered with fatty sauce (such as cheese or cream), are generally In-Betweens, while deep-fried vegetables (including French fries) are Empties.

Using the Field Test for Vegetables

Of course, all fresh vegetables are Smart! But if you sometimes buy pre-packaged veggies, use the field test to figure out which ones are Smart, In-Between or Empty. The label used in this example is from Broccoli and Cheddar Cheese Deli Soup. This is how you can use the field test to decide if this soup would be a good choice for your family:

1. Read the Ingredients list for fats. Milk, cream, butter and cheese are all sources of fat, so this vegetable does contain added fat.

2. Read the Nutrition Facts label for trans fat. It says "Trans Fat 1g." Because it contains trans fat, this soup is an Empty. Step 3 and step 4 are not necessary. Step 3 is included to show that this soup would be Empty even if it did not contain trans fat.

3. Find the Calories from Fat (190) and double them: 190+190=380. Compare the total Calories (280) to the doubled Calories from Fat (380). Total Calories are lower; so over half the calories in this soup come from fat. It is definitely an Empty. No need to do step 4.

Nutrition Facts
Serving Size: 1 cup (245g)
Servings Per Container: About 3

Amount Per Serving

Calories 280   Calories from Fat 190

% Daily Value

Total Fat 21g	**32%**
Saturated Fat 13g	**65%**
Trans Fat 1g	
Cholesterol 70mg	**23%**
Sodium 920mg	**38%**
Total Carbohydrate 14g	**5%**
Dietary Fiber 2g	**8%**
Sugars 5g	
Protein 11g	

Vitamin A 25%	•	Vitamin C 50%	
Calcium 30%	•	Iron 4%	

INGREDIENTS: Chicken stock, milk, broccoli, cheddar cheese (milk, cheese culture, salt, enzymes), cream, butter, contains 2% or less of: modified corn starch, enriched flour (wheat flour, niacin, reduced iron, thiamine mononitrrate, riboflavin, folic acid), salt, sugar, natural asiago cheese flavor (cheese (pasteurized milk, cultures, salt, enzymes), water, natural flavors, salt, sodium phosphayes, sodium citrate), water, cultured dextrose, chicken flavor (contains salt, egg, milk), annatto (as color), tabasco sauce (vinegar, red pepper, salt).

After reading this label, you will probably decide to buy a different type of soup! Soups can be a healthy way to eat vegetables, but not always. This one is high in fat and contains trans fat. (For more examples showing how to use the field test for vegetables, go to the Appendix.)

Fresh Vegetables

Fresh vegetables are, of course, an ideal food. Most grocery stores have a great selection. Alternatively, if you have a local produce stand or farmers' market, you might be able to pick up very fresh, recently harvested vegetables that keep even longer in your refrigerator.

Some fresh vegetables are now available pre-washed, pre-cut and ready to either eat or cook. Some of the cut-up vegetables you can find at many grocery stories include green beans, baby carrots, grated carrots, potatoes and broccoli. They are just as healthy and can make preparing vegetables much faster. However, keep in mind that pre-cut versions never last as long in the refrigerator as uncut ones, so plan to eat them soon after you buy them. Bagged lettuce, spinach and salad greens do last for about a week in the refrigerator and can make a before-dinner salad very easy. If you can afford these prepared veggies, go for it.

Frozen Vegetables

Frozen vegetables are just as healthy as fresh, and they keep a lot longer. They also have the advantage of being very quick to prepare. Try to keep a few bags of vegetables in your freezer at all times in case you run low on fresh ones or for nights when things are really rushed. Frozen vegetables are pre-washed and chopped and some are even mixed into interesting combinations. (However, if your children will already eat a combination of vegetables, all touching one another, you probably don't need this chapter!)

But watch out—some frozen vegetables contain added fats. For example, frozen French fries look innocent enough, but they are usually partially deep-fried in unhealthy oil. Other fat-filled frozen vegetables are either breaded (such as okra), fried (such as potatoes) or in a sauce (such as broccoli with cheese sauce). If you decide to buy a vegetable with added fats, try to find one made with healthy oils—and avoid the ones that contain partially hydrogenated oil, cream or butter. Use the field test to pick out brands lowest in added fats.

Canned and Bottled Vegetables

In general, canned and bottled vegetables are less tasty than fresh and have too much added sodium and too many preservatives to be as healthy as you'd like.

There are some, however, that taste great and are very popular, such as salsa, spaghetti sauce, canned tomatoes and soups. When buying spaghetti sauce, check labels for the brand with the lowest grams of sugar, sodium and fat. They vary wildly. For soup, pick those that are not called "cream of" anything unless clearly labeled "fat free." Canned and bottled vegetables and soups usually contain large amounts of sodium unless clearly marked "no sodium" or "low sodium." Particularly if someone in your family is on a sodium-restricted diet, be very careful to look at sodium content on the label of any foods in bottles and cans. Most canned and bottled vegetables contain very minimal added fats, and it is generally healthy fat. However, use the vegetable field test, or just pick those labeled "fat free" if you are unsure.

Deli Vegetables

Deli vegetables can be a wonderful time-saver—or a disaster. Some delis offer a vegetable deli tray packed with plain, fresh, cut-up vegetables and dip. (The dip is usually highly suspect—full of sugar, fat or both. Throw it out and make your own, if possible.) Other delis offer a salad bar where you can pick a selection of plain vegetables. Of course, avoid the fatty additions such as croutons, bacon and cheese. If you can afford them, these are great choices for taking to potlucks or just munching on at home when you don't have time to do the cleaning and cutting yourself.

On the other hand, the majority of prepared deli salads, soups and pre-cooked side dishes are loaded with fat, often including a big dose of trans fat. Unless the food has an Ingredients list or Nutrition Facts label so you can use the field test, you are better off finding your vegetables elsewhere.

Adding Healthy Fats to Your Vegetables

The body definitely needs some healthy fats! Children, especially, should never be put on a low-fat diet. Using healthy oils with vegetables is smart because it supplies the healthy fats and at the same time makes your vegetables taste great. Adding healthy fats to vegetables is an especially good idea when the rest of the meal is quite low in fats. However, the type of fat you choose is very important. Cook your vegetables with:

- Olive oil

- Canola (rapeseed) oil

Salad dressings, dips, mayonnaise and margarines containing these oils are also good choices, unless they have any hydrogenated, partially hydrogenated or trans fats listed on the Ingredients list. If one of the heart-healthy oils listed above has been partially hydrogenated or hydrogenated (a manufacturing process that makes the fat change from liquid to solid), you'll want to avoid it, too.

VEGETABLE IDENTIFICATION CHART

As you explore your vegetable options, beware of extra or unhealthy fat. Use this chart to help identify vegetables that are Smart or In-Between and avoid Empties. When in doubt, use the field test.

SMART	**Fresh vegetables** served raw, steamed, baked or roasted. **Frozen vegetables** packaged without added fats. **Canned and bottled vegetables,** canned or bottled salsa, tomatoes, plain corn, soups and tomato-based pasta sauces. **Deli-prepared raw vegetable plates, salads and vegetable soups** that do not contain trans fat and qualify as Smart using the vegetable field test.
IN-BETWEEN	**Vegetables made with small amounts of fats** that pass the field test. **Restaurant vegetables** with added oil, but not deep-fried. **Deli-prepared salads and vegetable soups** that do not contain trans fat and qualify as In-Between using the vegetable field test.
EMPTY	**Deep-fried vegetables** such as French fries, onion rings, fried okra, Tater Tots, bagged vegetable chips, potato chips, tempura and anything with a crispy, greasy breading. Any method of deep-frying adds too much fat to vegetables. **High-fat vegetables,** including vegetables made or topped with creamy sauces, lots of cheese, butter, margarine, regular sour cream or regular gravy. Also, mayonnaise-based salads. **Vegetables that contain trans fats,** including most frozen vegetables packaged in "butter sauces" and some deli soups. Look for partially hydrogenated vegetable oil on the Ingredients list.

Cooking Your Veggies Using Healthy Fats

Of course, the problem with all fats, even healthy ones, is that they are packed with calories. Each tablespoon of oil contains more than 100 calories. Used in excess, all those calories can fill you up too fast or lead to weight gain.

So limit the amount of fat you mix into your vegetables during preparation. A spray of cooking oil or a nonstick pan is always a good choice. Or use a small amount of olive, canola or nut oil—about one or two teaspoons for each family member is usually enough for stir-frying, sautéing and roasting. Measure it out a few times until you get a feel for how much to use. Use measuring spoons for this because they tend to be smaller than regular tableware.

Also, watch the mayonnaise! Fortunately, most mayonnaise is made with healthy fats. You might even be able to find canola oil mayonnaise, which is very high in healthy fats. Using it on a sandwich can be a Smart way to eat healthy fat. But, at about 1,600 calories per cup, any foods made with a lot of mayonnaise are just too high in calories. So, for salads and slaws, use a small amount (about one teaspoon per person), then replace the rest of the mayonnaise with plain nonfat yogurt, nonfat sour cream or low-fat buttermilk. Fat-free mayonnaise works well, too, if your family likes it.

A Closer Look at Types of Fats

Vegetables (and other foods) are often fixed and served with fats. Since fat is essential for the proper functioning of the body, it is important to eat some each day. Fats provide essential fatty acids that are not made by the body, so they must be obtained from food.

We need a balance of three types: saturated, monounsaturated and polyunsaturated. These three types vary in their amount of saturation (a technical term meaning how much hydrogen they contain). The saturation affects how the body handles the fat. See the Fat Identification Chart on page 52 for examples of each of these fats.

On the other hand, we do not need any trans fats. This type of fat, found in partially hydrogenated oils, raises bad cholesterol and lowers good cholesterol. Read more in "A Closer Look at Identifying and Avoiding Trans Fats" on page 144.

The bottom line: Most Americans already eat enough fat each day but need to have a greater portion of it come from healthier unsaturated fats.

FAT IDENTIFICATION CHART

Type of Fat	Main Sources**	Benefits	Problems
Unsaturated fats (Including **Mono-unsaturated** and **Poly-unsaturated**) Liquid at room temperature	*Best choices:* Nuts and nut butters Cold pressed olive oil Cold pressed canola oil *Other options:* Any olive oil Any canola oil Avocados Flaxseed oil Walnut oil Pumpkin seed oil Safflower oil Sunflower oil Soybean oil (if not hydrogenated) Vegetable oil or all-purpose oil (which is usually made of soy oil) Peanut oil* Corn oil*	Provides fat-soluble vitamins, calories and essential fatty acids Helps prevent heart disease: lowers bad cholesterol, may raise good cholesterol	High in calories
Saturated Fats Solid at room temperature	Animal fat Dairy fat Lard Cottonseed oil Palm kernel oil Palm oil Coconut oil Fully hydrogenated oils in packaged foods	Small amount needed to build body tissues and hormones	High in calories Raises total cholesterol, both the good and bad
Trans Fats Solid at room temperature	Partially hydrogenated oils (on labels, "partially hydrogenated" is often shortened to just "hydrogenated") Shortening Liquid shortening (used to fry foods in restaurants)	None for health Extends shelf life of packaged foods	High in calories Raises bad cholesterol while lowering good cholesterol, increasing the risk of heart disease.

*These oils contain more saturated fat than the other oils in this group.
**All naturally occurring oils and fats contain a combination of saturated, polyunsaturated and monounsaturated fats. Even olive oil and canola oil contain some saturated fats. The fats listed under "Main Sources" have been selected based on the main type of fat each contains.

Topping Your Veggies Using Healthy Fats

Adding fat on top of vegetables is a time-honored tradition because it tastes so good. And it is a good idea, since fats on top of food (rather than mixed in) are quite noticeable, and most people tend be satisfied with a reasonable amount. When each person adds the fat themselves, they can self-regulate their fat intake. But fatty toppings should generally be used only when the vegetables are either raw or cooked without fats (steamed, broiled, grilled, boiled). Toppings high in unsaturated fats include:

- **Nuts or seeds** of any type make a great, healthy addition to salads or other vegetable dishes. Try slivered almonds, chopped walnuts or pecans, or sunflower or pumpkin seeds.

- **Salad dressing** can be a great veggie topping as well. Experiment to find several your family enjoys . . . or make your own. Remember, salad dressing isn't just for salads. It can be used on cooked vegetables or as a dip, too. But, pick one that contains olive, canola, nut or soy oil.

A Closer Look at the Margarine Versus Butter Debate

If there is a nutrition topic that is confusing, it's "margarine versus butter." The simple answer is to eat what you like, but eat either sparingly.

Choosing a healthy margarine is difficult because there are so many types. Some of them claim specific health benefits (which are actually quite small) and some are lower in calories (usually because water is added). When selecting margarine, the liquid (spray) or soft tub varieties have less saturated fat and are considered better choices than the stick types as long as they are trans fat free.

Butters, on the other hand, are always high in saturated fats. When selecting butter, an alternative choice is one of the new spreadable blends that combines healthy unsaturated oil (usually canola or olive oil) with butter.

Both margarine and butter contain different amounts of unhealthy saturated fats and can add tons of calories to your diet with very little nutrition. Decide which tastes better to you, but use margarine or butter sparingly to make Smart foods tastier.

Topping Vegetables with *Just a Little* Saturated Fat

Many traditional veggie toppings are not very healthy. Worse, we like to add large amounts of them, and those calories add up. But there are ways to get almost as much flavor without filling yourself up with less healthy fats.

- A **butter-oil mix** is a great choice for people who love the taste of real butter. By combining butter with healthy oil, these spreads are lower in saturated fat than regular butter. Another advantage is that they stay soft in the refrigerator. I personally love these spreads because they taste much better than margarine and contain fewer additives. These spreads are located near the other butters and margarines at the grocery store.

- A soft or liquid **margarine** without trans fats is another option. Find one by carefully reading the Ingredients list on the package. Look for margarines containing at least some olive or canola oil. If you find the words "hydrogenated," "partially hydrogenated" or "trans fat" on the Ingredients list, choose something else instead.

- Try topping your vegetables with grated or melted **part-skim or 2% cheese**. Lower-fat cheeses are considered In-Betweens and add a nice dose of calcium and protein. Lower-fat cheeses include: most parmesan cheese, 2% cheddar, part-skim mozzarella and any other cheese labeled "2%."

- Some less-healthy fats can be used on vegetables as well if you limit the amount to about a teaspoon per person. To make the limited amounts feel like enough, use **toppings with very strong flavors**. Try crumbled or grated strong cheeses such as blue cheese or feta, or even bacon bits.

Toppings to Limit

- Don't use **butter sauces** because they are full of saturated fats and pour too quickly. Some people use butter-flavored sprays, butter sprinkles or butter flavoring. Or, instead of butter sauce, dab on a small amount of stick butter, healthy margarine or a butter-oil blend; you'll tend to use less total butter this way than you would with a butter sauce.

- Other toppings high in saturated fats are **cheese sauces, cream cheese, sour cream or crumbled bacon**. Replace cheese sauces with a sprinkle of grated strongly flavored cheese or some lower-fat cheese as discussed before. Or you can also find low-fat versions of cream cheese and sour cream that taste very good. Bacon bits in a jar can give you smoky bacon flavor without the fat of regular bacon.

You may decide to remove certain fatty toppings from the table altogether. This is a good idea if your family is in the habit of putting unlimited butter on their corn or uses an entire container of sour cream on their potatoes. By removing the topping and trying something new, you don't have to get into debates over quantities at the table. Experiment with other ideas listed below.

Nonfat Ideas for Great Toppings

When your meal includes plenty of fat in other foods, experiment with these nonfat toppings for your vegetables:

- Nonfat versions of sour cream or salad dressings
- Nonfat gravy
- Bottled barbeque sauce, ketchup or salsa
- Vinegars: Try some unusual types such as raspberry-infused and balsamic
- Fresh grated pepper: Kids love to use a pepper mill
- A sprinkle of plain salt or seasoned salt
- A sprinkle of a favorite spice blend
- Chopped or grated veggies such as carrots, green onions, parsley or peppers

Organic Vegetables

Organic vegetables present the same issues as fruits (see "Should You Buy Organic Fruit?" on page 33 and "A Closer Look at Selecting Organic Foods" on page 34). As with fruits, organic vegetables may be more expensive or harder to find. In any case, it's always best to eat vegetables rather than skipping them even if you can't find an organic choice or the organics cost more than you care to spend.

How to Get There: Actually Eating the Veggies

If getting your family to actually eat the three servings of vegetables is a challenge for you, you're not alone! Many families struggle with this problem. Don't give up! Keep offering the vegetables to your kids in a relaxed way and try some of the following ideas:

The Best Idea Ever for Getting People to Eat Vegetables

Here is the trick you've been looking for to get everyone eating vegetables! Serve vegetables before dinner every night: raw with dip, just plain, steamed or as a salad. Why?

- People will eat a surprising amount of vegetables just before dinner because most of us are hungry that time of day (especially if you've limited snacking).

- By partly filling up on vegetables, your family won't come to the table ravenous. Being less hungry will help them self-regulate portions of the main course and other foods.

- If the kids eat some vegetables before dinner, parents can relax if kids refuse other parts of the meal.

I have found that most kids prefer vegetables and dip as their pre-dinner vegetable. This is a good way to introduce new vegetables. Just put it out next to old favorites, but don't make them eat it. The exposure to the vegetable—and seeing other family members eat it—might eventually lead to your child tasting it.

Instead of vegetables and dip, you could also serve salad or something plain such as a bowl of cherry tomatoes, sliced cucumbers or a handful of raw sugar snap peas. It doesn't have to be fancy.

To take advantage of the mindless snacking urge, try serving everyone this first course while they're busy doing something else just before dinner: reading, chatting with you while you cook, coming home in the car or working on homework. If your kids watch TV before dinner, you're in luck. Children zoning out in front of the television will eat anything you give them. I tested this theory by watching my kids eat raw cauliflower dipped in hummus—something I don't even like!

Use Vegetables as the First Course

If you prefer, the family can enjoy the pre-meal vegetables together at the table before starting the rest of the meal. Although using raw vegetables is often faster, you can also use a cooked vegetable, leftover or canned vegetable soup, or even salsa and baked corn chips as your appetizer (as long as your family will actually eat the salsa—not just the chips!).

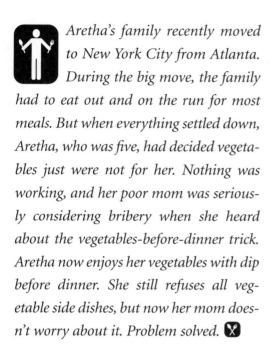

Aretha's family recently moved to New York City from Atlanta. During the big move, the family had to eat out and on the run for most meals. But when everything settled down, Aretha, who was five, had decided vegetables just were not for her. Nothing was working, and her poor mom was seriously considering bribery when she heard about the vegetables-before-dinner trick. Aretha now enjoys her vegetables with dip before dinner. She still refuses all vegetable side dishes, but now her mom doesn't worry about it. Problem solved.

Serving the vegetables when appetites are at their peak is a great way to get your hungry family to try something new. It is also a super delay tactic when dinner isn't ready. Most importantly, it's the best way to make sure that the spaghetti (or whatever your kids love) doesn't upstage the vegetables.

Finally, when you eat veggies together as a "first course," it also encourages one of the most important benefits of family meals—slowing down for good conversation with time to share thoughts about the day.

Getting Creative with Vegetables at Dinner

Another serving of vegetables can be served with dinner's main course. For this serving, you can always serve a traditional plain vegetable on the side. But, since some kids won't eat them that way, especially if they aren't used to them, you may have to become a master at adding vegetables to almost everything you cook. Remember, kids need to learn that they like vegetables. So make them more popular by mixing them into favorites.

There are many ways to add vegetables to your favorite main course dishes. Try adding:

- A few handfuls of finely chopped fresh or (drained) frozen spinach to the pasta sauce
- Grated carrots to the chili
- Corn, tomatoes or green peppers to the quesadillas
- Frozen peas or corn to whole-wheat macaroni and cheese or any other casseroles
- Spinach, tomatoes and cucumbers on sandwiches
- Grated zucchini or chopped onions mixed into lean ground meats for moisture
- Canned tomatoes to soups to stretch them—add frozen or leftover veggies, too
- Double the vegetables called for in recipes for soup, beef stew or burritos
- Extra vegetables (frozen, fresh or canned) to canned soups or stews

Some children might be unhappy when vegetables appear in their favorite meals. Remember, they decide for themselves if they would rather not eat something. Also, allow your children to eat around the vegetables if they want to. They may just need to get used to the idea of vegetables showing up in new places! The constant exposure may lead to sampling eventually.

The worst thing you can do, though, is to make a separate meal for one child, leaving the vegetables out. Doing so teaches that child (and the other children at your table) that refusing foods leads to a new meal along with special attention.

Microwaving Vegetables

This technique will not be featured in any gourmet magazines, but this is how I make vegetables for my family at least three times a week. Place some frozen vegetables, such as peas or corn, in a microwave-safe bowl. Add two or three tablespoons of water and microwave on high just until steaming, but not boiling, for about five minutes. Do not overcook! Drain off the water and enjoy.

Providing Instant Veggies

Whether veggies are packed in the lunch box, taken in the car or served before dinner, very few parents have enough time, energy and organization to create three gourmet vegetable dishes each day! That's why we all need instant veggies on hand at all times. Instant vegetables require nothing but washing—no slicing, dicing, sautéing or steaming. Here is a list of ideas:

- Baby carrots
- Cherry tomatoes
- Sugar snap peas (also called sweet peas)
- Bagged salad mixes (the darker the color, the more vitamins)
- Bagged baby spinach
- Small whole cucumbers
- Still-frozen peas and corn (gross, maybe, but little kids seem to enjoy them)
- Raw green beans

Almost Instant Veggies

Others vegetable ideas that require just a bit of preparation, including a good washing:

- Celery sticks with peanut butter
- Carrot sticks
- Pepper slices
- Cucumber sticks
- Tomato slices
- Jicama slices (if you haven't tried jicama, peel it like a potato and slice it into sticks)
- Radishes
- Raw broccoli with dip
- Raw cauliflower with dip

Serving Healthy Dips

Healthy dips contain very little saturated fat—but may contain healthy oils like olive or canola oil. You can mix up your own dips using nonfat sour cream or plain nonfat yogurt, perhaps mixed with a little canola oil mayonnaise. Other healthy dips might use beans, avocado, peanut butter or even tofu as a base. Check in the recipe section for some dip ideas. But I often just use a favorite salad dressing straight from the bottle.

Provisions: Ideas for Veggies to Serve

Here are some ideas for serving vegetables at lunch, snacks and dinner. Look for the ones with an asterisk (*) in the recipe section.

Lunch

- Pasta and Vegetable Salad*
- Veggie Roll-Ups or Sandwich*
- Salsa
- One Vegetable Salad*
- Mandarin Orange Salad*
- Veggies and Dip*
- Leftovers (salads, soups, stir-fries)
- Any instant vegetable (see previous section)

Before Dinner

- Veggies and dip
- Any raw vegetable
- Vegetable soup (canned or homemade)
- Salsa or mashed avocado with dipping vegetables and baked chips (if everyone will actually eat the dip!)

Vegetables with Dinner

- Veggies from the Freezer*
- Easy Garlic Broccoli*
- Enhanced Canned Soup*
- Salsa Bean Soup*
- Enhanced Spaghetti Sauce*
- Frozen veggies (microwaved or steamed)
- Grilled (or Baked) Sweet Potato Pouches*
- Twice-Baked Potatoes*

- Stir-fried veggies
- Steamed fresh veggies

* *In recipe section*

Vegetable Survival Tips

While exploring ways to add extra vegetables to your family's regular diet, you'll probably encounter a few obstacles. Here are ways to get through several common vegetable challenges:

Feeding the Veggie-Resistant Child

Some children and adults will say they don't like vegetables. But if you sit down and help them come up with a list, there are almost always a few veggies that they like. Try to include one of those favorite vegetables each day.

Although they might protest dramatically, do not stop serving a variety of vegetables to "veggie-resistant" children. Remember, it can take up to 20 exposures before a child is willing to eat a particular food. Although they beg for mercy, I make my poor kids have a disliked vegetable on their plate (usually it is pushed to the extreme edge of the plate) "just to look at"(see the"Just Look at It" rule in Chapter 3, on page 12). I don't make them eat it. The constant exposure combined with low pressure will often entice a child to eat a sample—eventually. Remember, forcing a child to eat vegetables will only turn the veggies into "bad guys." And kids, like adults, have the right to dislike certain vegetables.

Another important technique to use with veggie-resistant children is to feed them vegetables when they are most hungry. If they're starving when they come home from school or after sports practice, make it part of your daily routine to serve vegetables with a dip or celery with peanut butter. Or try giving them a big serving of vegetables as a first course, to eat before the rest of the meal is served.

An Adult Who Dislikes Vegetables

If vegetables disgust the adults at the table, the kids will probably copy that behavior. Ideally, adults will role model eating and enjoying heaping helpings of a variety of vegetables. But what if an adult in your family hates vegetables?

Many people grow up hating vegetables because of what they felt when they were kids, like traumatic experiences with overcooked vegetables: boiled canned green beans, mushy peas and limp broccoli. If you hate certain vegetables, try reducing the cooking time by a few minutes. You could also buy an electric vegetable steamer with a timer and let it cook—but not overcook—the vegetables for you. Vegetable steamers are located near the Crock-Pots and toasters in many big stores.

Jennifer, a busy mother of two young children, is also a college student. After reading this book, she decided her kids were not always getting enough vegetables. They usually skipped them at school and often refused them with dinner. She also knew that the kids were starving when they walked in the door from school. So she decided to make their afternoon snack veggies and dip. The first day she served it, her older child ran to her room crying, slammed the door and refused to eat. Jennifer, very wisely, resisted the urge to offer her daughter something else. The next day she again offered the veggie snack, and this time her daughter ate it while scowling and asking for something else. Jennifer held out. By the third day, her daughter just ate the vegetables without comment. Within a week, her daughter seemed to actually enjoy her after-school veggies—and Jennifer enjoyed the smug satisfaction of a motherhood victory.

Also, consider cooking less well-liked vegetables in a new way. Steaming, stir-frying and sautéing vegetables can sometimes change an old vegetable enemy into a new favorite. Putting veggies on the barbeque grill can also give them an amazing new flavor. Check out the recipes section for specific ideas.

If most people in your family really dislike a certain vegetable, you certainly don't have to serve it. There are so many vegetables available, and so many ways to serve them, that your family is sure to find plenty that they really do like.

If you need more vegetable ideas, check out a cookbook from the library, read cooking magazines, go online for recipes or take a cooking class. Just don't give up on vegetables because you never liked them before!

Eating Potatoes and Other Starchy Vegetables

Recent diet trends have confused people about starches and "carbs." But potatoes are *not* a dangerous species to be avoided in the veggie wilds! In fact, when baked or mashed without a lot of added fat, potatoes are a great (and usually popular) option. And, if the kids will eat the potato skins, they will get a good dose of fiber.

Potatoes are considered a "starchy" vegetable just like sweet potatoes, yams, peas, corn, lima beans and winter squash. Any of these foods can count as either a vegetable or as a whole-grain substitute. Potatoes and corn usually fit into a meal better as a grain substitute. But I find that peas, winter squash and lima beans work well as vegetables. This choice is really up to you.

Missing Vegetables

Serving your vegetables at the same times each day makes getting your three servings much more likely. However, some days are just too complicated for real meals, let alone vegetables. On those (hopefully rare) days, you can eat extra fruit to replace the missed veggies.

Also, if your kids are refusing all vegetables at the moment, do not give up! Be sure to continue to offer the veggies consistently. Meanwhile, be sure they have their fruit three times each day. That will make up for some of the nutrients and fiber they are missing from veggies.

Lunch-Box Vegetables

When you pack vegetables in a lunch box for kids, pack their favorites! They will be more likely to actually eat them.

Also, make sure the veggies you pack are still fresh when your children eat them. Pack dressings and dips in separate containers to avoid making the vegetables soggy, and add ice packs or something frozen (such as a plastic container of frozen skim milk!) to keep the vegetables cool on hot days.

Here are a few vegetables that travel well. You might also pack some healthy dip:

• Baby carrots
• Cucumber slices

>
> **A Closer Look at "Glycemic Index"**
> The "Glycemic Index" (GI), or the newer term "Glycemic Load" (GL), both refer to the idea that we can overwhelm our insulin production organ—the pancreas—by eating too many carbohydrates, especially Empty ones that are high in refined flour and sugar. Both the GI and GL measure how long it takes for carbohydrates in food to break down and enter the bloodstream as "blood sugar."
>
> Recently many popular diets have confused people by misapplying these ideas along with information about insulin and lists of "low GI" foods. The advantage of these lists is that they often eliminate foods with lots of added sweeteners. The disadvantage is that the lists also eliminate certain very healthy foods. The Glycemic Index is simply not an important consideration for healthy people, including children, who eat a balance of Smart foods that include plenty of fruits, vegetables, whole grains and other healthy foods.
>
> However, if someone in your family has diabetes or requires a special diet, follow your healthcare provider's recommendations.

- Green, red, yellow and/or orange pepper slices
- Celery sticks (with or without natural peanut butter)
- Cherry tomatoes
- Bean sprouts
- Sugar snap peas
- Leftover salads
- Quick salad of baby salad greens, with or without other veggies, plus small container of dressing
- Thermos of leftover soup or stew
- Sandwiches with lots of veggies such as lettuce, tomatoes, grated carrots or sliced cucumbers
- Container of salsa with baked corn or tortilla chips

Eating Vegetables in School Lunches

Many school lunch programs are starting to emphasize vegetables. If your children eat school lunches, find out if healthy vegetables are served every day.

Then, try to find out if your child actually eats the vegetables. Some high schools have nice salad bars, but these aren't always a hungry teen's first choice.

If your child isn't getting the vegetables in his school lunch, I recommend that you pack your child's lunch. That way, you can include healthy foods that you know he will—or at least might—eat. If you cannot pack lunches, try to work in an extra serving of vegetables as a snack after school or before bed.

Finding Veggies When Eating Out

If your family eats out often, getting your three servings of vegetables can be a big challenge. The problem is that vegetables in a restaurant are often fried, dripping with mayonnaise, soaking in some fatty sauce or overcooked! The worst so-called "vegetables" are side dishes such as macaroni and cheese or fried cheese sticks. These are absolutely not veggies—these are Empties!

Eating a meal full of Empties once in awhile is fine. However, if you eat out more than once a week, your kids may be missing valuable Smart vegetables that they need for good health. If your family is already in the habit of ordering Empties and won't change, you may be forced to eat at home more often.

But, before giving up on restaurants, try finding a few restaurants that serve real vegetables. Ask about how vegetables are made and what is put on top before you place an order. You can ask for fats, such as cheese or salad dressing, to be served on the side or not put on the food at all.

Some other strategies:

- Order a salad before the main meal. Remember: The darker the lettuce, the more vitamins. Look for actual veggies in the salad because cheese, bacon bits and croutons don't count—except as calories!
- Eat veggies, such as baby carrots, in the car on the way to the restaurant.
- Order a side of Smart vegetables with your dinner, and ask them not to overcook the veggies or add fats. Often, the server can even bring these vegetables out before the rest of the meal.
- Select a dinner item that includes lots of vegetables but is not fatty.
- Plan to eat more veggies at another meal at home.
- Eat fruit for dessert at home after the meal.

Major Points of Interest
What to Keep in Mind about Vegetables

As you practice adding vegetables to your daily routine, remember:

- Offer your family vegetables at least three times a day and at the same times each day to create a vegetable-eating habit. Most people prefer having vegetables for:
  - Lunch
  - Just before dinner or as a first course
  - Dinner

- Choose vegetables without too much added fat. Use the vegetable field test to find low-fat vegetables.

- If you add fats to vegetables, use mostly healthy fats such as olive oil, canola oil, nuts and seeds. Limit saturated fats and avoid partially hydrogenated oils (which contain trans fats).

- Get your children to eat their vegetables by using adult role modeling, feeding them veggies when they're most hungry, serving the vegetables your family enjoys most and adding veggies to favorite dishes.

- Don't turn vegetables into "bad guys" by bribing or forcing your children to eat them. Simply offer them.

- Practice having both vegetables and fruits 3 times a day for about one week. You may notice that your family members are better able to self-regulate other types of foods and that they have less room for eating Empties.

DAILY ITINERARY (after Week 2)	Fruits	Veggies			
Breakfast	✔				
Lunch	✔	✔			
Dinner		✔✔			
Snacks/Desserts	✔				

Pick mostly Smart choices. Try to limit In-Betweens to one per meal or snack.

After completing Week 2, your family will have started a truly healthy new habit—eating more vegetables and fruits!

Navigating Dairy Foods

Yogurt, yogurt tubes, yogurt snack packs, organic yogurt, yogurt drinks, low-carb yogurt, European yogurt, whipped yogurt—the variations on this dairy "species" seem endless, and that's just the yogurt. Dairy foods are important for getting calcium and protein, but they can seem overwhelming to pick out with the tremendous variety available in stores today.

That is why, during Week 3, you'll learn exactly how to identify the Smartest dairy choices from the tangle of fatty, sugary imposters. Once you know what to look for, you can swap out any Empty dairy foods you normally eat for better choices. Also, if you need to, you can add some extra servings of Smart dairy. Your goal, as with fruits and vegetables, is to create the habit of giving your family healthy dairy foods three times each day (or four times for teens).

As always, your kids may sometimes leave these servings untouched. If that happens occasionally, don't worry about it. If they rarely get their dairy, this section has strategies that will help. Of course, if you have a milk allergy in your family, follow your doctor or dietitian's advice on how to replace the missing calcium and protein.

Why Eat and Drink Dairy Foods?

Milk and foods made from milk are great ways to get many things your body needs for good health. Here are some reasons for everyone in your family to have dairy foods every day:

- Dairy foods provide calcium needed to grow strong bones and help prevent osteoporosis and bone fractures. (Getting calcium is important throughout life since 40 percent of adult bone mass is developed during the pre-teen and teen years.)
- Most dairy foods, including milk and yogurt, are fortified with vitamin D that helps the body absorb calcium. Vitamin D can also be absorbed by going outside on sunny days—but remember the sunscreen!
- Vitamin D in dairy products also helps keep blood phosphorus and calcium levels in balance, important in many body functions including blood pressure regulation.
- Nonfat dairy is a healthy, low-calorie way to add protein needed to build muscles, bones, cartilage, skin, blood, enzymes and even hormones.
- Milk can replace other higher-calorie Empty beverages such as sodas, lemonade or sweet tea.

A Daily Itinerary:
Planning When You'll Eat Dairy

For most people, having some milk or other dairy food with breakfast and lunch is fairly easy. I recommend having a third serving for a snack or as dessert. But you might prefer to simply add a glass of milk with supper. Just

DAILY ITINERARY 3 Nonfat Dairy Foods a Day*		
Breakfast	✔	With breakfast (or in coffee for adults).
Lunch	✔	Pack or buy with lunch.
Dinner		Optional, and as occasional replacement for protein foods.
Snacks/Desserts	✔	Nonfat dairy options can replace Empty snacks and desserts.

*NOTE: Teens need four servings of dairy per day. Let your family self-regulate. Some kids may turn down all or part of some servings.

be sure to decide on a routine so that offering dairy foods three times each day will become a habit.

Remember, as you work on getting enough Smart dairy into your diet, keep eating those fruits and vegetables. Also during this week, start having no more than one fruit, vegetable or dairy In-Between for each meal and snack. Of course, you don't have to have In-Betweens—you can always stick with all Smart options!

A Closer Look at How Much Calcium Children Need
The American Academy of Pediatrics recommends the following milligrams of calcium each day:

- For ages three to four: 500 milligrams
- For ages four to eight: 800 milligrams
- For ages nine to 18: 1,300 milligrams

To give you an idea of what that means, each of the following contains about 300 milligrams of calcium: one-and-one-half ounces of cheese, one eight-ounce cup of milk and one eight-ounce cup of yogurt.

Many other Smart foods, including fish, beans and leafy greens, provide additional amounts of calcium. Plus, fruits and vegetables provide vitamins that increase the absorption of calcium into the body.

Most of the calcium your child eats gets stored in the bones (99 percent), while a small amount is used for other things such as blood pressure regulation. About 40 percent of lifetime bone mass is accumulated during adolescence. So a healthy diet that includes adequate calcium throughout childhood establishes the foundation for healthy bones throughout life.

How to Identify Smart Dairy Foods— And Avoid Empty Ones

Granted, identifying Smart and In-Between dairy foods is something of a science—but one you can easily learn. Next time you make a grocery store expedition, you'll be equipped with a new way to navigate confidently through the overgrown yogurt (and milk, ice cream, cheese and pudding) sections of the store.

Spotting Smart Dairy Foods
- **Identifying features:** Nonfat or low-fat (1%); low in added sweetener
- **Best aspects:** Easy to serve; some versions can be used for dessert or treats
- **Number of servings to offer:** Three (four for teens)
- **Varieties:**
  - Nonfat milk
  - Nonfat yogurt
  - Low-fat soft cheeses (cottage cheese, cream cheese)
  - 2% and part-skim hard cheeses (cheddar, Swiss, parmesan)
  - Variations made from one of the above

A Closer Look at Fat in Dairy Products

Whole milk is about 4 percent milk fat by weight. The current recommendation for dairy foods is to choose either nonfat or low-fat (1%) products for adults and children age two or older. That's because the fat in dairy foods is mostly saturated fat, the type of fat linked to heart attacks and strokes later in life. However, children under age two need this type of fat for their development.

While 4 percent doesn't sound too bad, you need to know that 4 percent fat almost doubles the total calories in milk and other dairy foods. This is because fat doesn't weigh much (it's light and fluffy), but it is very high in calories. Drinking all those fat calories in whole (4%) milk and eating them in other fat-based dairy foods (cheese, butter, cream, half-and-half) can make people get too many calories and be too full to eat other healthy foods. Also notice in the milk comparison below that reduced-fat (2%) milk or dairy is healthier than whole milk, but it is still considered a high-fat type of milk.

MILK COMPARISONS

Milk	Other Names	Total Calories for One 8 oz. Cup	Saturated Fat Calories for One 8 oz. Cup
4%	Whole Milk Full-Fat Red-Capped Homogenized	150	72
2%	Reduced-Fat	130	45
1%	Low-Fat Light	120	23
Skim Milk	Fat-Free Nonfat	90	4.5

Scouting Out Smart Dairy Foods

In your search through the many aisles of dairy products at the grocery store, always begin by looking for one of these words on the package: "nonfat," "skim" or "fat free." These terms are used mostly for milk, but you'll also see them on cottage cheese, ice cream, yogurt, cheese, pudding and sour cream. Low-fat (1%) dairy is also considered a Smart choice and may be more appealing for families who really dislike nonfat.

The next identifying characteristic of Smart dairy products to look for is no added sweetener. Many common nonfat or low-fat dairy products, such as yogurts, flavored milks and low-fat ice cream, *do* contain sweeteners. Read the Ingredients list if you aren't sure. Look for sugar, corn syrup or any of the sweetener words listed in "Words used for Added Sweetener" on page 29. Nonfat and low-fat dairy foods that contain some added sweetener, but not too much, are In-Betweens. If a product contains lots of sugar, even if it is nonfat, it is an Empty.

Unfortunately, deciding if a dairy product is In-Between or Empty can be confusing. The grams of sugar listed on the Nutrition Facts label include

---

Field Test for Dairy

1. Find a product labeled "nonfat," "fat-free" or "low-fat." For cheese, skip to step 4.

2. Read the Ingredients list.
   - If there is **no sweetener** listed* on a low-fat dairy food, it is a **Smart dairy.**

3. Compare the total number of grams of sugar** on the Nutrition Facts label to the Percent Daily Value (%DV) for calcium.
   - If the **sugar is LESS than the calcium,** it is an **In-Between dairy.**
   - If the **sugar is MORE than the calcium,** it is an **Empty dairy.**

4. For cheeses, find lower-fat products labeled as "part-skim" or "2%," or with nonfat or 2% milk in the Ingredients list.
   - **Lower-fat cheeses are In-Betweens.**
   - **Regular cheeses are Empty.**

Dairy products often contain an artificial sweetener, such as Splenda or NutraSweet. Many parents choose to avoid feeding their children artificial sweeteners.
**Remember, grams of sugar on Nutrition Facts labels include both the added sweeteners and the naturally occurring "milk sugar" called lactose.*

both the added sugar and the naturally occurring "milk sugar" called lactose. Lactose is a natural, healthy part of all milk products and doesn't "count" as an Empty sugar. This labeling practice is confusing and annoying.

Fortunately, you can use the field test to figure out if a dairy food is Smart, In-Between or an Empty. This simple test ensures that the food you're considering has a significant amount of calcium in it. In some cases, a food will pass the test only because it is calcium fortified, but that food is still an In-Between choice. Also, remember that this test is only a guideline! If your family's favorite dairy food is within a gram or two of qualifying as an In-Between, go ahead and count that food as an In-Between choice.

Cheese

Cheeses deserve a special mention. Cheese is packed with protein and calcium. And, for many people, cheese is a favorite way to consume dairy. Unfortunately, cheese gets about half its calories from saturated fat, plus another quarter of its calories from other types of fat. In fact, it contains so much fat that regular cheese is an Empty.

But don't go feed yourself to the wolves over the thought of giving up cheese! There is a solution: Try 2% or part-skim cheeses, such as part-skim mozzarella, 2% American, 2% Colby, 2% cheddar and most parmesan cheese (even when it is not labeled part-skim). Lower-fat cheese contains between 1/3 and 1/2 less saturated fat compared to regular cheese and has fewer total calories. Although most lower-fat cheeses still get just over half their calories from fat, they are a great way to get protein and calcium. So all low-fat cheeses are In-Betweens.

And, of course, regular cheese can be enjoyed as a treat or added to Smart foods in limited amounts (about one ounce or a one-fourth cup grated per person) to make the combination an In-Between.

Using the Field Test for Dairy

If they are unsweetened, all nonfat and low-fat dairy products are Smart. However, many dairy products do contain sweeteners that make them either In-Between or Empty. Here is how to use the field test for dairy to decide if this nonfat vanilla yogurt is an Empty or an In-Between:

Nutrition Facts
Serving Size: 1 cup (227g)
Servings Per Container: about 4

Amount Per Serving	
Calories 190 Calories from Fat 10	
	% Daily Value
Total Fat 2g	**4%**
Saturated Fat 1g	**8%**
Trans Fat 0g	**0%**
Cholesterol 15mg	**5%**
Sodium 150mg	**6%**
Potassium 500mg	**14%**
Total Carbohydrate 31g	**10%**
Dietary Fiber 0g	**0%**
Sugars 28g	
Protein 11g	**21%**

Vitamin A 0%	•	Vitamin C 0%
Calcium 35%	•	Iron 0%

Percent Daily Value are based on a 2,000 calories diet. Your daily values may be higher or lower depending on your calorie needs:

		Calories:	2,000	2,500
Total Fat		Less than	65g	80g
Sat Fat		Less than	20g	25g
Cholesterol		Less than	300mg	300mg
Sodium		Less than	2,400mg	2,400mg
Potassium			3,500mg	3,500mg
Total Carbohydrate			300g	375g
Dietary Fiber			25g	30g

INGREDIENTS: Cultured pasteurized lowfat milk, crystalline fructose, natural vanilla, pectin, natural flavor, active cultures (L. Bulgaricus, S. Thermophilus, L. Acidophilus, L. Bifidus, L. Case)

1. The front of the carton says "nonfat yogurt."

2. Read the Ingredients list. It says "crystalline fructose," a sugar word. So this is not a Smart dairy. It is either Empty or In-Between.

3. Look at the Nutrition Facts label. Notice that the "% Daily Value" for calcium (35%) is a higher number than the grams of sugar (28g). The calcium is higher than the sugar, so this yogurt is an In-Between.

Since this yogurt is an In-Between, it is a great choice for a flavored yogurt. Other brands contain so much sugar or corn syrup that they are Empties. Some brands even contain Splenda, so read the ingredient list if you want to avoid feeding your kids artificial sweeteners (see A Closer Look at Artificial Sweeteners on page 31). (For more examples showing how to use the field test for dairy food, go to the Appendix.)

Empty Dairy Foods for Special Treats

Many foods, such as ice cream or pudding, are Empties because well over half their calories come from sugar. However, the low-fat versions of any of these foods are great as treats because, unlike soda or candy, they do contain *some* nutrition from their milk content. Likewise, cheese makes a great treat since it contains protein and calcium along with the saturated fats, unlike butter or sour cream.

Buying Organic Dairy Products

Organic dairy products, like organic fruits and vegetables, do not contain more minerals or nutrients. And, as with any food, the fact that it is organic

DAIRY IDENTIFICATION CHART

The chart below shows which dairy foods are usually Smart, In-Between or Empty. However, the amount of sugar and fat vary by brand, so always read the label and use the field test.

SMART	**Nonfat milk,** also called skim or fat-free milk **1% milk,** also called low-fat **Nonfat plain yogurt** **Nonfat plain cottage cheese** **Evaporated nonfat milk** **Nonfat buttermilk** **Nonfat sour cream**
IN-BETWEEN	**Whole** and **2% milk** **2% or part-skim cheese,** including most parmesan cheese. Comes in many flavors, including cheddar, American and mozzarella. Look for grated, plain, string cheese or cubes. **Homemade low-fat pudding** made with less sugar. Very few commercial brands pass the field test. **Nonfat flavored yogurts and cottage cheese** that pass the field test. **Hot chocolate and chocolate milk** depending on the brand. Use the field test. **Macaroni and cheese** only when it is made with 2% cheese and nonfat or low-fat milk.
EMPTY	**Butter** **Cream** **Cream cheese** (Low-fat cream cheese is widely available.) **Half-and-half** **Regular sour cream** (Nonfat sour cream or a healthy oil is a better choice.) **Regular full-fat cheese** **Macaroni and cheese** when made with regular full-fat cheese, including most boxed mixes and restaurant versions. **Ice cream popsicles and sandwiches** often contain partially hydrogenated vegetable oil. Plus, they are generally very high in sugar and fat. **Ice cream** is usually high in sugar. Low-fat ice cream makes a better empty treat than regular or premium ice cream. **Frozen yogurt** is usually very high in sugar and is sometimes high in fat. **Squeezable or kids' yogurts** usually contain more sugar than "adult" yogurts. Use the field test to check. **Pudding** (packaged or instant)

does not make the item healthy. Some organic dairy products are Empties and In-Betweens because they contain lots of sugar or fat.

However, organic meat, poultry, eggs and dairy products do come from animals that are not given antibiotics or growth hormones and are fed only pesticide-free foods. That is a good thing, since there are some concerns about the effect on human health from hormones and pesticides. And overuse of antibiotics is being blamed for causing some strains of harmful bacteria to become resistant to antibiotics.

However, organic dairy foods, meats, poultry and eggs may be more expensive. Also, in some areas, Smart low-fat organic options are simply not available. If you have to make a choice, choose Smart foods over Empty organic foods.

How to Get There:
Drinking (or Eating) Enough Smart Dairy

Three servings a day can seem like a lot of milk. Try these ideas to make sure your family gets and enjoys plenty of dairy:

Never Run Out

Try not to run out of milk—much easier said than done, of course. Pick containers of milk with the latest expiration date and buy plenty. If you end up with milk that's about to expire, you can always make pudding or milkshakes to use it up quickly.

Also, keep some nonfat dry milk or evaporated skim milk on hand for when you do run out of milk. Even if your family doesn't drink reconstituted milk (mine won't!), you can add dry or evaporated milk to pancakes, oatmeal, casseroles or soups. Have nonfat yogurt, cottage cheese or cheese on hand, too. These can be used instead of milk when you run out or just need some variety.

The Easiest Source—A Simple Glass of Nonfat Milk

Getting in the habit of offering everyone a glass of milk at meals and snacks is an easy way for most families to fit in daily servings of healthy dairy.

The Next Easiest Source—Sneak Extra Dairy into Foods

If your family doesn't like to drink milk, apply your survival instincts and add the milk to other foods. Here are a few of my favorite ideas:

- Add an extra serving of milk to hot chocolate, pudding and smoothies (see the recipe section) by stirring in a few spoonfuls of nonfat dry milk. The extra milk will also add creaminess to low-fat foods.
- Use evaporated skim milk instead of cream in sauces, soups and casseroles.
- Place nonfat cottage cheese in a food processor or blender to remove lumps, then use it to replace about half the regular cheese in lasagna, tuna noodle casserole and macaroni and cheese.

Calcium in Non-dairy Foods

If you are concerned that your family is not always eating enough dairy food, you can supplement their calcium intake with other foods. One great source of calcium is canned salmon with the small bones crushed. Other high-calcium foods include greens, beans, tofu and almonds.

A Closer Look at Using Calcium-Fortified Foods

Many foods, including breakfast cereals, soy foods, rice milk and juices, may be fortified with calcium. Studies show that these foods work well as a calcium source as long as they also provide vitamin D. Be certain to read the package carefully, especially if you are relying on these products as a primary calcium source for your family.

However, remember that juices *do not supply protein*. In addition, many calcium-fortified foods are In-Betweens or Empties. If you are relying entirely on calcium-fortified foods for your child's calcium intake, you should talk with your healthcare provider. A diet review can help identify how much usable calcium your child is getting, if your child might be getting too much (an upper limit for children and adults is currently 2,500 mg. per day) or if a supplement is needed.

In-Betweens—Sweet Treats That Add Dairy

Sweetened dairy foods make the perfect treat after school or for dessert as In-Betweens. My kids really love the Banana Milkshakes, Almost Instant Pudding, Healthier Hot Chocolate, Super Smoothie and Sorbet described in the recipe section of this book. You can also serve flavored nonfat yogurt or nonfat chocolate milk as quick In-Between options.

Take Dairy Food with You

Freeze smoothies in small plastic lidded drink containers available at grocery and other stores. Or pack nonfat milk using the same containers with Milk Cubes (see recipe on page 202). Kids never seem to mind if these drinks are still slushy when they drink them. These cold drinks have the added benefit of helping to keep the other packed food cold, too. You'll have to pack a straw, of course. Some other great traveling dairy ideas:

• String cheese (pick low-fat or part-skim versions)
• Flavored nonfat yogurt with a spoon or fruit slices for dipping

For the Adults: Nonfat Dairy in Coffee or Tea

Adults may be able to get the dairy they need by adding plenty of nonfat milk to their coffee or tea. Coffee shop fans can get dairy by ordering nonfat lattes or cappuccinos.

Of course, half-and-half is *so* good! The problem is that it's high in saturated fat. If you want it, limit yourself to about one tablespoon a day. But beware: Even that amount adds up to about two pounds of weight gain in one year—or 10 extra minutes in the gym three times a week. If you don't want those extra calories, try nonfat half-and-half or just use nonfat milk.

Adults should also be aware of fancy coffee and tea drinks because they often contain lots of sugar and high-fat dairy. Order your lattes or cappuccinos "skinny" (made with nonfat milk) and forget the sweetener-packed "flavors" most days. Also, you should definitely avoid specialty coffees from machines because they usually contain a big dose of unhealthy trans fat and tons of sugar.

Provisions:
Ideas for Dairy to Serve

Here are some quick ideas for offering three servings of dairy each day. The ideas with an asterisk* are in the recipe section of this book.

Breakfast Ideas

- Glass of nonfat milk
- Super Smoothie*
- Healthier Hot Chocolate Mix*
- Hot Flavored Milk*
- Fruit and Oats*
- Warm Fruit Sundae*
- Tropical Yogurt*
- Coffee shop "skinny" latte or cappuccino (adults)
- Cold cereal with milk

Lunch/Supper

- Glass of nonfat milk
- Flavored milk
- Flavored nonfat yogurt
- Nonfat cottage cheese
- Low-fat string cheese
- 2% cheese quesadilla
- Pack-n-Go Berry Dessert*
- Milk packed with Milk Cubes*

Dessert/Snacks

- Glass of nonfat milk
- Sorbet*
- Almost Instant Pudding (Chocolate, Vanilla)*
- Banana Milkshakes (Chocolate, Peanut Butter)*

- Fruit slices dipped in nonfat yogurt
- Flavored nonfat yogurt, cartons or tubes
- Fruity Yogurt*

* In recipe section

Dairy Survival Tips

As easy as dairy products are to track down in the wilds of your grocery store, they often present obstacles for families. A few survival tips might help you elude some of these common dairy challenges.

My seven-year-old has recently decided he hates drinking milk. I have tried switching brands, using 1% instead of skim and serving it in what I thought were cool new cups. Nothing has worked. I assume that soon he will start drinking it again, but in the meantime I am only serving plain milk to the family once a day. I give him a little, even knowing it will be wasted. For the other dairy servings, we are having nonfat yogurt, pudding, smoothies, 2% cheese, hot chocolate and sometimes milk cunningly added to oatmeal or soups. He is ending up with a decent amount of calcium from these dairy foods and from other Smart foods he eats, so I don't bug him about the milk. This way, I have plenty of energy to bug him about brushing his teeth, combing his hair, picking up his toys and not tracking mud into the house!

Your Family Doesn't Like Plain Milk

If your family isn't excited about drinking milk, look for ways to make it more appealing. For example, try the Smart recipes for banana milkshakes and warm vanilla milk in the recipe section. You might also experiment with different brands of milk. The food the cows eat actually influences the taste of the milk, so some brands appeal more than others to sensitive palates.

You can also create "double" milk servings by adding nonfat dry milk to recipes calling for milk. Try some of the recipes in this book, including double milk pudding or healthy hot chocolate, or make up your own creations. You might sometimes substitute other dairy products, such as nonfat yogurt and cheese, to still get the calcium. (Some will be In-Betweens.)

Your Family Prefers Whole Milk

If your family drinks whole milk right now, they are getting too much saturated fat. It's time to make the change, but most families like to do it slowly.

When Dad had a heart attack, the Posey family had to make changes in their diet. They were all used to eating whatever they wanted. The kids—David, age 10, and Anna, age 14, especially disliked the idea of changing to nonfat milk because they said it tasted "like water." The refrigerator soon contained a variety of milk types: whole milk for the kids, 2% for Dad and nonfat for Mom. One day Mom got tired of buying and throwing out all that milk, so she mixed 2% and nonfat together and announced that everyone had to start drinking the same milk. Within two months, the whole family was drinking nonfat milk, and the protests had stopped. Later that year, David accidentally picked whole milk for lunch at school and actually couldn't drink it. He announced to his family that it had tasted "slimy" and "gross." 🅧

Start by switching from whole to 2% milk. You can even mix them together for awhile to make your own 3% version. Give everyone a chance to adjust to the lower fat levels, then start buying 1%. If you stop there, you have done a great thing for the health of your family! But, if you can, go all the way to nonfat. Just make the changes gradually.

If your family gripes, explain the need for lower-fat milk. If the long-term danger of heart disease doesn't convince your family to change their milk choices, remember that just switching from three eight-ounce glasses of whole milk to skim milk can save adults in the family from gaining 19 pounds in one year! It can help children avoid unnecessary weight gain, too.

Your Family Loves Regular High-Fat Cheese

Actually, my own family really loves regular high-fat cheese! And they have made it very clear that they don't like many of the reduced-fat versions.

The problem is that just a one-inch cube of cheese (picture four dice) contains about 28 percent of the saturated fat needed in a day and over 100 calories. And to most of us, eating that amount of cheese feels like almost nothing!

Usually, I serve "real" cheese with Smart whole grains or beans and make it our In-Between for that meal or snack. I just don't serve other foods high in saturated fats on the days we have cheese.

I do sometimes sneak in some low-fat cheese when it's mixed in with other foods. For example, the difference isn't noticeable when using low-fat cheddar in burritos or part-skim mozzarella on pizza. Also, the kids seem to like any cheese in the form of a stick, even part-skim.

You're Worried That Your Child Is Too Skinny

Many people think that thin kids, very active kids or rapidly growing teens should eat high-fat dairy. First, before you get too worried that your child is underweight, talk to his doctor. There are many different body types, and some kids are healthy even when they look a bit thin. In any case, unless your doctor has a good medical reason for feeding him saturated fat, a skinny kid doesn't need high-fat dairy any more than the rest of us do.

If you want your thin child to gain some weight, you can increase his calories by offering him healthier higher-calorie alternatives with his regular

A Closer Look at Dairy Allergies and Lactose Intolerance

If you think a family member has problems eating or drinking dairy products, talk with your healthcare provider. A dairy allergy is a reaction to the proteins in milk and milk products that often shows up in infancy but may later go away. Lactose intolerance (pain, bloating or discomfort when eating dairy) is caused by lack of an enzyme that helps break down the natural sugars in milk. Both problems should be properly diagnosed and treated so that the child or adult can still get enough calcium and protein.

Since many foods are made with a dairy product combined with other ingredients, it is important to find out why someone is not tolerating dairy. Many "milk problems" turn out to be sensitivity to another food or a chemical used in food production. If someone in your family cannot eat diary, get help in discovering the reason. A great source for more information is www.kidshealth.org.

food: extra whole grains, extra starchy vegetables such as corn or healthy fats such as peanut butter, walnuts, avocados and dips made with olive or canola oil. Remember, though, that forcing food on a thin kid usually doesn't cause him to eat particularly well. He will almost always eat a healthier amount if you just offer the food.

Your Child Isn't Getting Low-Fat Milk at School

Many new laws require that nonfat milk and water be served in schools. Yet with all the health problems associated with high-fat foods and sugary drinks, it is amazing that some schools still sell kids high-fat milk, sugary chocolate and "strawberry" milk, soda and my personal pet peeve—those so-called "fruit drinks."

Children should be offered only nonfat milk and water with their lunch! If they have juice with lunch (and it should be 100% juice), that's their one In-Between for that meal. If your kids choose their own beverages at school, they're more apt to pick the healthier milk if they are used to getting it at home. However, your child will be fine with one glass of whole milk or flavored milk a day—just count it as the In-Between choice for that meal or snack.

But, if your child eats many of her meals in a childcare setting or at school, check to make sure that nonfat or low-fat milk and other nonfat or low-fat dairy foods are served. If you aren't happy with the school's milk policy, request that they change it. If they don't want to make a change, see if they will let you provide your own milk for your child. Also, consider sending a letter or talking with the principal if nonfat or low-fat milk is not available with lunch.

Finding Dairy in a Restaurant

Most restaurants offer milk, and many of them now have nonfat or low-fat milk. Even whole milk is a better choice than a soda. Ask if milk can be substituted for the drink in the kids' meal. If not, just order water.

Beware of restaurant foods that feature cheese or cream, such as macaroni and cheese. These foods usually contain way too much fat. Combined with white pasta and no veggies, this type of meal is just plain Empty! Read "Week 6: Escaping from Empties" for some ideas on getting around this problem.

Finding Milk as You Travel

If you're traveling, you can often pick up milk in grocery stores, gas stations and some quick stops. On road trips, I often buy low-fat chocolate milk at gas stations. Served with some fruit from home, it is a much healthier treat than candy or chips. You can also ask for milk instead of a soda or juice on airplanes and at most places where you eat.

Major Points of Interest
What to Keep in Mind about Dairy Foods

As you practice adding nonfat dairy to your daily routine, remember:

- Keep eating those fruits and vegetables!
- Offer your family nonfat or low-fat (1%) dairy at least three times a day. Be sure to serve it at the same times each day to create an eating routine. Most people prefer having dairy for:
  - Breakfast
  - Lunch
  - Snack or dessert
- Choose dairy without saturated fat: nonfat or skim has the least. 1% dairy has more fat but is still considered low fat.
- Choose Smart dairies without added sugar or other sweeteners.
- Look for In-Betweens that have a higher Percent Daily Value (% DV) of calcium than grams of sugar. But aim for having only one In-Between choice at each meal or snack.
- The easiest way to offer your children dairy is a glass of nonfat milk.

DAILY ITINERARY (after Week 3)	Fruits	Veggies	Dairy Foods		
Breakfast	✔		✔		
Lunch	✔	✔	✔		
Dinner		✔✔			
Snacks/Desserts	✔		✔		

Pick mostly Smart choices. Try to limit In-Betweens to one per meal or snack.

Tracking Down Whole Grains

Grains are a huge part of diets the world over, and many of the world's most delicious foods are made from grains: breads, pastas, tortillas, muffins, cereals—even beer. In recent years, these "carbs" have been widely blamed for obesity. However, the problems associated with grains come from either the excessive use of refined grains or from all the sweetener and fats added to them. Whole grains prepared alone or with other Smart foods, on the other hand, are extremely healthy. Even enriched refined grains are good In-Betweens, if they aren't full of sugar and fat.

Fortunately, there are plenty of whole grains at almost all grocery stores. But unfortunately, these whole grains are hidden among imposters with healthy-sounding claims on the labels. To complicate the search, even whole-grain foods are sometimes packed with added sweeteners, fats or both. Tracking down Smart whole grains takes savvy, patience and a few easy-to-learn identification techniques.

Of course, even after you locate real whole grains, the challenge isn't over. A big part of this step is likely to be experimenting with brands and types of whole grain until you discover some that your family really enjoys eating.

Even If You Already Eat Whole-Wheat Bread, This Section Is Important for You

Important guideposts abound in this section, so please don't assume you're already doing this step without reading through it. Your family needs whole grains in other foods besides just bread, including pasta, cereal, rice and crackers. Plus, many bread packages use sneaky words such as "multigrain," "wheat," "contains whole grains" and "made with whole grains" to mislead consumers into thinking they're buying whole grain when they aren't.

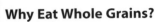

Why Eat Whole Grains?

Whole grains can benefit everyone in your family, from those wanting to control their weight to athletes. There are several reasons to eat whole grains every day:

- Research has linked whole grains to reduced risk for cancer, heart attack, stroke, obesity and diabetes.
- Whole grains are an excellent source of fiber that helps you feel full without overeating.
- They supply B vitamins, iron, calcium, magnesium, chromium and other nutrients.
- Whole grains contain 10 times the vitamin E found in refined grains.
- They provide more than twice the protein, potassium, zinc, copper and selenium found in "enriched" wheat flour.

A Daily Itinerary: Planning When You'll Eat Whole Grains

Most people already have some form of grain for breakfast, lunch and dinner. If you're used to eating grains at these meals, you can just switch any of your current refined choices for Smart whole-grain alternatives that don't contain too much fat or sugar. Or you might prefer swapping some of your old refined-grain choices for totally different foods—ones that are whole-grain, of course.

During this week, you'll work on making sure your family has healthy grains at least three times every day. At first, this sounds very different from the "official" six to 12 servings of grain foods listed in many other places. But, these sources are using very tiny serving sizes: one-third of a muffin or a half cup of pasta, for example. Surely only about 12 people in the United States actually eat those serving sizes! Likewise, I don't know a single parent willing to serve their kids six to 12 different grain foods a day. So I find it much easier to think of "servings" as the number of times you actually offer the food to your family. Exact portions of whole grains—and of all Smart foods—can be left to each person's own self-regulation.

For most families, whole grains fit most naturally into their eating plan at breakfast, lunch and dinner. You could, of course, have whole grains as a snack, as well. If your family still wants to eat some refined grains, those work well as In-Betweens. As always, though, find a pattern that works for your family and stick with it.

Of course, don't stop eating your fruits, vegetables and dairy, too. And remember to pick just one In-Between food for each meal or snack.

DAILY ITINERARY 3 Whole Grains a Day		
Breakfast	✔	Use whole-grain breakfast options.
Lunch	✔	Pack whole grains in lunch boxes; order when available in cafeterias and restaurants.
Dinner	✔	Have as part of the main dish or serve as a side dish.
Snacks/Desserts		Optional for snacks or in desserts.
Let your family self-regulate. Some kids may turn down all or part of some servings.		

How to Identify Smart Whole-Grain Foods–And Avoid Empty Ones

Before beginning your search for whole grains, let's look at how to identify them.

Spotting Smart Whole-Grain Foods
- **Identifying features:** Contain at least one-half whole grains; do not contain excess sugar or fat, or any trans fat
- **Best aspects:** People love grain foods
- **Number of servings to offer:** Three or more
- **Varieties:**
    - Whole-grain baked goods (such as bread, buns, bagels, English muffins and pitas)
    - Whole-grain pasta
    - Whole-grain breakfast cereals and oatmeal
    - Popcorn and baked chips
    - Brown rice
    - Starchy vegetables (potatoes, corn)
    - And many more!

The Definition of "Whole Grain"

A whole grain is the seed of a plant. A whole grain contains all the parts of this seed: the bran, the germ and the endosperm. Together, they provide a perfect balance of carbohydrate, protein, a little healthy fat, vitamins and minerals. In fact, scientists are still discovering new beneficial elements in whole grains.

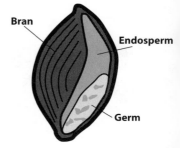

"Refined" grains have had the bran and germ taken out. Removing those two parts from the grain removes most of the fiber, protein and nutrients. Sometimes manufacturers try to compensate for this removal by mixing vitamins back in to create "enriched" or "fortified" foods. The problem is that they do not add in all the protein, fiber or other nutrients they removed, resulting in a grain that is much less healthy to eat. However, these refined grains can still be part of a healthy diet when used as your one In-Between for a meal or snack.

Don't Get Tricked by Labels

Most foods that make claims such as "wheat bread," "multi-grain," "contains whole grains," "seven grain" or "made with whole grains" are *not* really whole-grain foods at all. In fact, they may or may not contain any whole grains. "Wheat" usually means *refined* wheat flour—not whole-grain wheat. In most cases, breads, rolls, muffins, rice (unless it is brown rice), corn products, bagels and even things labeled "spelt" (just a type of flour) are not whole-grain foods. If a product doesn't actually say on its label that it is 100% whole grain, you will have to look more carefully before jumping to that conclusion.

Sugars and Fats

Many grain foods, particularly those marketed to children, have excessive amounts of sweetener, fat or both. Too much sugar or fat turns a Smart whole-grain food into an In-Between or even an Empty. Likewise, an enriched refined-grain food will go from In-Between to Empty if it is full of sugar or fat.

Finding Smart Whole Grains

The search for whole grains may not be as hard as it seems once you have an easy field test. What you are looking for is a grain that contains lots of whole grain, but not lots of fat or sugar. Fortunately, whole grains always contain fiber, so the amount of fiber in a grain product is a very helpful clue as to how much whole grain it contains.

Healthy and good-tasting grain foods are out there, but tracking them down the first time or two can take some searching. Give yourself 10 extra minutes at the grocery store each time you plan to find a new type of Smart grain food (bread, pasta, cereal, etc.).

Field Test for Whole Grains

1. Find a package that reads: "whole grain wheat" on the front of the package OR one that lists a whole grain first on the Ingredients list. If neither is true, skip to step 3.

2. Look at the Nutrition Facts label. Compare the number of grams of fiber to the number of grams of sugar and fat.
   • If a whole-grain food has **MORE fiber than sugar and fat,** it is a **Smart grain.**

3. If the Ingredients list starts with a refined grain, or if it is whole grain with too much sugar or fat to be Smart (from step 2), double the grams of fiber and compare that number to the grams of sugar and fat.
   • If **the sugar or fat is LESS than double the fiber,** it is an **In-Between grain.**
   • If **the sugar or fat is MORE than double the fiber,** the food is an **Empty.**

Using the Field Test for Whole Grains

Tracking down healthy whole grains is easier with the field test. And one of the best places to use the field test is on the cereal aisle. The following example shows how to analyze a box of cold, frosted cereal by using the field test:

1. The front of this package only says "Whole Grain" (not 100% whole grain) but the Ingredients list has "whole grain wheat" listed first.

2. Look at the Nutrition Facts label. Notice that the number of grams of fiber (6) is lower than the grams of sugar (12), though it is higher than the grams of fat (1). Since there is more sugar than fiber, this cold cereal is not a Smart grain.

3. Double the fiber: 6+6=12. Compare double fiber (12) to sugar (12). Since they are the same, this cereal squeaks under the wire as an In-Between.

Nutrition Facts

Serving Size: about 24 biscuits (52g)
Servings Per Container: about 9

Amount Per Serving **Cereal**

Calories 200   Calories from Fat 10

	% Daily Value
Total Fat 1g	2%
Saturated Fat 0g	0%
Trans Fat 0g	0%
Polyunsaturated Fat 0g	0%
Monounsaturated Fat 0g	0%
Cholesterol 0mg	0%
Sodium 5mg	0%
Potassium 200mg	6%
Total Carbohydrate 48g	16%
Dietary Fiber 6g	24%
Sugars 12g	
Other Carbohydrates 30g	
Protein 6g	

Vitamin A 0%	•	Vitamin C 0%
Calcium 0%	•	Iron 90%
Thiamin 25%	•	Riboflavin 25%
Niacin 25%	•	Vitamin B6 25%
Folic Acid 25%	•	Vitamin B12 25%
Phosphorus 15%	•	Magnesium 15%
Zinc 10%	•	Copper 10%

INGREDIENTS: Whole grain wheat, sugar, high fructose corn syrup, gelatin

The conclusion? Though many kids' cereals are Empties, this one is an In-Between because it contains a lot less sugar than other brands. And did I mention that it is frosted? (For more examples showing how to use the field test to find healthy whole grains, go to the appendix.)

Store-Baked or Restaurant-Baked Grain Foods without Nutrition Facts Labels

Unfortunately, current laws do not mandate that food baked on-site in grocery stores, bakeries or restaurants have standard nutrition labels. That's why these items may have no label or just have a list of ingredients. Many of these foods appear to be whole grain but are only dyed brown or have some added sawdust (cellulose for fiber). As mentioned previously, packages containing refined-grain bakery products often have misleading claims such as "wheat bread" or "seven-grain bread."

You can talk with the baker or ask for a list of ingredients, but expect to be told they don't have one, especially in restaurants. When in doubt, assume that most sweet-tasting bakery foods, such as muffins and cookies, are Empties. On the other hand, most breads and bagels are In-Betweens.

Home-Baked Grain Foods

If you bake at home, you can easily make Smart or In-Between foods by finding a great recipe or modifying an old one to make it healthier. (If you bake often, you might write the following guidelines on an index card and tape the card to the inside of the cupboard where you keep your baking stuff.)

To bake Smart grain foods use:

- At least half whole-grain flour—of course, more is better.
- Up to 1/8 cup (2 tablespoons) sugar, honey or other sweetener for each cup of flour or other grain.
- Up to 1/8 cup (2 tablespoons) fat for each cup of flour or other grain.

GRAIN IDENTIFICATION CHART

Because there are literally thousands of grain products and recipes, the examples of foods given on this chart are not absolutes! Some chips are Smart, while some muffins are definitely Empties. The only way to know is to use the field test to look at the Nutrition Facts label and Ingredients list.

SMART	**Whole-grain bread products,** including bread, pita bread, English muffins, rolls, buns (hot dog and hamburger), muffins and quick breads. **Whole-grain crackers** that pass the field test. Look for reduced-fat or "baked" versions. **Whole-grain cold breakfast cereals** that pass the field test. Most Smart breakfast cereals are not sweetened. **Whole-wheat pasta** **Whole-grain pancakes and waffles** that are either homemade or pass the field test. **Whole-grain cooked cereals** such as oatmeal, Cream of Wheat. **Popcorn** that does not contain partially hydrogenated vegetable oil and passes the grain field test. **Brown rice** of any variety, including instant. Wild rice is also a whole grain. **Brown rice cakes, corn cakes and popcorn cakes** that do not contain too much sweetener. **Foods made with stone-ground cornmeal,** including baked corn chips, corn tortillas, muffins and breads made with whole cornmeal. **Grains cooked whole,** including quinoa, bulgur wheat, millet, amaranth and barley. **Starchy vegetables** make great whole-grain substitutes. Choices include steamed corn, baked or mashed potatoes and sweet potatoes.
IN-BETWEEN	**Whole-grain cold breakfast cereals and packaged instant oatmeal** if they qualify using the grain field test. **Some granola bars** **Pizza** unless it is loaded with Empty toppings such as pepperoni, sausage or extra cheese. **Most breads, rolls, buns, bagels, muffins, biscuits and other baked goods** that do not have a whole grain as the first ingredient. **Baked potato chips, baked corn chips, crackers and pretzels** unless they contain partially hydrogenated vegetable oil. **Enriched white rice** **Enriched white pasta**

GRAIN IDENTIFICATION CHART (CONTINUED)

EMPTY

Most cold breakfast cereals and granola, including the vast majority of "kid's" cereals.

Cereal bars, energy bars, nutrition bars, granola bars and other "bars" unless they pass the field test as In-Betweens.

French fries

Potato chips, corn chips, cheese puffs, nachos and similar snack items

Cookies, cakes, pastries, pies and other desserts

Macaroni and cheese unless it is made with whole-grain pasta and low-fat cheese.

To bake In-Betweens use:

- All refined flours if you prefer. But try adding whole-grain flour.
- Up to 1/4 cup sugar per cup of flour or other grain.
- Up to 1/4 cup fat per cup of flour or other grain.

In general, replacing white flour with "white whole-wheat" flour tastes best to me—and is less noticeable to my kids. (See www.feedingthekids.com for specific brand names.) This type of whole-grain flour has all the benefits of whole grain but has a milder taste, a lighter color and a good texture. It is made from a naturally occurring strain of wheat that has less of the tannins and phenolic acid that give most whole-wheat flours their distinctive flavor and brownish color.

Healthy Toppings and Spreads for Grain Foods

When you are making the switch to whole grains, I suggest you do not take favorite toppings away at the same time! See "Empty Toppings on Whole Grains," page 108.

On the other hand, grains, like vegetables, are a great place to *add in* some healthy fats to your family's diet. But add the extra fats to the food at the table. Don't mix or cook them in since they will be less noticeable that way. Then, let individuals choose the amount of fat to add so that your family will learn to self-regulate quantity.

When you add healthy fats to a Smart food, the food remains Smart. Here are some examples of Smart fats:

- Nuts and seeds, such as almonds, walnuts, sunflower seeds
- Nut butters, such as peanut butter, almond butter, cashew butter, tahini
- Olive oil
- Sesame oil
- Hummus or other bean dips
- Avocados or guacamole made without sour cream
- Mayonnaise, especially canola oil mayonnaise
- 2% or part-skim cheese, including parmesan

Other fatty toppings contain more saturated fats or sugar. These toppings are Empties on their own but can be combined with a Smart food to make an In-Between choice for that meal or snack.

- Butter or, a better choice, butter-oil blend
- Cheese
- Cream cheese
- Jelly
- Honey
- Maple syrup

Some other Smart toppings don't add healthy fat, but they do add great taste and, in some cases, extra nutrition. However, try to find brands with the lowest amounts of sodium:

- Mustard
- Ketchup
- Salsa
- Spaghetti sauce
- Unsweetened fruit, applesauce or fruit butters

How to Get There: Eating More Whole Grains

If you look hard enough, you'll find that almost every grain-based food you love has a whole-grain equivalent. In some cases, though, you might have to do some taste tests to find a brand or recipe that you really love. Your family probably doesn't love every refined-grained product available either! So don't give up on whole grains if you try one or two that your family rejects—keep trying.

Whole-Grain Breads

Whole-grain bread is a great way to give your family a big dose of healthy nutrition—if you find (or make) Smart bread.

Of course, the typical store carries a dizzying array of breads and rolls disguised as whole grains. They might be labeled as:

- Enriched: white flour with some vitamins mixed in
- Wheat: simply flour, almost always white flour, from the wheat plant
- Unbleached: white flour that wasn't bleached (most flour is bleached, which is one more step in the refining process)
- Spelt: refined wheat flour from the spelt plant (unless it is whole spelt)
- Multi-grain: a mix of several types of flour, usually refined flours
- Organic: no pesticides or herbicides were used to grow the plants, but usually the flour is still refined

Remember that only the words "whole wheat" mean whole wheat! For multi-grain loaves, look for the word "whole" before any grain (except oats, which are almost always whole).

My family will eat some brands of whole-grain breads and won't eat others. Your family probably won't like every brand either. Buy only one loaf at a time, and keep trying. While you're experimenting, also try some whole-wheat pita bread, whole-wheat bagels, whole-wheat buns and (my favorite) whole-wheat English muffins. If your family doesn't seem to like *any* whole grains, read "Your Family Doesn't Like Whole Grains," page 107 for ideas.

A Closer Look at Carbohydrates: Innocent or Guilty?

Have you noticed how various foods or food groups become wildly popular and then unpopular? Most recently, carbohydrates ("carbs") were the "bad guys." Just a few years ago, it was fats. Usually these ideas originate in a popular diet book. However, the truth about any fad diet is that people lose weight because they are eating fewer calories—not because they have eliminated a whole type of food!

Nutrition experts encourage eating whole grains and other healthy carbohydrates such as fruits, vegetables and nonfat milk. They also discourage eating overly refined carbohydrates: those made with refined white flour and refined sugars. These fill you up without giving you the nutrition you need, and it's easier to gain weight from too many calories. Many popular refined carbohydrate foods also contain high-calorie unhealthy fats such as trans fats. Examples are pastries, cakes, cookies, pies, croissants, chips and crackers.

Whole grains, on the other hand, contain a balance of some healthy fat, protein and fiber along with the carbohydrates. Most people who eat whole grains find their intake of food easier to self-regulate because the fiber and protein in whole grains are filling. A growing child definitely benefits from some Smart whole grains every day. Moreover, if an adult wants to lose weight, eating a balance of Smart whole grains along with lots of fruits and vegetables, lean proteins and healthy fats is the best way to do it.

If you make your own bread by hand or in a bread machine, replace at least half the white flour with 100% whole-grain flour. There are many great bread recipes on the Internet, and there's an easy whole-grain bread recipe in the recipe section of this book. Most kids love baking bread, and there is nothing like warm bread right from the oven!

Whole-Grain Cereals

Ah, the breakfast cereal aisle. The major manufacturers know that we want to feed the kids whole grains for breakfast, so they're now adding a sprinkling of whole grain to their cereals—along with the usual mountains of sugar, corn syrup and food dye. Then, they flaunt this on the package with "Contains Whole Grains" or something similar. Ignore those claims! Most packaged cereals are Empties—sad, but true.

Fortunately, there are a few good choices out there. Start by scanning the box fronts for the words "whole grain." Then, flip the box over and read the Ingredients list and the Nutrition Facts label following the field test for grains.

After reading about its benefits, Jill decided that the time had come to switch her family to whole-grain bread. She searched the store shelves and found one made with 100% whole wheat. The next day, she served it to her daughters. Her 10-year-old liked it OK, but the eight-year-old ate exactly one bite. Unfazed, Jill picked out a different brand of bread the next time. Again, the older child ate it and the younger one wouldn't. Starting to feel frustrated, Jill quizzed her daughter. After a bit of discussion, Jill figured out it wasn't actually the bread itself that her eight-year-old disliked—it was the "chunks," also known as nuts, which happened to be in both brands. Sure enough, when Jill bought a nut-less loaf, both kids ate the bread. The family has happily eaten whole-grain bread ever since. ✖

You will soon find that the vast majority of breakfast cereals, even organic or those in the health food section, are Empties because they contain many more grams of sugar than fiber. Just to put that in perspective, a cereal with 16 grams of sugar per serving has four full teaspoons of sugar in each serving. That's not a great way for your child to start the day.

But there are several nationally available Smart breakfast cereals, even including a few kids' cereals. There are also quite a few good In-Between cereals that contain about twice as many grams of sugar as fiber. You can make one of those cereals the In-Between for breakfast by having it with nonfat milk and fresh or frozen fruit, such as bananas or blueberries. Visit www.feedingthekids.com for a list of some of your Smart and In-Between cereal options.

Many sugary cereals are fortified with a long list of vitamins and minerals. These are not part of the food; they are either mixed in or sprayed on. You might as well feed your kid a bowl of sugar with a vitamin pill on top. If you're seriously concerned about vitamins, feed your child a vitamin supplement recommended by your healthcare provider, and find a breakfast cereal that contains Smart whole grains.

Of course, oatmeal is a great Smart grain and one of the very best break-fast choices. The soluble fiber in oatmeal is thought to actually lower cho-lesterol levels. Plain oatmeal, instant or regular, can be quickly cooked in the microwave or on top of the stove. But watch out: Most flavored instant oat-meal contains a ridiculous amount of sugar—about four teaspoons per packet! If you want flavored instant oatmeal, try the recipe for homemade instant oatmeal in this book.

Oatmeal in the form of granola, granola bars or the newer oatmeal breakfast bars are also usually loaded with sweetener, and in some cases, trans fats. As you know by now, cut through the dense camouflage by read-ing the labels. There are one or two Smart granola items out there, and they're great for snacks and packing in lunches.

If your kids are really into sugary cereals, don't surprise them with a bowl of a new healthier cereal one morning. If they are old enough, let them help you locate an In-Between cereal at the store. You'll be glad to have the help, and they'll be much more likely to try it. If your kids are still quite young, try offering them the new cereal as a snack to get them used to the new food at a more relaxed time.

Usually, an easier way to make the transition to a whole-grain breakfast is to have something other than cereal. Try whole-grain English muffins, toast or bagels. If you have time, make whole-wheat waffles, pancakes or French toast. Or, on weekends, make an enormous batch of whole-grain muffins or Breakfast Bars (see recipe section) that can be frozen for quick weekday breakfasts. If you have a bread maker, set it to have a warm loaf of cinnamon nut bread (at least half whole wheat, of course) ready to tempt everyone in the morning.

Whole-Grain Pastas

Kids love pasta! My own kids eat pounds and pounds of it every year. With a food this popular and quick to cook, you need to find a whole-grain ver-sion your family likes. For kids who are less than thrilled with veggies and protein foods, whole-wheat pasta is a great way of ensuring that they get some fiber, protein and nutrients. Of course, if your family really loves white pasta, just use it as your In-Between for that meal.

Some brands of whole-wheat pasta have a strong flavor or a strange texture that many people (like me) don't like. Search the Internet to find a few ideas for good brands. You can also visit a health food store to find a better selection, and ask someone there for recommendations. Once you find a tasty version, you probably won't hear many protests. I have even fed several of my kids' unsuspecting playmates whole-wheat pasta without getting a single negative comment. Again, visit www.feedingthekids.com for some specific brand names.

For a reason I can't fathom, at least one excellent brand of pasta is made from a blend of white flour, bran and wheat germ. In effect, the manufacturer has taken apart a whole grain and then put it back together again. Strange as it may be, these pastas contain all the goodness of whole wheat, taste great and qualify as Smart pasta.

Colored "vegetable" pastas, however, are almost never Smart! They are just white pasta lightly stained with pretty vegetable colors. They are usually not whole grain, and they contain such a tiny amount of vegetables that they aren't any better for you than regular white-flour pasta. So count the spinach pasta as an In-Between unless it is whole wheat.

When changing pasta types, don't expect your family to like every brand, but do keep experimenting. If you're lucky—or your kids are still little—the family may eat the new pasta and not say a word about it. Sometimes offering spaghetti sauce, meatballs or a sprinkling of parmesan cheese will convince doubters.

Rice

White, enriched rice looks like a whole-grain food because you can see what look like the whole little grains, but white rice is not whole grain. It has been polished to remove the bran and the germ. This process leaves it pretty much empty of nutrition, except what is added back in to make the rice "enriched." Enriched white rice is an In-Between.

Brown rice, however, is a Smart choice. You can find it in instant, regular, basmati and every other way that white rice is sold. It has a nutty flavor and slightly firmer texture than white rice. Most people seem to like it, so the switch shouldn't be too hard.

Jo Ann was always torn when it came to rice for her rice-loving family. On the one hand, brown rice is healthy. On the other hand, white rice cooks much faster. So she cooked brown rice on the rare occasions when she was home before dinner and remembered to put it on the stove in time. She also occasionally served white rice when she wanted dinner on the table fast. The kids didn't seem to notice what type of rice they had—they just wanted to have rice more often. The answer to her dilemma became apparent during a recent shopping trip. Located just down the shelf from her usual rice selections, she found instant brown rice that cooks just as fast as the white rice. Now, Jo Ann's family very happily eats rice several times a week. ✗

Regular brown rice does take about twice as long to cook. If time is a factor, try the instant variety—it is quick, healthy and quite good. Electric rice cookers can also speed up the cooking time for regular brown rice.

Many people, especially children, won't even notice the switch to brown rice. If you think your family will notice, cook it with a bouillon cube or serve it with sauce.

Cornmeal and Grits

Many corn-based foods are real comfort foods. Unfortunately, cornmeal is usually de-germinated because the corn oil in the germ spoils too quickly for long storage. Therefore, corn products (cornbread, muffins, chips, corn tortillas, grits, polenta, cornflakes) are rarely whole grain.

If you bake your own cornbread, corn muffins, hush puppies or other cornmeal-based foods, look for "whole cornmeal" or "stone-ground cornmeal." Unfortunately, these are very hard to find! If you are lucky enough to find whole-grain cornmeal, store it in the freezer since it spoils quickly.

Even if you can't find whole cornmeal (my grocery store doesn't carry it), you can always replace unhealthy fats and dairy ingredients in your baking and replace all the white flour with either white whole-grain flour or whole-wheat pastry flour. Depending on the recipe, you will still end up with a food that is half whole grain and therefore a Smart grain. Otherwise, just count cornmeal-based foods as In-Betweens.

Grits and polenta are often made with de-germinated corn, particularly the instant versions. Unless you can find whole-grain versions, they are not Smart whole-grain foods. However, the "quick" and "regular" versions contain enough nutrition and fiber that you can consider them In-Between choices.

Corn chips, corn tortillas and cornflakes are definitely available in stone-ground or whole-corn flour versions. You may need to look in the health food section of the store to find them, though. If you eat these foods often and can't find them in your regular store, try going to any health food store to stock up.

Whole-Grain Crackers

Whole-grain crackers may be the easiest way to get kids started eating whole grains. Most kids really like them, and most stores have a nice variety to choose from.

A few well-known brands of crackers are whole grain and don't contain any dangerous fats. Most of these crackers let you know this with labels that read "NO TRANS FAT!" and "100% WHOLE GRAINS!" Still, check the nutrition labeling.

If you can't find a good whole-grain cracker on the regular cracker aisle, check the health food section. You can usually find many Smart choices there.

Whole-grain rice cakes can be a nice alternative to crackers. Many brands are now available made with brown rice or popcorn; both are kid-friendly Smart choices. If you get the flavored ones, don't forget to check the fat and sugar content—some are healthier than others.

Kids love them, but graham crackers aren't Smart. Graham crackers are no longer commonly made out of the whole-wheat graham flour that gave them their reputation as a health food. And many brands today contain partially hydrogenated oils. Check the health food section for healthier types, but there are very few available.

Starchy Vegetables

As I mentioned in the vegetable section, you can use vegetables such as potatoes, corn, peas and winter squash as whole-grain substitutes.

Whether baked, mashed or boiled—russet, sweet or golden—potatoes can replace other whole grains at dinner. In general, they should be prepared with as little fat as possible because people like to add cheese, butter or sour cream to them at the table. Whenever possible, scrub the potatoes but do not peel them. The peels actually contain more nutrients than the interior part. Mashed potatoes, homemade oven-baked fries and even potato soups are delicious with peels included. Some people enjoy the skins on baked potatoes, too.

Sweet potatoes and yams (I'm not going to even try to explain the difference, if there is one) are even more nutritious than regular potatoes. Most people do peel sweet potatoes because the peel is tough, though edible. Sweet potatoes can be mashed, roasted, oven-fried, baked and used in stews just like regular potatoes. They are much sweeter and may change the flavor of a recipe. Give them a try; some children actually prefer their sweeter flavor.

Corn is another great whole-grain substitute, served as corn on the cob, a side dish made from frozen or canned corn or as an addition to other dishes. Just watch the flavorings! Butter on the corn, or making a cream sauce for it, transforms it from a Smart food into an In-Between. If you add lots of any fat, especially the saturated type (i.e., butter), it can even become an Empty. My family likes to eat corn topped with a "light" butter/canola oil blend, which makes the corn our In-Between for that meal.

Chips

Chips range widely from Smart choices to In-Betweens to Empties. As always, read the labels to find the best brand.

Baked corn chips are a popular Smart choice. Make sure your brand contains "stone-ground" or "whole" cornmeal; many baked chips are made out of de-germinated cornmeal. Baked corn chips usually qualify as Smart food, though a few are In-Betweens.

Baked potato chips are a popular In-Between or Smart option, depending on the chip. For the healthiest chips, look for high-quality brands that are made from whole potatoes. I will certainly admit that baked chips don't taste as great as the "real" deep-fried potato chips that my family loves. However, they are much healthier as an everyday option.

You'll find out more about chips in "Week 6: Escaping from Empties."

Other Whole Grains to Try

An ideal diet contains a variety of whole grains. Most people end up using the more common whole grains: wheat, corn, oats and rice. That is absolutely fine. On the other hand, if you want to experiment, here are a few interesting grains to try. A simple Internet search or a book on whole grains will give you recipes for each of them:

Barley can be found near the rice in most grocery stores. It is easily added to soups that have a long cooking time. The most nutritious form is called "whole barley" because the outer layers are left intact. There is also "pearled barley," the kind most common in regular grocery stores. It is mild tasting and softens with cooking.

Quinoa (KEEN-wah) is essentially a tiny seed. It is the only grain that is a "complete protein"—the same quality protein found in milk or meat, which is great for people who do not eat meat. Quinoa can be prepared just like pasta: Add two parts water to one part quinoa in a large saucepan, and cook for about 15 minutes. Each seed pops open and looks like a curly sprout. Quinoa makes a great change of pace as a side dish. It's quite bland in flavor, so you can add any spicing your family enjoys such as pasta sauce, salsa or soy sauce.

Amaranth, millet and spelt are all good, healthy grains as long as they are used whole or as whole-grain flours. You will often see them on Ingredients lists for cereal, breads or crackers.

Provisions:
Ideas for Grains to Serve

Whole-grain versions of the following are all great choices. The ideas with an asterisk (*) are in the recipe section of this book.

Breakfast
- Instant Oatmeal*
- Fruit and Oats*
- Breakfast Bars*
- Banana Bread Muffins*

- English Muffins*
- Pancakes*
- Toasted whole-grain bread topped with peanut or almond butter
- Whole-grain English muffins topped with melted part-skim cheese
- Whole-wheat bagels
- Whole-grain cold cereal

Lunch or Dinner

- Orange Juice Hummus* with whole-grain crackers
- Salsa-Bean Dip and Chips*
- Warm Bean Dip and Chips*
- Baked potato chips
- Sandwich on whole-grain bread (PB&J, turkey, ham)
- Tuna-Cheese Burgers*
- Whole-grain pasta or brown rice
- Whole-wheat spaghetti (see Enhanced Spaghetti Sauce*)
- Whole-grain rolls, muffins or biscuits
- Quinoa and Tomato Soup*
- Instant Mini Pizzas*
- Baked or mashed potatoes
- Corn or peas
- Mashed sweet potatoes
- Twice-Baked Potatoes*
- Pizza with crust made from Great, Great Bread*
- Carrot Cake Whole-Wheat Pancakes*

Snacks

- Trail Mix*
- Banana Bread Muffins*
- Oatmeal Cookies*

- Breakfast Bars*
- Baked corn or potato chips
- Popcorn or rice cakes
- Whole-grain crackers

In recipe section

Whole-Grain Survival Tips

Switching to more whole grains might feel like a big project calling for lots of adaptive behaviors. Here are a few tips for surviving common problems that may crop up during the process:

Your Family Doesn't Like Whole Grains

Most people don't hate whole grains as much as they think they do! Try these ideas if your family seems whole-grain resistant:

- First, make sure they really dislike whole grains: I've fed whole-grain waffles, pasta, rolls, pizzas, crackers and muffins to some of the world's pickiest eaters (so labeled by their own moms). I didn't mention the whole grains, and they didn't notice.
- Use a "whole" different whole-grain food to add a little biodiversity to your family's provisions: Add in new whole grains in ways that don't directly compete with the old favorites. Try switching from:
    - A favorite Empty cereal to whole-grain English muffins with low-fat cream cheese and jelly
    - White bagels to a whole-grain cereal with berries on top
    - White dinner rolls to brown rice
    - White sandwich bread to whole-wheat pitas
    - Regular pasta to whole-wheat pasta in a new and different shape
- Make an irresistible whole-grain treat such as fresh-baked whole-wheat bread, a stack of steaming pancakes, warm cookies with milk or hot muffins. Chances are that your family will eat these goodies without complaint! Make sure you let them know (*after* they eat it) that they just enjoyed a whole-grain food.

• Jump right in: If all else fails, let yourself run out of the Empty choices and just start offering whole grains. If family members actually notice, explain your reasons for switching to a healthier food. If you decide to use this strategy, I recommend not taking the kids shopping with you for a few weeks!

Empty Toppings on Whole Grains

It seems that every whole grain has an Empty waiting to jump on top: bread and butter, pasta and alfredo sauce, mashed potatoes and gravy, bagels and cream cheese, pancakes and syrup! Of course these toppings can be problems when used in excess, but while you're working on the whole-grain step, don't try to remove all your favorite toppings, too. If you always serve gravy with your rice, just make the switch to brown rice at first. This is a step-by-step process, and too many changes at once could make eating miserable for everyone. Swapping and switching some of your Empties will happen during Week 6, so try not to worry about these for now. Meanwhile, remember that grain foods are a wonderful place to add in healthy fats as toppings.

Baking with Whole-Wheat Flour

If you like to bake from scratch, you can easily add whole-grain flours. To start with, I find that most recipes still taste great and have a nice texture if I replace half the white flour called for with whole-wheat flour. You can gradually experiment with using more and more whole-wheat flour—or start collecting whole-grain recipes. As I mentioned earlier, I love to bake with "white whole-wheat" flour because of its mild taste and light texture.

For baked goods leavened with eggs, baking powder or baking soda, such as pancakes, waffles, biscuits, batter breads, cookies or muffins, try using whole-wheat pastry flour or white whole-wheat flour for at least half of the total flour. These flours add whole-grain nutrition but still let the foods rise well. If you can't find these types of flour at your regular store, go to a health food store and stock up. They'll keep for a long time if tightly wrapped in the freezer.

For foods that depend on yeast to rise, such as pizza crust, bread or rolls, white whole-wheat, stone-ground whole-wheat and whole-wheat bread flour are all great options. Again, try using about half whole wheat in place of the regular flour.

If you want to, you can also experiment with adding other whole grains such as spelt flour, rolled oats, oat flour or even soy flour. Start replacing the regular flour with just a quarter-cup or half-cup, then try upping the amount the next time you bake.

Finding Whole Grains in Restaurants

Most rolls, buns or breads in restaurants are made from white flour. Restaurant rice or pasta is rarely whole grain, though it is usually enriched. These would all be In-betweens, except that many restaurants add lots of sweetener and unhealthy fats, making them Empties.

If you eat out frequently, your family needs to hunt for restaurants that offer some Smart foods that all of you enjoy. Fortunately, more and more restaurants are starting to serve healthier grains. You can now sometimes find brown rice, whole-grain pasta and whole-wheat rolls. Visit www.feedingthe kids.com for restaurant suggestions.

Packing Whole Grains On the Go

There are lots of easy ways to pack whole grains to carry for lunch or snacks.

- Whole-grain crackers
- Breakfast in a Bag (in the recipe section)
- Whole-grain rice or popcorn cakes
- Sandwiches made with whole-grain bread
- Homemade whole-grain goodies such as cookies (in the recipe section)
- Some granola bars (watch carefully for sugar and trans fat!)

Major Points of Interest
What to Keep in Mind about Whole Grains

Congratulations! If you have reached Week 4, your family is well on the way to a truly healthy diet. Don't get discouraged in your search for delicious whole grains for your family—they really are out there. You may need to take some extra time and do some experimenting to make these changes stick.

As you practice switching and swapping for more whole-grain foods, remember:

- Continue eating your fruits, vegetables and low-fat dairy foods.

- Offer your family whole grains three times a day (or more often) and at the same times each day to create an eating routine. Most people prefer having whole grains for:
  - Breakfast
  - Lunch
  - Dinner

- Try to swap whole grains for refined grains for snacks, too.

- Choose Smart whole grains with more grams of fiber per serving than grams of sugar and fat.

- Choose In-Between grains that have either whole grains or enriched flours and have no more grams of sugar or fat than double the number of grams of fiber.

- Any food with trans fat is always Empty.

DAILY ITINERARY (after Week 4)	Fruits	Veggies	Dairy Foods	Grains	Proteins
Breakfast	✔		✔	✔	
Lunch	✔	✔	✔	✔	
Dinner		✔✔		✔	
Snacks/Desserts	✔		✔		

Pick mostly Smart choices. Try to limit In-Betweens to one per meal or snack.

As always, try to include no more than one In-Between choice for each snack or meal, which you can choose from fruits, vegetables, dairy or grains. After completing Week 4, your daily food plan will include the foods on the chart above, along with extra servings of these or other food, plus Smart fats, toppings and treats.

Hunting for Smart Proteins

Good news: Since your family is now eating the Smart foods from the first four weeks (most of the time), you are already getting a fair amount of healthy protein from nonfat dairy foods and whole grains. Even the fruits and vegetables you eat contain some protein.

However, having two servings of protein-dense foods a day is still a good idea. Most people already do that. Unfortunately, many of the common protein foods in the store and at restaurants are very high in saturated fats. Your expedition this week will take you on a hunt through all the fatty choices to get to leaner, Smarter proteins.

Fortunately, there are many healthy protein foods and many simple, tasty ways to prepare them, so remember that this step is definitely not about deprivation! Also, portion size can be much more flexible with healthier protein choices. So the big meat-eaters at your table can have enough to feel full and satisfied without damaging their health.

> **Why Eat Protein Foods?**
> Protein provides the building blocks for the body. There are many good reasons to eat healthy types of proteins every day:
> - Protein is used to build and repair blood, skin, bones, muscles, hormones and almost every other body part.
> - People who eat a protein at each meal report feeling more satisfied and full until the next meal, making them less likely to eat Empty snacks.
> - Many Smart protein sources are loaded with B vitamins, including riboflavin, B6, niacin and thiamin, and many contain vitamin E, iron, zinc and magnesium.
> - Plant-based proteins (such as nuts and seeds) and fish contain heart-healthy fats.
> - Beans provide protein along with "soluble" fiber that helps soak up cholesterol.

A Daily Itinerary: Planning When You'll Eat Smart Proteins

Many people have a serving of meat, beans or soy for both lunch and dinner. If that is already your schedule, you just have to find Smart protein choices that can replace any less-healthy protein foods your family eats now. You can also add a protein for breakfast or for snacks. As always, just figure out what works best for your family.

DAILY ITINERARY		2 Protein Foods a Day
Breakfast		Optional.
Lunch	✔	Pack in lunches, serve leftovers from dinner, or order at restaurants.
Dinner	✔	Use as main course or as part of another dish.
Snacks/Desserts		Optional.
Let your family self-regulate. Some kids may turn down all or part of some servings.		

During this week, remember to select no more than one In-Between choice for each meal or snack. And, of course, keep eating your fruits, vegetables, dairy foods and whole grains, too. In fact, your family will get protein from those foods as well.

How to Identify Smart Protein Foods–And Avoid Empty Ones

Spotting Smart Protein Foods
- **Identifying features:** High in protein, low in saturated fats
- **Best aspects:** Satisfying and filling
- **Number of servings to offer:** Two or more
- **Varieties:**
    - Extra-lean beef, ham, lamb
    - White skinless poultry
    - Fish and seafood
    - Beans
    - Soy foods
    - Low-fat dairy
    - Nuts
    - Eggs

In general, the healthiest proteins contain the least amount of saturated (animal) fat. But, since most protein sources contain a mixture of saturated and unsaturated fats, you will need to limit the total fat you eat from protein sources. The field test on the next page will help you find Smart lower-fat protein foods.

An In-Between protein can be used as a substitute for a Smart protein if you are willing to make the food your In-Between for that meal. Some In-Between protein choices include lean meats (as opposed to *extra*-lean meats), skinless dark-meat poultry, skin-on white-meat poultry, eggs, nuts (unless used as a healthy fat topping on vegetables or grains) or any of the Smart proteins prepared with added sweetener or added saturated fat.

Empty proteins get more than 50 percent of their calories from fat, and most of the fat is saturated (the fat associated with heart disease and stroke). Because they're Empties, they should be eaten only rarely or used as a flavoring in an otherwise healthy dish. Empty proteins include all types of fatty meats, such as regular ground meats, many luncheon meats, sausage, bacon and fried fish or chicken.

Many healthy protein sources exist that we don't always think about. The following section offers a bit more information on some of the protein choices just waiting to be discovered by your family.

Field Test for Meats, Beans and Soy Foods*

1. Find the number of calories from fat on the Nutrition Facts label. Double that number. **

2. Find total calories on the Nutrition Facts label. Compare double the fat calories to total calories.
   - If the **total calories are LOWER than the fat calories doubled,** the food is an Empty (because over half the calories in the food come from fat).
   - If the **total calories are HIGHER than the fat calories doubled,** it is **at least an In-Between.** But, it could be Smart . . . so, do step 3.

3. Next, triple the fat calories and compare it to the total calories in one serving.
   - If **the total calories are HIGHER than the fat calories tripled,** the food is **Smart** (because less than 33 percent of the calories come from fat).

For other protein foods, such as nuts and eggs, see the protein identification chart on pages 124-125.

**If you prefer, round all numbers to the nearest 10 for easier math.*

Using the Field Test for Meats, Beans and Soy Foods*

Beans, skinless chicken or turkey breasts, fresh seafood and meats labeled as extra-lean are always Smart choices. But many other types of meat are Empties or In-Betweens. The field test for protein will help you locate the leaner meat products that may be hidden among fattier choices at the grocery store. This label came from a package of frozen chicken strips. Here is how to use the field test to decide whether to buy it:

Nutrition Facts	
Serving Size: 3oz (84g)	
Servings Per Container: 8	
Amount Per Serving	
Calories 200 Calories from Fat 70	
	% Daily Value
Total Fat 8g	12%
Saturated Fat 1.5g	9%
Trans Fat 0g	0%
Cholesterol 35mg	12%
Sodium 790mg	33%
Total Carbohydrate 14g	5%
Dietary Fiber 0g	0%
Sugars < 1g	
Protein 18g	
Vitamin A 0% • Vitamin C 0%	
Calcium 6% • Iron 4%	

INGREDIENTS: chicken breast strips with rib meat, wheat flour and bleached wheat flour, water, contains less than 2% of salt, modified corn starch, spices, soybean oil, dried whey, sodium phosphate, garlic powder, leavening (sodium aluminum phosphate, sodium bicarbonate, monocalcium phosphate), dextrose, dried garlic, dried yeast, dried onion, extractives of annatto and paprika, xanthan gum, fumeric acid. Breading set in vegetable oil. **Contains wheat, milk and gluten.**

1. Find the calories from fat on the Nutrition Facts label: 70. Double them: 70+70=140.

2. Find the total calories: 200 for one serving. The total calories (200) are higher than double the calories from fat (140), so these chicken strips are at least an In-Between.

3. Now triple the calories from fat by adding another 70. 140+70=210. The total calories (200) are less than triple the fat calories (210), so these chicken strips are not Smart. But they are an In-Between (from step 2).

*For other protein foods, such as nuts, eggs and dairy foods, see the protein identification chart on pages 124-125.

This example shows how packaged meats can vary by brand and type. I have found that most kids are just as happy with these In-Between chicken strips as they would be with traditional high-fat nuggets. So before you give up a favorite type of Empty meat, try using the field test to see if you can find an In-Between or Smart version that your family enjoys.

(For more examples showing how to use the field test to analyze protein foods, see the Appendix.)

Finding Extra-Lean Meats

The key to buying meat is to learn to find extra-lean choices. Several clues can help you identify the characteristics that will lead you to these Smart choices.

If the meat has a label, look for the term "*extra* lean" on it. Extra-lean meats have only 5 percent fat by weight or less. But 5 percent fat by *weight* usually means that about 30 percent of *calories* will be from fat, which is pretty good for meat. If the meat doesn't say "extra lean" on the package, use the field test to figure out whether it is Smart, In-Between or Empty.

Unfortunately, not all meat has nutrition labeling. However, even without labeling you can still find a lean choice. First, when picking out meat, look for a piece with few visible white globs, dots or streaks of fat (marbling). Then, no matter how lean the cut, always trim off all visible fat before cooking. Finally, know the leanest cuts for your favorite types of meat:

Pork: Think loin! The leanest pork choices include pork loin, sirloin, tenderloin and center loin.

Beef: Pick top loin, top sirloin, round steaks and roasts (round eye, top round, bottom round, round tip), chuck shoulder and arm roasts. Beef is also graded by the amount of fat: "prime" meats have the most fat marbling! Save family arteries and money by selecting "choice" or "select" cuts. So for beef, remember round, loin and shoulder—and *not* prime!

Poultry: Look for skinless white meat without many globs of white fat. Skinless white chicken or turkey breast meat is always extra lean, even if it isn't labeled as such. Although they are cheaper, the dark meats in drumsticks and thighs are In-Betweens because they are higher in fat, even if they are skinless. Wings are mostly just fatty skin, so they are Empties.

Picking Ground Meats

Ground meats are often labeled by percentage "lean" or percentage "fat free." However, these percentages refer to how much fat is in the package based on weight, not calories. Because fat is lightweight compared to the moisture in the ground meat, these percentages can be misleading. To pick a Smart ground meat, you need to find a ground beef that gets less than 30 percent of its calories from fat. That means the ground meat must be at least 94 percent fat free by weight. Ground meat in packages labeled with the American Heart Association check mark or labeled with the words "extra lean" are less than 30 percent fat by calories. If the ground meat has a Nutrition Facts label, you can use the field test to see if it is Smart or In-Between.

If ground meat does not have a label, assume it is high-fat—because it usually is. Eighty percent lean is the standard for ground beef, which means it gets 72 percent of its calories from fat. Even 90 percent "lean" ground meat gets half its calories from fat!

It might be surprising to learn that all types of ground meats, including turkey, chicken, buffalo and elk, are usually very high-fat foods. In fact, they are generally just as fatty as regular ground beef, and the fat in all these

---

A Closer Look at Cholesterol

Cholesterol is a wax-like substance that circulates in your bloodstream carrying various fats. The body needs it to make cell membranes, some hormones and vitamin D. When the body produces too much of it in the liver, it circulates in the blood and collects in the blood vessels to form a blockage that can result in heart attack or stroke.

LDL (stands for Low-Density Lipoprotein) cholesterol is often called the "bad" cholesterol because it stimulates cholesterol production and then carries it into the arteries. HDL (stands for High-Density Lipoprotein) cholesterol is known as the "good" cholesterol because it picks up excess cholesterol and brings it back to the liver, so HDL is like a "cleanup crew" for your arteries. You can see why you want to eat a diet that helps your body produce lots of good HDL and less LDL.

Your food choices and exercise habits can influence both your bad (LDL) and good (HDL) blood cholesterol levels. Some people, however, inherit genes that crank out too much cholesterol, and these people usually need both special cholesterol medication and a healthy lifestyle. An overall healthy diet with lots of fiber is the best way to manage cholesterol levels for most people.

The biggest problem foods that raise LDL-cholesterol levels are those with saturated fats in them, such as fatty meat and dairy, palm oil and coconut oil. Also, hydrogenated fats (healthy fats turned into saturated fats by a manufacturing process) affect the body exactly like natural saturated fats. Of course, the worst fats are the partially hydrogenated oils that contain trans fats. Trans fat makes the liver crank out too much LDL cholesterol and can even lower your good HDL cholesterol. Always read nutrition labels for "saturated fat" and "trans fat" so your family can eat well to lower risk for future disease.

meats is mostly saturated fat. So, use the field test on all ground meats. If the meat does not have a Nutrition Facts label, assume the meat is an Empty.

Hot Dogs, Sausage and Bacon

Bacon is made from the belly of the pig. Unless the pig does sit-ups, this is a very fatty part of the animal. Most bacon is well over 50 percent fat, as measured by calories, including bacon made from turkey (or any other animal). A few manufacturers have recently come out with low-fat bacon. I have yet to find anyone who actually likes it . . . but feel free to give it a try! Bacon may be a food that should just be enjoyed, in its full-fat form, as a very occasional treat or used in small amounts as a flavoring. For a more frequent, Smart replacement for bacon, my family enjoys Canadian bacon.

Sausage and hot dogs are traditionally made from the leftover bits and pieces of various animals, usually pigs, cows and sometimes turkeys. These leftover parts are usually high-fat. Fortunately, many of the low-fat sausages and hot dogs do taste good. Just be sure to use the field test to find Smart or In-Between choices. Also, look for brands that contain less sodium.

A Closer Look at Nitrites

Nitrites are found in many cured meats such as deli meats, bacon, hotdogs and sausage. They are added as a preservative and to allow meat to retain a pink or red color. The Food and Drug Administration and the U.S. Department of Agriculture believe that nitrite is a safe ingredient and is not associated with cancers in humans at the levels recommended for use.

The American Cancer Society says that some studies have linked eating large amounts of preserved meats to increased risk for colorectal and stomach cancers, but this association might not be due to the nitrites. Studies have also shown that nitrites can be converted in the stomach to carcinogenic nitrosamines, but eating fruits and vegetables has been reported to partially block this process.

Still, some parents choose to avoid nitrites just to be safe. However, most cured meats contain very little of these chemicals, and meats without them are quite expensive. Whatever you decide, make sure to buy lean lunch meats—and offer fruits and vegetables at meals!

You can also check out the vegetarian sausages, hot dogs and bacon available in the "natural foods" freezer section. These are often high in sodium but lower in saturated fat. They taste surprisingly good. The hot dogs, pre-shaped sausages and sausage crumbles are easiest to use.

Lunch Meats

As a rule, buy lunch meats made from a whole chunk of meat, not from parts pressed together into a roll. As with hot dogs and sausage, "parts" used to make lunch meats are usually high in fat. Examples of high-fat deli meats include pastrami, salami, pepperoni and all the "rolls."

Instead, look for extra-lean turkey breast, chicken breast, ham, roast beef or corned beef. If you are buying these meats at the deli counter, ask the person doing the slicing for a look at the Nutrition Facts label to double-check that you are making a lean choice.

Beans

Beans, whether canned or made from dried beans, are certainly a Smart choice. They are full of fiber and high in protein. However, check various brands of beans to find the one with the lowest sodium content, then drain and rinse the beans before using them.

If you buy pre-flavored beans, such as refried beans, pork and beans or baked beans, make sure your favorite brand does not contain more sugar per serving than protein. Also look for brands with little saturated fat, no trans fat and lower sodium content.

Fish and Seafood (shrimp, crab, oysters, lobster, scallops, etc.)

Some fish and seafood do have more than 30 percent of their calories from fat. However, all seafood and fish are Smart because the fat they contain is mostly healthy fat. Canned fish is also a Smart choice. Just look for the words "packed in water" because fish "packed in oil" is much higher in calories.

Of course, it is possible to transform fish and seafood into Empties by deep-frying (also called breading). Fried popcorn shrimp, breaded fish and fish sticks are all Empties.

> **A Closer Look at Which Types of Fish Are Safe for Kids**
> In general, fish and shellfish (shrimp, lobster, crabmeat) are great types of Smart proteins that contain healthy fat (called omega-3 fatty acids). The federal government published three recommendations in 2004 for selecting and eating fish or shellfish for young children (and pregnant women):
>
> 1. Do not eat shark, swordfish, king mackerel or tilefish because they contain high levels of mercury.
>
> 2. Eat up to 12 ounces (two average meals) a week of a variety of fish and shellfish that are lower in mercury. Five of the most commonly eaten fish that are low in mercury are shrimp, canned light tuna, salmon, pollack and catfish. Another commonly eaten fish, albacore ("white") tuna, has more mercury than canned light tuna. So, when choosing your two meals of fish and shellfish, you will want to limit albacore tuna to six ounces (one average meal) per week.
>
> 3. Check local advisories about the safety of fish caught by family and friends in your local lakes, rivers and coastal areas. According to the U.S. Environmental Protection Agency (EPA), if no advice is available, you should feel comfortable eating up to six ounces (one average meal) per week of fish you catch from local waters, but shouldn't consume any other fish during that week. Please note that the numbers in the advisory are averages; your child might eat more fish one week and less the next without harm.
>
> For information on current lists of safe fish and other details, visit the FDA food safety Website at www.cfsan.fda.gov or the EPA Website at www.epa.gov. For a convenient clip-and-carry wallet card that lists kid-safe fish along with "endangered" species of fish, visit the Monterey Bay Aquarium Website at www.mbayaq.org and click on "Seafood Watch" for your area.

Soy Foods and "Fake" (Vegetarian) Meats

If you like them, many types of soy, including plain tofu, tempeh and whole soybeans (also called edamame), are good Smart protein options. They contain plenty of protein, fiber, vitamins and healthy fats.

Other soy foods, such as "fake meats," "soy chips," soy milk and various soy-based protein bars, are also available. The fake meats include everything from breaded "chicken" fillets to sausage to pepperoni. My family likes some of these "meats" pretty well as meat alternatives. However, all these foods have many other things added to the soy, so always read the labels and use the protein field test to locate Smart soy foods.

In any case, soy is not necessary for a healthy diet—and soy's health benefits have not been scientifically proven. This means you don't need to bother feeding your family soy if they really don't enjoy it!

Eggs Are an In-Between Food

For years, eggs have had a bad reputation for being high in cholesterol. Now we know that high blood levels of cholesterol come more from eating saturated fats and trans fats than from eating the cholesterol itself.

Eggs are now considered an In-Between choice to be enjoyed in moderation unless you are specifically trying to lower your cholesterol intake. Eggs are packed with high-quality protein and other nutrients and are fairly low in saturated fats.

Egg whites do not contain saturated fat and are a Smart choice. In fact, if you use two egg whites for every whole egg, any egg dish becomes Smart.

When picking eggs, there is little difference between types. White or brown eggs are basically the same. Also, the term "free range" on eggs only means that the doors of the cage were opened for at least five minutes a day and doesn't really affect the egg quality.

Of course, as with all proteins, how you fix the eggs is important. Fried in lots of butter or made with tons of added cheese, eggs can go from being an In-Between food to an Empty. Also, if a few eggs are used in an otherwise Smart dish, the food can still be considered a Smart food.

Nuts

Nuts and seeds are high in calories because they are high in fats. Fortunately, these fats are mostly unsaturated, healthy fats. Plus, nuts contain protein and fiber. However, because nuts are so high in fat, they should be used in moderation in the same way you use other fats. Nuts make Smart toppings, spreads and additions to baked goods. However, plain nuts eaten as a snack should be treated as an In-Between.

Choices include: walnuts, peanuts, natural peanut butter (ground peanuts plus salt only), cashews, almonds, pecans and pistachios. Seeds include pumpkin, sesame and sunflower. Of course, chocolate- or sugar-coated nuts are Empty treats.

PROTEIN IDENTIFICATION CHART

In general, always look for protein foods low in saturated (animal) fats. Just as with grains, give yourself some extra time at the grocery store the first few times you plan to hunt for new, leaner choices.

SMART

Skinless white-meat poultry, including skinless chicken or turkey breasts, whole or filleted, bone in or boneless.

Sliced deli meat coming from whole pieces of extra-lean meat: turkey breast, chicken breast, ham, corned beef and roast beef.

Fish and seafood of any type—fresh, frozen or canned (water-packed is best); not deep-fried, breaded or canned in oil.

Extra-lean ground meats, including beef, ham, turkey, chicken, buffalo and elk. Pick those labeled "extra lean" or that pass the field test.

Extra-lean cuts of beef, game, pork/ham, including loin and round, that pass the field test. Look for the lower-fat "choice" or "select" cuts, not the higher-fat "prime."

Beans, including canned or cooked dried beans without added sweetener or fat.

Soy in the form of tofu, baked tofu, edamame and tempeh. Choose from the many "fake" meat products, such as veggie burgers and soy sausage.

Egg whites contain most of the protein in the egg, without the saturated fat and cholesterol found in the yolk.

Low-fat and nonfat hot dogs, sausage and bacon that pass the field test.

Canadian bacon

Nonfat, low-sugar dairy (See Week 3.)

Whole grains (See Week 4.)

As always, read the labels! Look for dry-roasted or raw nuts, not oil-roasted. Beware: Many nuts are roasted in hydrogenated or partially hydrogenated oils. And many pre-packaged trail mixes (even healthy-looking ones) are also coated in these unhealthy oils.

Also read the Ingredients list on your peanut butter. This should read simply: "peanuts, salt." Too often, peanut butter contains sugar and partially hydrogenated oils. The same rule applies for any other nut butters, such as cashew or almond. Any natural nut butter may develop a layer of healthy oil on top when stored. This is normal. Just pour off the oil, or, before you open it, store the jar upside down to mix in the oil. (Make sure the lid is on tight before using this trick!)

PROTEIN IDENTIFICATION CHART   (continued)

IN-BETWEEN

Whole eggs cooked without much added fat.
Nuts, seeds and nut butters that do not contain hydrogenated or partially hydrogenated oils or sweetener. A few examples include peanut butter, peanuts, almonds, almond butter, walnuts, cashews, sunflower seeds and pumpkin seeds. (Nuts can also be added to other Smart foods as a Smart fat.)
Dark chicken or turkey meat with or without the skin (although removing the skin takes away a lot of the fat). This includes thighs and drumsticks.
Higher-fat red meat without obvious fat seen on edges and "marbling" (fat streaks or globs you can see in the meat).
"Lean" ground meats, including beef, pork (ham), turkey and chicken. Lean meats are 10% fat by weight, which equals 50% fat by calories!

EMPTY

Bacon, except Canadian bacon or low-fat bacon.
Hot dogs and sausage, except some lower fat and vegetarian varieties. Use the protein field test to check.
Fatty cuts of steak, including rib-eye, porterhouse, flank or other steaks with visible fat marbling.
Chicken wings
Pepperoni
Salami, pastrami, baloney and "deli loaves"
Regular (most) ground beef
Regular (most) pork
Deep-fried meats such as fried chicken or chicken nuggets
Fish sticks unless they pass the protein field test as Smart or In-Between.
Peanut butter or nuts containing sweeteners or trans fats
Candy-coated nuts or seeds, including yogurt and chocolate-covered nuts.

How to Get There: Eating Healthier Proteins

Meat can be an emotional issue for many people. Not having big portions or full-fat versions seems almost insulting, let alone leaving meat out of some meals entirely. As you know by now, the most important thing to do is make sure whatever proteins you do choose are Smart. My husband will never eat just one hamburger the size of a deck of cards, which is the "correct" portion size; however, he will eat two or three extra-lean burgers fortified with grated zucchini—after some cajoling the first time!

Keep Extra-Lean Meats Moist

A major issue with leaner meats is keeping them moist. Here are several tricks to try:

- Mix grated zucchini or carrots into extra-lean ground beef (or other ground meat) for burgers, meatballs or meatloaf. It adds moisture and a vegetable at the same time. This is a great way to get a serving of vegetables into the kids. See Healthy Hamburgers in the recipe section.

- Add sauces to extra-lean meats: pasta sauce, low-fat gravy, barbeque sauce or ketchup.

- Use moist cooking methods, whenever possible, for extra-lean meats and fish: try poaching, steaming and pan-frying using a nonstick pan.

- Add extra-lean pork, steak and chicken to moist dishes such as stew, soup and chili.

- Thoroughly cook—but try not to overcook—extra-lean beef, pork or skinless poultry. (To be honest, I often do over-cook extra-lean meats, so I know for sure that overcooking dries it out! If you do overcook, add a sauce as mentioned above.) Go to www.feedingthekids.com for a list of websites on food safety.

My husband really loves hamburgers. We used to not eat them often, though, because of the high fat content. We tried extra-lean hamburgers, but they were just too dry for his taste. One day, I came across the idea of adding moisture to lean ground meats in the form of grated zucchini. As I set to work that evening, industriously grating zucchini, my husband wandered into the kitchen. (You need to understand that my husband was traumatized as a child by excessive zucchini eating thanks to his mom's yearly bumper crops of zucchini from her garden.) "What is your plan with that grated zucchini?" he asked, glancing toward the ground beef on the counter and somehow correctly guessing my ingenious idea. I smiled and told him I just wanted to try it once. When I served up the green-speckled hamburgers, everyone (including me) was a bit doubtful. But after a few tentative bites, we were all very pleasantly surprised that they were moist— and still tasted like real burgers. "So, does this make hamburgers a Smart food?" my husband wanted to know. Yup.

Feeding Fish to Kids

Many kids dislike fish. I can't guarantee they will ever eat it, but since it's such a great protein source, here are some ideas to try:

- Pick mild fish. Go for trout or cod, or ask the person at the fish counter which fish is mildest. Also, be sure to ask how fresh the fish is. Old fish is smelly, slimy and bad tasting!

- Serve canned tuna or salmon instead of fresh fish. It is mild and can be turned into patties, salads and sandwiches.

- Don't add lots of fabulous herbs, spices or sauces to the fish. In fact, serve it with ketchup, barbeque sauce or even ranch dressing for dipping.

- Serve it breaded using the variation on the recipe for Chicken Nuggets in the recipe section of this book.

- Keep trying. Kids may just surprise you and eat it after enough exposures, especially if you don't cook them a separate meal to replace the fish.

Soy Foods, Fake Meat and Beans

The very idea of tofu or vegetarian "meat" makes some people squeamish. However, vegetarian products really can taste good. See if your family is willing to give them a try! It's true that tofu can be bland and mushy if it isn't made well. Some people find pre-baked, pre-flavored tofu easier to use in sandwiches and other dishes. Soy products such as burgers, "dogs" and sausages are also a good way to eat soy.

Although we eat tofu or fake meats occasionally, my family prefers edamame (ed-ah-MAH-meh). Edamame are just boiled whole soybeans that are traditionally served as an appetizer or snack in Japan. They count as both a protein and a vegetable, and they are fast and easy to fix—just boil or microwave them as directed on the package. Edamame are sold in the natural foods frozen section of most grocery stores and are available shelled and unshelled. Kids love the type with shells; they can squeeze the shell and pop the soybeans into their mouths.

Beans such as kidney, black and pinto are also super-healthy protein foods. As with soy, you may enjoy trying pre-made bean foods such as fat-free refried beans or canned baked beans. Beans can also be added to many foods, including quesadillas, soups, chili, salads and nachos. You'll find some kid-approved bean recipes in the recipe section of this book.

If you are interested in learning to cook with tofu or beans, look for a good vegetarian cookbook. Vegetarians are the experts because they eat beans and soy nearly every day!

Provisions:
Ideas for Proteins to Serve

Most people already have their favorite protein foods and should just try switching to Smarter versions of any less-healthy ones. Still, a few extra ideas never hurt. The listings with an asterisk (*) are in the recipe section of this book.

Lunch

- Sandwich with low-fat deli meat
- Salmon Salad*
- Peanut butter on whole-grain bread
- Nuts
- Tuna-Cheese Burgers*
- Warm Bean Dip and Chips*
- Orange Juice Hummus* with veggies
- Hard-boiled eggs
- Leftovers from dinner
- Low-fat hot dogs
- Baked Beans

Dinner

- Easy Orange Chicken*
- Beef Stew*
- Quinoa and Tomato Soup*
- Grilled, broiled or steamed extra-lean beef, chicken or turkey

- Plain Fish*
- Salmon Patties*
- Black Bean Salad*
- Beans and Rice*
- Salsa Bean Soup*
- Edamame*
- Chicken Nuggets*
- Lower-fat frozen chicken strips or patties
- Lower-fat frozen fish sticks or patties
- Healthy Hamburgers*
- Pancakes*
- Low-fat sausage

* *In recipe section*

Protein Survival Tips

With all the Empty meats out there, switching to leaner proteins can some-times feel like a journey through uncharted territory. The following tips should help you find the right path for your family:

How Much Meat Is a Healthy Portion?

The current recommended adult serving for all meat is three to five ounces, which is about the size of a deck of cards or regular bar of soap. This usual-ly feels too small to an adult meat-lover. And small children are supposed to have even less, about one to three ounces of meat per day.

But before your meat-lovers run screaming into the wilderness, let them know that there is some good news: If you are truly following all the other guidelines in this book and you select extra-lean Smart meats, your family can have larger serving sizes of meat sometimes. So rather than restrict the meat intake for each member of the family, just buy a reasonable amount of extra-lean meat—about four to six ounces per person—and try not to worry too much about serving size.

> ### A Closer Look at Calories in Meat
> Most meat is higher in calories than other foods, making meat one way that some people eat too many calories too often. For example, chicken is about 50 calories per ounce, and fatty red meats can reach 100 to 125 calories per ounce. (Compare this to many fruits and vegetables that are about 15 to 25 calories per ounce.) But many people have come to think that meat portions of eight to 16 ounces are normal and now eat these restaurant-sized portions at home, too.
>
> The problem with this is that a 16-ounce steak contains more than 1,600 calories! That's about the number of calories you burn in a five-hour workout at the gym or running nonstop at the playground. In addition, research shows that we tend to eat whatever we are given on a plate—even if it is too much food. Most of us will eat the entire meat portion given to us regardless of the size and number of calories. The solution is to start with smaller portions and use mostly Smart meats—then let people come back for seconds.

If your family's meat portions are regularly more than around a quarter pound per person (four ounces), try sometimes using meat as a flavoring instead of the main course. You can do this by serving more stews, soups, casseroles and sauces made with meat. That way, your family gets to enjoy the flavor of meat but will end up with smaller portion sizes. These mixed foods automatically balance the family's meat intake with the vegetables and grains they usually contain.

No matter how you choose to serve it, every parent knows that meat is one of those foods that kids eat in strange quantities. One day your kid won't eat any, and the next day she wants hers and yours, plus the meat you were going to serve as leftovers the next day. Just let her self-regulate (unless you don't have enough). With Smart foods, including lean meats, children get signals from their bodies about what they need!

Empty Meats—The Ones That Taste So Good

Who can resist the smell of bacon? Many of us who eat meat have a real emotional attachment to particular types of meat. It can be hard to change to leaner forms when it means giving up old favorites.

Meredith is a bright, active and highly opinionated three-year-old. Sometimes she likes the meat the rest of the family eats and other times . . . she won't even try it. Her mom wisely doesn't comment but also doesn't prepare Meredith a different meal. One night, after several meatless days, her mom served the family Chicken Nuggets (see recipe section). Meredith ate 12 nuggets! Her mom watched in amazement. The next day she ate the four leftover pieces. Then, the following day, Meredith went right back to her meat-rejecting ways. But her mom doesn't worry—she knows Meredith will fill up on meat again when she is good and ready. Meanwhile, both Meredith and her mom just relax and enjoy eating together. ✗

It's easier to change if you really believe in what you're doing. The saturated fats in Empty meats are a health hazard to your family when eaten frequently. In fact, intake of excessive animal fat has been associated with obesity, cancer, heart disease, inflammatory arthritis, diabetes and chronic pain.

Try transforming Empty meats into In-Betweens by mixing them with beans, leaner meat, whole grains or vegetables. A little bacon could go on top of a salad or in an otherwise healthy sandwich. Sausage in small quantities makes a wonderful addition to many dishes. If you use only part of a package, put the rest in the freezer for later use.

Getting "Deep-Fried" Satisfaction without Deep-Frying

Deep-fried meats are often family favorites: chicken nuggets, popcorn shrimp, fried catfish. Whether an old family recipe, store-bought or a fast-food version, deep-frying turns any meat into an Empty choice. The crispier the meat after cooking, the more oil has been absorbed by the food. Deep-frying a food causes the total calories to double, triple or quadruple.

Don't believe all the myths you hear about some deep-fried foods being lower in calories. Fried foods absorb huge amounts of oil regardless of the frying temperature or how quickly they are deep-fried. Even using healthier oils does not stop the food from being very high in calories.

Worst of all, many restaurants and delis use cheap, partially hydrogenated vegetable oils called "liquid shortening" to deep-fry foods. A potato turned into French fries can have as much unhealthy saturated fat as a fatty piece of steak. Obviously, that reason alone makes most deep-fried restaurant foods terribly unhealthy and something to avoid.

Besides being unhealthy, fried foods are just too hard to self-regulate. Most kids and adults can easily eat much more oil in a fried food than they would normally eat if the oil were added to the top of the food. For example, an order of ten chicken nuggets has about as much fat as five teaspoons (almost two tablespoons) of oil—more than most of us would pour on a salad. Nobody needs all those extra calories. Of course, fried foods can be an occasional special treat or served in very small portions but should not be eaten routinely as part of a healthy diet.

The good news is that you can replace many of your favorite deep-fried foods with healthier versions. There are many other ways to get a similar

---

 A Closer Look at Getting Protein without Eating Meats

Protein sources are classified as "complete" or "incomplete" depending on how many of the 22 most important amino acids they supply. The body can actually "manufacture" nine of these. However, the 13 others must be supplied by your food and are called "essential amino acids" (it's "essential" that you eat them). Protein from animal sources, including meat and milk, tend to contain all these essential amino acids, so they are called "complete proteins." However, these sources often contain saturated fat, so picking lean, low-fat or nonfat types is important. Protein sources that lack one or more of the essential amino acids are called "incomplete proteins." These are usually plant sources of protein such as fruits, vegetables, grains, beans and nuts.

The good news is that eating a variety of Smart foods throughout the day will supply more than enough protein. In fact, the body can store amino acids from various foods and use them later. Therefore, the idea of having to worry about proteins by combining certain foods (for example, beans and rice) at the same meal is not necessary—unless you want to do it because it tastes good! It is also not necessary to have meat at every meal or even every day. Please note: If your family is strictly vegan (no eggs, milk or meat), you will need to be more careful and should seek additional nutrition support.

crispy texture and some of the delightful taste associated with deep-frying. You can bake a food in the oven (oven-frying) or lightly pan-fry food in a small amount of oil (pan-frying). Try the healthy Chicken Nuggets in the recipe section of this book. Or, if you prefer, hunt through the frozen, breaded meat section of your grocery store. A few fish sticks and breaded chicken breast fillets pass the protein field test as In-Between—or even Smart—protein choices.

Beans, Fake Meats and Tofu Don't Always Sound So Great

If your family doesn't eat beans now, check the recipe section for some great bean recipes that are kid-approved and easy to make. Even if you don't like beans, you might be surprised how much your kids do! Many kids like them because beans have a mild flavor, are easy to chew and can be turned into fun dips.

If you are somewhat bean-resistant yourself, start by replacing some meat with beans in your favorite recipes (chili, casseroles, soups, salads). You can always sneak more beans into a taco, enchilada or quesadilla. Or try eating a bean-based dip or hummus with your pre-dinner vegetables.

As for fake meats and tofu, you can have a very healthy diet without these items if you prefer. The main soy food I really recommend for families is edamame because children love it so much. (See the recipe section in this book for more ideas.)

If Your Kids Refuse Healthy Proteins

There is no reason to bribe or force your children to eat their meat (or anything else, for that matter). People can do well without a lot of meat, nuts or beans. So remember not to offer to substitute an Empty choice (such as deep-fried chicken nuggets) if your kids refuse the protein choice at a meal.

Your child will be fine because you are serving a variety of other healthy foods during the day. Many other foods such as whole grains and dairy contain plenty of protein. If you are still concerned, serve high-protein foods that are nothing like meat: pancakes (made with whole-grain flour, milk and eggs), peanut butter and jelly sandwiches on whole-wheat bread or home-made muffins with nuts. You might even attempt bean dip or a tofu smoothie as a snack.

Cautious eaters may have an easier time with utterly plain, recognizable, un-spiced foods, such as baked chicken or oven-fried fish. Also, remember that ketchup or barbeque sauce is not just for chicken nuggets. Serve it with fish, baked chicken or even eggs if that's what it takes. (Yes, ketchup and other sauces contain sweeteners and salt, but usually not enough to worry about.)

Continue to offer new foods with the confidence that your kids will eventually try them. For the vast majority of children, a protein-rejection stage will eventually pass as long as you continue to role model enjoying the healthy stuff yourself.

Proteins On the Go

If you need to pack proteins, here are a few quick Smart ideas:

- PB&J—using natural peanut butter, of course
- Peanut butter and fruit—try bananas, apple slices, diced dried apricots or raisins
- Smart deli meats in sandwiches or roll-ups
- Nuts
- Hummus with veggies or whole-grain crackers for dipping
- Bean salads
- Tiny cans of tuna
- Beef jerky (I prefer the nitrite-free varieties)
- Any nonfat dairy from Week 3

Many healthy proteins must be refrigerated. If you are packing them for a lunch, try freezing a smoothie in a lidded plastic bottle to use for cooling the whole meal. Or simply include a small ice pack.

Finding Smart Proteins in Restaurants

Smart proteins can be found in most restaurants, but they can be hard to spot on the menu. With all meats, ask that they leave off or serve on the side things such as cheese, butter, gravy, special sauces and other very high-calorie toppings when ordering.

Always ask if the meat is deep-fried, even if it is on a salad. I've been fooled many times, thinking I was ordering a healthy option and ending up with deep-fried food. Watch for words such as "fingers," "sticks," "nuggets," "breaded" or "popcorn"—these are Empties. Grilled, broiled or steamed are words that imply a healthier cooking method.

Hamburgers are always a favorite and are actually a healthier option than anything fried. Most fast-food restaurants use lean hamburger to avoid shrinkage during cooking, so the meat is an In-Between. The killer is usually the burger portion size: Have you noticed how big burgers are these days? Order a regular burger—not double, triple or monster!

Pork and steak eaters can look for the lean cuts discussed earlier. When in doubt, look for a loin cut or ask your server for the leanest cut offered.

Beans and nuts can be harder to find. Sometimes a vegetarian bean dish is offered, but often the beans are full of added fats or cheese. If you aren't sure what you're getting, ask.

In general, kids' menus are made up of the very worst protein choices the restaurant owners could find (fried chicken nuggets, hot dogs, mac and cheese), so I almost never order off the kids' menu for my children. Two small kids can split an adult portion of a more healthy choice, or they can each order an adult serving of what they want and you can take the leftovers home. This strategy has several other advantages: They don't get a free soda, they don't get a free cookie and they don't get an annoying free toy that the dog eats when you get home.

A Closer Look at Health Concerns about Meat

Mad cow disease, bird flu, salmonella, E-coli—these are just a few of the health concerns about meat. Many of these concerns are based partly on reality and partly on media hype. If you become worried, check with reputable sources such as the Centers for Disease Control (www.cdc.gov) or your healthcare provider so you get the facts.

The most important thing you can do to protect your family is to treat raw meat and eggs with respect: Don't allow the juice to drip in the refrigerator, on the floor or on clean serving dishes. You should also wash dirty cooking surfaces, utensils and cutting boards with hot, soapy water. Cook all meats thoroughly, and make sure meats you are served in restaurants are also cooked well. Probably most importantly, teach your family to always wash their hands well before eating.

Major Points of Interest
What to Keep in Mind about Proteins

As you continue to hunt down and offer your family Smart proteins, remember these points:

- Pick proteins lower in fats and added sweeteners—and never use any that have trans fats or partially hydrogenated oils, of course.
- Most people serve healthy proteins for:
  - Lunch
  - Dinner
- Enjoy a variety of Smart proteins such as extra-lean meats, fish, seafood, soy and beans.
- Remember that many other foods your family is now eating offer protein: dairy, whole grains and vegetables. So if your kids won't eat many high-protein foods, double-check that they are getting a variety of other healthy foods.
- While working on this step, continue to eat fruits and vegetables! Also remember to use low-fat, low-sugar dairy and whole-grain foods.

DAILY ITINERARY (after Week 5)	Fruits	Veggies	Dairy Foods	Grains	Proteins
Breakfast	✔		✔	✔	
Lunch	✔	✔	✔	✔	✔
Dinner		✔✔		✔	✔
Snacks/Desserts	✔		✔		

Pick mostly Smart choices. Try to limit In-Betweens to one per meal or snack.

Now that you have added all these healthy foods to your family's diet, you may want to post this daily itinerary on your refrigerator as a reminder of what to include in each meal or snack.

After Week 5, your daily Smart eating pattern now contains all the additions needed in a healthy diet. Enjoy the foods listed on the Daily Itinerary on the previous page, along with healthy fats, toppings and an occasional treat.

As you complete this step, take a moment to congratulate yourself and your family. You have come a long way. You can now march confidently into the wilds of the grocery store and identify the healthiest, Smartest foods available no matter how well camouflaged they are among the Empty pretenders. You have figured out ways to add all these wonderful foods to your family's meals. This is one of the most amazing gifts you could ever give your family. Great job!

WEEK **6**

Escaping from Empties

Finally, the time has come for the last leg of your journey: getting away from some of the Empties lurking around your otherwise fantastic diet. Of course, you aren't going to do away with *all* of them. Keeping a few Empties in your life serves two very important purposes in your lifelong eating adventures. First, they're fun. Second, having a few Empties around keeps kids from being overly fascinated with them.

Remember: Empties are foods that have very little or no nutritional value, just calories. A food is an Empty when it contains lots of sugar, excess or unhealthy fat, or both. Plus, as you certainly know by now, any food containing partially hydrogenated oil is automatically an Empty no matter what else it contains.

Your Empty Goal

Before jumping into this step, please understand that the goal is *not* to get rid of Empties entirely. That would be totally unrealistic and overly restrictive. But eating too many Empties can cause several problems:

- You get too full to eat healthy foods.
- You gain weight from eating too many calories.
- Or both! You are too full to eat healthy foods *and* you gain weight.

It is a balancing act to decide how often you eat Empties, what serving sizes you eat and when you serve them. The first sign that you're eating too many Empties or that you're eating them too close to mealtimes is that your family is not hungry for the healthy foods that you serve at regular meals and snacks. When treats are interfering with nutrition, you need to cut back! When Empties crowd out Smart foods, the next sign you notice could be unhealthy weight gain.

Most families should limit themselves to no more than one or two Empties per day. In general, these Empties should replace an In-Between at a regularly scheduled meal or snack.

Of course, all Empties are not created equal! When choosing a fun Empty for the family, look for ways to make the treats a bit healthier when you can. Low-fat ice cream contains calcium, so it has more nutrition than a soda. A granola bar is a better treat than a trans fat-filled doughnut.

Stay Upbeat

It is important to keep this step upbeat and not let it become a war in your family. With any luck, your family has probably already eliminated some junk foods to make way for all the Smart and In-Between foods you've added.

And you may have already found satisfying substitutes for many of the Empties you've given up. During this week, you can find more substitutes.

Finally, most people in your family may have some buy-in for getting rid of Empties. Your teenager may want better sports performance and more muscles, your preschooler might feel clever and grown-up if he helps the family get rid of Empties and your school-age child may enjoy reading labels and helping you discover great substitutes for Empties. Adults, of course, can understand the long-term health and weight consequences of giving up most Empty foods. Be sure to be lavish with your praise every time one of your kids (or an adult in your household, for that matter) figures out a way to eliminate an Empty without feeling deprived.

Also, remember that you get to keep your favorite Empties! You may decide to eat them less often or eat them instead of a less favorite junk food. Or, you might find clever ways of mixing your favorite Empties with Smart foods to create In-Betweens.

Why Cut Out Most Empties?

Empties seem normal because so much of our diet is made up of them, but they are unhealthy. If someone in your family needs more reasons to eat fewer Empties, here are a few:

- Empties have almost nothing in them but calories—they do not contain nutritious things the body needs to grow and thrive.
- Empties make you full so you don't want all the Smart foods your body needs to prevent disease and feel great.
- Empties are linked with diseases such as diabetes and obesity.
- Empties are often made with the cheapest, unhealthiest types of fats, including partially hydrogenated oils, which contain trans fat. These fats can set the stage for heart disease later in life.
- Empties often leave you feeling bloated, tired and sluggish. When people change to a mostly healthy diet, they often notice a major increase in energy.
- Empties can lead to excess weight gain. They are high in calories, served in large quantities and very hard to stop eating once you start!
- High-calorie Empties are especially hard on kids, who need fewer calories than adults because they have smaller bodies and need lots of nutrition because they are growing.

How to Identify Empties

In general, Empties are made out of sugar and other sweeteners, or unhealthy or excessive fats. A doughnut is the ultimate example because it contains plenty of both, with a little refined flour to hold it together!

If you are suspicious that a food is an Empty, read the Ingredients list. If the first ingredient is a type of sweetener or some form of fat, the food is an Empty (unless it is a healthy fat used to top a Smart food). Also, if the food contains partially hydrogenated fat, it is an Empty. On the other hand, if the first ingredient is Smart or In-Between, draw on your species identification skills from past weeks to determine if the food overall is Smart, In-Between or Empty.

> ### Spotting Empties
> - **Identifying features:** Made of mostly sugar or saturated fat—or contain trans fats (partially hydrogenated oil)
> - **Worst aspects:** Fill you up without providing vitamins, minerals, fiber or protein
> - **Best aspects:** Attractive to almost everyone; taste good; add fun to our diet
> - **Number of servings to offer:** Less is better—most days just one
> - **Varieties:** Lurk near many Smart and In-Between foods, often imitating their packaging; thrive in soda and snack machines, many restaurants and cafeterias, gas stations and movie theaters; enjoy tempting you at parties

Empties Made with Sugar

Sweeteners, including sugar, corn syrup, honey and all the other sweeteners listed in the chart "Words Used for Added Sweetener" (on page 29), are in lots of foods. People are naturally drawn to sweet tastes, and children seem to absolutely crave sugary foods. You have probably noticed that the more sugary foods you eat, the more you seem to crave.

However, our bodies do best when the majority of the sugar we consume comes from foods that contain naturally occurring sugars, such as the "fructose" in whole fruits and the "lactose" in nonfat dairy. These foods are easier to self-regulate because the sugars are balanced with some combination of fiber, vitamins, minerals and proteins. Eating these foods can help you feel full and well nourished so your body can more easily say "stop."

On the other hand, foods containing lots of added sweetener are often hard to stop eating because they taste sweet but aren't as filling. Without fiber, protein or nutrients, your body may not register the calories until you have overeaten. For example, picture your child drinking a regular 12-ounce can of soda or lemonade: It takes only a few minutes to drink, but a single can contains about 10 percent of the calories a typical seven-year-old needs for the entire day! On the other hand, for the same number of calories your child could have an apple, a handful of baby carrots *and* some baked potato chips.

> ### A Closer Look at Sugar: Is It Really Bad?
> Refined table sugar is often seen as "very bad" or "dangerous" and is often rumored to be the cause of illnesses such as diabetes. Neither is true. However, all types of sweeteners (even honey, molasses and maple syrup) have close to the same number of calories and behave the same in the body. Calories from sugary foods add up quickly because sugar, in all forms, has about 800 calories per cup. You can get huge numbers of calories in just a few swallows or bites.
>
> These sugary Empties are linked with weight gain that, in turn, is related to developing type 2 diabetes and other health problems. Sugary foods also fill children up, reducing their appetite for more nutritious foods. For all these reasons, the best way to use sweeteners is in small quantities with Smart foods. Sweeteners used this way can actually help some people enjoy nutritious foods such as fruit or whole grains.

The easiest way to keep the sugary Empties at bay is to simply not bring them into your car, house or any other place where you like to snack. If you do buy them, go with the smallest package you can find.

Empties Made from Fats

All people need some fat each day. The problem is, fat adds lots of calories to foods, without making the food seem larger or take longer to eat. That is why foods that contain excess fat are Empties. These excess fats are added to foods in several ways. They are mixed into the food (such as ice cream or creamy salads), used for deep-frying (such as doughnuts, French fries, fried chicken and potato chips) or served as part of the food (such as foods that come loaded with cheese sauce or butter).

Foods containing partially hydrogenated oils and too much saturated fats are also Empties. Read more on these fats in "A Closer Look at Types of Fat" on page 51 and "A Closer Look at Identifying and Avoiding Trans Fats" on page 144.

While small servings of fat-laden Empties are fine as occasional treats, many Empties now come in gigantic portion sizes. A single burger that used to be 300 calories is now often available as a double, triple or "supreme" burger that can contain over 1,000 calories—mostly due to extra meat, cheese and sauces. Baked goods that used to be two or three ounces in size are now commonly six to 10 ounces. For example, a standard two-ounce muffin with 200 calories has grown to a five- or six-ounce muffin that contains 500 or more calories. Servings this large contain more calories than any adult needs, so you can see why they are too big for kids.

There are many strategies for cutting back on fat-filled Empties without feeling deprived. In many cases, you can swap higher-fat choices for lower-fat versions (see Substitutions for Empties chart on page 151). A great example is buying lower-fat ice cream in place of regular or premium versions. You can also buy smaller amounts of higher-fat treats so that each person eats less. For example, pick a smaller bag of chips or buy just a few croissants rather than a whole dozen. On the other hand, your family should occasionally get the chance to indulge in a large serving of fatty Empties. You might be surprised when you see your children naturally self-regulate how much of it they eat.

A Closer Look at Identifying and Avoiding Trans Fats

This rule is simple: Reduce your intake of trans fats found in "partially hydrogenated" oils and shortening. Research shows a direct, proven relationship between eating trans fat and elevated levels of the bad (LDL) cholesterol that can lead to heart disease. Although heart disease usually occurs later in life, children can start building plaque in their arteries at any age.

Trans fat is hard to avoid, however. It is still in many common foods such as cookies, chips, margarine, crackers, ice cream bars, fried foods, salad dressings and many processed foods. Parents should remain aware that most restaurants use numerous products that contain trans fat, including the fat used to make fried foods such as French fries and chicken fingers. You should check with the restaurant about the fats they use, but it is safe to assume that the vast majority of fried restaurant foods do contain trans fat. When possible, read food labels and Ingredients lists carefully.

The government now requires that trans fats be listed on Nutrition Facts labels, so don't buy products unless they say "0 grams." But stay alert: There is a labeling loophole that allows manufacturers to add up to 0.5 gram of trans fat per serving and still claim "0 grams." You can recognize this type of product by reading the Ingredients list for the words "partially hydrogenated" or even "hydrogenated" because some manufacturers leave off the word "partially." Put those products back on the shelf. There is almost always a similar food available that does not contain trans fat.

But the best day-to-day solution to avoiding fatty Empties is to find Smart, lower-fat replacements for fatty foods. Then serve a healthy fat at the table so it can be added as a topping or flavoring. When kids add their own Smart fats, they can self-regulate the amount they need of toppings, such as salad dressing or nuts. When healthy fats are added to a Smart food, the food remains Smart.

Toppings higher in saturated fats, such as butter, cheese sauce, whipped cream or sour cream, should be used less often and in smaller quantities. But they can still be served at the table for everyone to add to their own food. When less-healthy toppings are used in moderation, the resulting combination will be your In-Between for that meal or snack. On the other hand, using large amounts of toppings high in saturated fat turns Smart and In-Between foods into Empties.

How to Act around Wild Empties

Empties should be a fun, interesting part of life. They should not be allowed to take over your life or be treated with fear, but they also should not be banned. I like to think of Empties as somewhat wild animals that you can tame and then keep around as pets. Here are a few ideas for taming the Empties in your life so you can continue to enjoy them in small amounts:

Stay Relaxed (Show No Fear)

Stay calm about eating junk food, and control what you can control. My children are fed trans fats at birthday celebrations at preschool, and they are given sodas and candy when visiting other homes. Sometimes our family grabs fast food after hiking all day because we are starving on our way home. As a parent, you just have to make whatever changes you can without creating stress, embarrassment and discontent in your household!

Don't Allow the Empties to Take Over Your Home

If you surround yourself with Empty foods they will take over your diet. Instead, surround yourself with Smart and In-Between foods. As you have added in a healthy variety and quantity of fruits, vegetables, low-fat dairy, whole grains and lean proteins, many Empties were probably crowded out and therefore eliminated. For example, serving fruit for dessert removes the ice cream you might have had otherwise. Packing whole-grain crackers in your child's lunch box eliminates the potato chips they could have eaten for lunch. And the Smart foods you add into your diet will balance out some of the negative effects of junk food.

Eating Fewer Empties Should Be about Health, Not Losing Weight

Keep the focus in a relaxed way on your "family value" for eating well most of the time. Always avoid telling your kids that they can't eat Empties because they need to watch their weight.

Remember, eating Empty foods means that you're not eating Smart foods. Children will grow into a healthy weight if they are allowed to self-regulate with healthy foods most of the time and have the occasional single serving of an Empty.

Children should not have to worry about the shape of their bodies! They should learn to love their bodies by taking good care of them, listening to their own hunger cues and exercising for fun.

Be a Role Model about Your Own Weight

Be a role model for positive attitudes toward your weight. If you're always worried about your weight, research shows that you can pass this worry on to your children, especially daughters.

Although we don't always realize it, we're serving as role models for our kids just as much with our negative actions as with the positive ones. So try not to role model ignoring your own hunger cues by being hungry and then grumpy, or going on and off diets. Instead, role model snacking on a banana rather than a bag of chips, turning down the extra cupcake at a school picnic or ordering water instead of soda when you eat out. These behaviors will show your kids positive eating behaviors that will, in turn, naturally lead *you* toward a healthier weight as well. Most importantly, these choices will also teach your children that you value good nutrition and enjoy healthy eating!

How to Tame the Empties

Empties will always be a part of your life. But here are strategies that should help keep them under control:

Don't Keep Empties Around

Here is a nugget of truth: If you buy it or bake it, you and your family will eat it—all of it. If you don't want to eat an Empty, don't have it around. Realistically, plenty of Empties will come into your life from parties, friends, work, school and church (among several hundred other places). So you really don't need to buy or bake many of your own.

Go with Small Quantities

When you do buy or make Empties, go with a quantity that the family can safely polish off quickly. Even if the party-size bag of chips is cheaper, or you have a two-for-one coupon, your family is better off with a smaller amount of an Empty around. If you are baking chocolate chip cookies, just make half a batch. With lesser quantities, you can serve the treat with a smile and just let everyone eat until it is gone. This way, you don't have to be the bad guy who tells them to stop.

Go Ahead—Throw Empty Foods Away

People are shocked when they find out I do this, but I do throw away food that I don't want in my house. I have thrown away an enormous box of doughnuts, the Halloween candy my kids didn't like and gave to me, bakery cupcakes, unhealthy peanut butter—anything that contains trans fat or is just not a good Empty to have lying around the house.

Eliminate Your Least-Favorite Empties First

Take a minute to think about the Empties you and your kids have had in the past two or three days. Did you eat any Empties you didn't really enjoy that much? Maybe a hot dog, a not-too-great cookie, a soda or a too-large dish of macaroni and cheese? The ones you don't really like are definitely the ones to give up first! Any time you decide to eat an Empty, you should *really* enjoy it.

When my order of Girl Scout cookies arrived this year, I just happened to be researching trans fats for this book. The box claimed "0g trans fat per serving." But the Ingredients list told a different story! The cookies contained partially hydrogenated oil, the type of oil that contains trans fat. Obviously, the cookie manufacturer was taking full advantage of the loophole in the labeling laws for trans fats. This loophole allows foods with up to 0.5 gram trans fat per serving (in this case just two cookies) to be labeled as "0g trans fat." So my kids and I talked about it. We even tasted a few cookies. Then, together, we decided to throw the rest away. That might sound extreme, but I knew from vast personal experience that if we had them in the house, we would slowly (or, more likely, quickly) consume all that trans fat, sugar, white flour, glycerin and artificial coloring. I don't want my children eating a food known to cause heart disease—or all those Empty calories! To soften the blow, we celebrated our happy hearts and blood vessels with a better Empty treat, some low-fat ice cream . . . which actually tasted just as good as the cookies.

Double-Check the Foods You Eat Often

Over the next few days, read the Ingredients list for any product you or your kids eat often. If the ingredients make it an Empty, start looking for a Smart or In-Between substitute food. There are many great options out there. In the past five weeks you've begun to tame the wilds of the grocery store, so this part of the adventure may be easier.

But watch for clever camouflaging! Things such as energy drinks, pretzels, graham crackers, cheese crackers, granola bars, energy bars, animal crackers, bagels, muffins and fruit chews are commonly believed to be healthy choices, but in most cases, they are actually Empties! Lots of breakfast bars, toaster pastries, cereals and instant oatmeal packs are made out of a combination of Empties and chemicals. Those popular pre-packed lunches are usually full of Empties, too.

Really LOVE Your Empty Choices

When you eat Empties for special treats, you can eat them without guilt. Go ahead and pick something that you and your family really *love*. I use a scale of one (least favorite) to 10 (favorite—"to die for") to rank an Empty. If it isn't a nine or 10, then think hard about wasting your health on a so-so Empty.

"Earn" Your Empties by Eating More Smart Foods

If you know your family will be eating a lot of Empties later in the day, offer only Smart foods before and after. You can do this before birthday parties, class parties and cookies from Grandma. You might even have a week of extremely healthy foods prior to a vacation. This should be done casually, never as a bribe or punishment. Simply serve your family their favorite Smart foods before they go and then let them enjoy the treats.

Don't Get Fooled by Cost

Are you sometimes tempted to buy foods because they are so inexpensive or because you have a coupon? That is a very common trap that even very good food trackers can fall into. The fact is that parents don't buy cigarettes for their children when they go on sale, and they don't let them watch X-rated films because they have a two-for-one pass to the theater. So follow that same logic with Empties: Don't buy junk food just because it is cheap, free or a special offer.

Living with Lurking Empties

Empties are built into our lives in many ways. The challenge is to find healthier routines that satisfy our eaters.

Snacks

Hopefully, by now your family is used to regularly scheduled snack times and isn't munching all day. Because kids often eat a lot at these snack times, snacks should be healthy. Admittedly, there are a lot of delicious Empty snack foods that tempt us all: chips, ice cream bars, candy bars, sodas, granola bars, cookies and so on. However, Empty treats are *not* a good every-day habit. Here are five ideas for improving snacks:

SUBSTITUTIONS FOR EMPTIES

Getting rid of Empties is *much* easier when you swap them for something else that your family enjoys. Fortunately, Weeks 1 through 5 have already made you an expert at switching and swapping foods. And here are a few more ideas:

	Common Examples	Healthier Possibilities
SUGAR-FILLED EMPTIES	Sugar, maple syrup, honey, fruit sauces	Use to top Smart foods to make an In-Between. Or use natural applesauce or other unsweetened fruit.
	Icing, glaze	Powdered sugar sprinkled on top
	Soda, juice drinks, energy drinks	Water, 100% juice, Cold Herbal Tea,* bubble (carbonated) water, Bubble Juice*
	Nonfat (but sugary) popsicles	100% juice popsicles
	Granola and most kids' breakfast cereals	Oatmeal or other whole-grain cereals with less sugar
	Granola bars, nutrition and energy bars	Breakfast Bars or Breakfast in a Bag*
	Cookies, cakes, muffins (even low-fat versions)	Oatmeal Cookies,* Banana Bread Muffins*
	Ice cream and frozen yogurt	Almost Instant Pudding,* Sorbet,* or low-fat ice cream or yogurt
	Graham crackers or animal crackers	Whole-wheat crackers or popcorm cakes
	Yogurts (some brands)	Other lower-sugar brands or plain yogurt mixed with fruit
	Chocolate milk (some brands)	Other lower-sugar brands, Healthier Hot Chocolate* or plain milk
	Sweetened fruit or fruit in syrup	Fresh or frozen fruit or fruit canned in 100% fruit juice.
	Fruit chews and Roll-Ups™	Fresh fruit or fruit leather made from 100% fruit.

In recipe section

SUBSTITUTIONS FOR EMPTIES (continued)

Many fat-filled Empties can be easily swapped for lower-fat choices. Here area few examples.

FAT-FILLED EMPTIES

Common Examples	Healthier Possibilities
Butter, margarine or lard	Butter/oil blend, applesauce for baked goods
Sour cream, cream cheese	Low-fat or nonfat versions
Half-and-half	Fat-free half-and-half or nonfat milk
Whipped cream	Light canned whipped topping
French fries	Some brands of frozen fries, Twice Baked Potatoes*
Fried chicken, chicken nuggets	Some brands of frozen chicken "strips," Chicken Nuggets*
Chips (potato, corn, cheese puffs)	Baked corn chips or baked potato chips
Sausage, hamburgers, hot dogs	Healthy Hamburgers,* veggie burgers or extra-lean meat
Mayonnaise	Mustard, plain nonfat yogurt, nonfat sour cream, catsup, light mayonnaise or regular mayonnaise in limited amounts
Cheese sauce and nachos	Salsa, lower-fat cheese and baked corn chips
Buttered popcorn	Low-fat popcorn (without trans fat)
Croissants and doughnuts	Whole-wheat English muffins or bagels
Pies and pastries	Same pie but without the crust
Cheese quesadillas with sour cream	Whole-wheat quesadillas with 2% cheese & non-fat sour cream
Bacon	Canadian bacon

* In recipe section

1. Don't keep junk food around; it's too easy to grab.

2. Keep healthy snacks with you if you'll be away from home at snack time.

3. Keep easy-to-serve snacks, such as fruit, nonfat yogurt, baked chips, crackers and nuts, in your home at all times.

4. Have a supply of Smart drinks on hand: herbal tea, bubble water, milk and plain water. Also, have a water bottle for each family member so you can take along water when you leave home.

5. Keep a supply of bottled water in the trunk of your car for times when you forget the water bottles.

Liquid Candy

Beverages are a necessary part of your diet, so they should be healthy. Beware, though: All beverages are not created equal. As we talked about in Week 1, many contain enormous amounts of sugar. These include sodas, part-juice drinks, sports drinks, energy drinks, sweetened ice tea, lemonade, vitamin "water" and drinks made from mixes.

These sugary drinks often fill kids up so that they don't want milk or healthy foods. In addition, these drinks can cause both kids and adults to become overweight! Many parents don't think about the hundreds of extra calories added to a meal or snack with sugary drinks. To put these beverages in perspective, here's a scary statistic: Drinking one soda or other sugary drink each day raises a kid's risk of obesity by 60 percent.

There are many healthier things for everyone in your family to drink:

- Water, ice water

- Water with a splash of lemon, lime or cranberry juice

- Nonfat milk

- Seltzer water or carbonated water (without sugar) with a splash of juice

- Herbal teas (cold or hot)

When you eat away from home, order water or milk! Decide ahead of time not to order lemonade or a soda for your children, even if a drink comes free with the meal. Here is why: The drinks are usually brought to the table first. The kids are hungry and bored, and will gulp down the drink. Then, when the food arrives, everyone is already full and doesn't want to eat. If your child is "starving" or needs a distraction, ask if the server can bring out water and a side vegetable or salad right away.

With older children, soda drinking is often out of a parent's control and is often best ignored. They may purchase sodas with their own money or drink it at friends' houses. If you're worried about the amount of soda your teens are consuming, though, try helping them calculate how much money they would save in a month if they just drank water. They might end up preferring to spend that money on something else. If they are looking for caffeine—and many teens are—you might offer to supply them with healthier caffeinated alternatives such as cold green tea or iced coffee made with lots of nonfat milk.

Some families turn to diet drinks to avoid the sugar and calories in regular sodas. The problem with diet drinks is that they condition children to expect sweet beverages, which might cause them to reject water and milk. Plus, many people do not give children diet drinks because they contain artificial sweeteners. Instead, my family enjoys full-sugar soda as a very occasional treat. Read more about artificial sweeteners in "A Closer Look at Artificial Sweeteners" on page 31.

Vitamin-Fortified Drinks

The trendy new vitamin beverages and powdered mixes are a particular disservice to children. By drinking several of these beverages in a day, children can easily get an over-dose of vitamins. At the same time, they are drinking extra sugar. All kids, and adults for that matter, would be better off with water. If you believe that your children need more vitamins, talk to their pediatrician about giving them a multivitamin.

"Adult" Drinks: Beer, Wine and Liquor

For many adults, there is just no substitute for a glass of wine or bottle of beer. These drinks can certainly be part of an overall healthy diet. However, they are Empties because they contain calories with very little nutrition and no fiber or protein.

Adults trying to lose weight should consider the amount of alcohol they are drinking each day. These calories add up quickly. Reducing the number of alcoholic drinks can result in some amazing weight loss. Beer has about 150 calories a bottle, wine has about 120 calories in a six-ounce glass and liquors have about 100 calories per shot (without mixers). Just to put those numbers in perspective, adding one drink a day to your regular diet, without any other changes, would cause you to gain about 12 pounds per year. On the other hand, if you have one or more daily drinks now and decide to cut back, you can shed those pounds without any other changes. If you decide to have a daily drink, be sure to compensate for the extra calories with exercise or cutting back on other Empties.

Old Favorite Main Dishes

If some of your favorite dinners are Empties, don't give up on them. Instead, start looking for ways to change them into In-Betweens or even Smart foods.

- Add whole-grain foods! See Week 4 for specific suggestions.
- Cut sweetener in half. You probably won't notice the difference.
- Replace saturated oils or shortening with healthy oils. This may affect the texture of some pastries and biscuits, but keep experimenting!
- Cut the amount of cheese in half and use a stronger-flavored cheese such as sharp cheddar.
- Use low-fat cheese.
- Sprinkle the cheese on top where it is most noticeable.
- Replace cream with nonfat evaporated milk.
- Replace sour cream, cottage cheese or yogurt with nonfat or low-fat versions.
- Find oven-fried recipe versions for any deep-fried foods. Recipes can be found in cookbooks or on the Internet.

Healthier Baked Foods

If you are a baker, your family is very lucky! Make them even luckier by transforming your baked goods into healthier ones. When you bake from scratch you are in control, so trade out some of the Empty ingredients for healthier ones in your favorite recipes.

- Again, go for whole grains! See Week 4.
- Cut the fat by at least one third. Then, substitute a healthy oil or margarine for solid shortening or butter. Applesauce works, too.
- Cut the sweetener in half—most people never notice.
- For an extra nutritional boost, add nuts, raisins, oatmeal, apple chunks, wheat germ, wheat bran or even nonfat dry milk.
- Make sure that chocolate chips, candies, icing and baking mixes do not contain any partially hydrogenated oils.

Empty Toppings

So many healthy foods taste even better with Empty toppings, such as butter, whipped cream, cheese sauce, maple syrup, chocolate syrup, jelly, gravy, sour cream, cream cheese, cream or half-and-half and even just sugar.

If your family is very attached to some of these toppings, you have several options:

- My favorite technique is to find a Smart topping to replace the Empty topping. Then, everyone can self-regulate quantities. Here are a few Smart toppings:
    - Salad dressing made with olive oil or canola oil
    - Nuts
    - Avocados
    - Parmesan cheese or other low-fat cheese
    - Mayonnaise
- Another idea is to replace a favorite Empty topping with a different topping that has less saturated fat than the original version: a canola oil and butter mix, lower-fat gravy, low-fat (or nonfat) sour cream, low-fat cream cheese, nonfat half-and-half, light whipped cream, etc. When you use these better-for-you versions to top Smart foods, you create an In-Between.
- Replace the topping with something less calorie-dense. You might find that your family is perfectly happy sprinkling powdered sugar over their pancakes so they end up eating fewer Empty calories than if you poured on the syrup.

- Serve each person his or her own "supply," then put the bottle or jar away. For example, give each person a few pats of butter, and then take the butter off the table.

- Cut back on how often you serve the food that goes with the topping (serve oatmeal for breakfast instead of toast and butter if the butter feels like a big issue).

Avoiding Empties On the Go

The best way to avoid grabbing Empties when you're out and about is to have Smart food with you. Take your own popcorn and water to the movie, take your own sandwiches to the football game and take your own snacks on a car trip.

Consider keeping a small stockpile of healthy food in the car or in your bag, just for emergencies. A few choices for this include whole-wheat crackers, healthy granola bars, dried fruit chews, raisins and bottled water.

Tracy was involved in setting up an Earth Day booth for kids. Her group wanted to ask kids quiz questions and give out rewards for correct answers. Of course, Tracy got pretty irritated when candy and soda were suggested, and the environmental group didn't want to hand out plastic items that would end up in the landfill. Finally, they decided to ring a loud bell for correct answers. The kids were delighted with their "reward," and the group was satisfied that they had made the children feel happy and proud without junk foods or plastic prizes.

If you do get stuck away from home with a bunch of hungry children, stop at a grocery store instead of a fast-food restaurant. Some whole-wheat crackers, string cheese, a kid-sized nonfat yogurt, baby carrots or a bunch of bananas are all much healthier than buying Empties.

As we've talked about in previous weeks, control what you can control, and then relax. You will never be able to control everything your family eats. If they eat well at home, occasional treats will not hurt them. If the treats are so frequent that they are interfering with eating Smart foods or you are noticing excess weight gain, have a family brainstorming session to think of ways to avoid so many Empties.

Survival Tips: Avoiding Empty Pitfalls

Decreasing Empties is easier when great-tasting, healthier foods keep people full and happy. But there will be challenges!

You Don't Want to Deprive Your Family

Stay confident that you are not depriving your child by reducing the number of routine Empties or saving Empties for an occasional treat. Kids don't need Empties to keep them happy or entertained; there are thousands of other ways to make children happy. Plus, a child's enjoyment of food doesn't have to be directly related to sugar and fat content.

You are teaching your kids to love a variety of foods—Empty, Smart and In-Between. Helping your kids be healthy and fit is certainly not deprivation!

You Don't Want to Deprive Yourself

Adults don't need Empties either, but sometimes it feels like we do. Adults have been eating Empties for a longer time, so it can actually be harder for adults to change long-standing eating routines. But it is just as important for adults to focus on adding healthier foods while decreasing Empties. Remember, reducing Empties in your diet is an excellent way to manage weight, stay vibrant, avoid the health problems associated with aging and provide support for the healthy life you want for your children.

If you do start to feel deprived, take a moment to analyze why. Are you cutting out the wrong Empties? It is easier to give up the Empties you'll miss the least. For example, I would really miss chocolate candy if I gave that up, but I have cookies and cake less often without feeling deprived at all. If you have a few Empties that give you great joy, definitely keep them in your life and enjoy them.

Your Kids Aren't Convinced They Like Healthy Food

If you have kids who believe they only love junk food, you might want to put some time and energy into proving them wrong! Pretty much everyone likes some healthy foods. Here are a few ways to convince your doubting children that healthy food is fun:

- Visit a berry farm and pick fresh strawberries or blueberries.
- Bake some whole-wheat bread together.
- Make homemade pizza.
- Grow cherry tomatoes in the summer and let the kids eat them right off the vine.
- Make chicken soup together—let the kids chop up the vegetables (I bet they'll eat a few)—and take it to a sick friend or relative.
- Eat watermelon in bathing suits on the lawn and then wash off with a hose.
- Go to a farmers' market and let the kids pick out fresh vegetables for a salad.
- Let your older child select a healthy recipe, find the ingredients in the store, make it and serve it to the family.
- Let your child catch her own fish and cook it that day.

Also, point out times when your kids really enjoy healthy food, even if it is just a glass of skim milk or a ripe peach. They will learn to see themselves as people who enjoy "good for you" food.

The reality is that many kids will not mind giving up most of their Empties if the Empties are replaced with fun, and of course good-tasting, healthy choices. Giving up Empties is often much harder on the parents than the kids for reasons that go beyond the food itself. Parents have to change their routines, give up some of their own comfort foods and find new ways to make the kids and adults smile. Fortunately, knowing that you're giving your whole family the gift of health can make this an easier transition.

Major Points of Interest
What to Keep in Mind about Empties

As you plan your family's escape from eating too many Empties, keep these ideas in mind:

• Empties are foods that contain excess sugar and/or excess or unhealthy fats.

• Many people find that eating a variety of Smart and In-Between fruits, vegetables, low-fat dairy foods, whole grains and lean protein foods fills them up and reduces cravings for Empties.

• Empties are fine as occasional treats. But when kids (or adults) overeat Empties they don't feel hungry for healthy food and/or gain weight from consuming too many calories.

• Reduce your family's exposure to Empties by not keeping them around the house (or car), skipping Empties you don't really love, buying smaller quantities and finding satisfying substitutes for some Empties.

• But keep your very favorite Empties! Everyone should get to enjoy some Empties as treats or as taste-enhancing additions to Smart foods.

Keeping on Track . . . or Finding Your Way Back

During the last six weeks, you have learned to identify the best foods for your family and have discovered ways to serve Smart foods that your family actually enjoys. Hopefully, you have a daily itinerary that makes feeding your family easier as well as more healthful. You have given your children the gift of eating well and are also teaching them how to feed themselves and, someday, perhaps your grandchildren!

But let's face it: Despite the amazing journey you've begun, it's not like you have packed your bags and moved to a different planet—one where there are no temptations, holidays or stressful times. You still have to deal with all the crazy things life throws at you, including plenty of opportunities to give up on Smart food and eat lots of junk food.

The reality is that absolutely everyone gets sidetracked sometimes. Finding ways to get back into your healthy routine is part of the whole process. This section will provide some tools for orienting yourself on those occasions when you get trapped in the food wilds and have to find your way back to your healthier routine.

> **A Closer Look at Working Together for Lasting Change**
> Common sense tells us that people like to have a voice in what they eat. Research backs this up: People are more cooperative when they feel in control. When people (kids included) are given a choice, they tend to feel like their ideas and preferences are respected. If you are meeting resistance about eating healthier foods, make certain to listen well. And then offer to involve the unhappy or frustrated family members in planning, shopping or even cooking. Keep in mind that changing eating habits takes time, experience and flexibility.

First Aid for Common Problems

When you run into a glitch in your eating plan, it's easy to get discouraged. But you can treat the vast majority of these problems with just a bit of first aid. You'll probably recognize several of the following common traps and pitfalls. Consider these first-aid tips to get past them:

A New Research Study Seems to Undermine Your Efforts

The daily news is full of new studies and new books about health and food. But a research study is not valid just because the media reports it. In fact, the basics of good nutrition—eating Smart foods—have not really changed much in the past 20 years. Don't stop eating a type of food, or start eating a lot of a particular food, based on just one study you hear about. Before you change your eating patterns based on "new" research, do some research yourself. Ask your doctor, pediatrician or registered dietitian, or check with respected and non-extreme web resources, such as a U.S. government food website like www.usda.gov.

Mom Has PMS

Hormones can make life feel very difficult, so make a plan ahead of time—when you're in a good mood—for these tough times! You might plan to eat at your favorite healthy restaurant, serve easy whole-grain and no trans-fat frozen meals, eat leftovers from the freezer or have your spouse or teenagers cook.

Eating Well Feels Like Too Much Work

You might hit a time when finding and eating Smart foods just feels like too much work. Planning, shopping and cooking can feel much harder when you're low on energy. This weary feeling happens to almost every parent at times, but it does go away. Just don't give up! Forgive yourself for any Empty days and make a plan to get back on track. Also, remember that Smart foods do not have to be gourmet! Whole-wheat pasta, scrambled eggs or sandwiches on whole-wheat bread are just a few easy but Smart choices.

Healthy Food Seems Boring: Feeling Deprived and Missing the "Good Stuff"

Normal, normal, normal! A healthy diet should include some special treats. Beware of making these treats so rare and so special that you give your kids the message that you're all somehow making a big sacrifice so you can be healthy. This strategy can backfire by focusing on the treat as the preferred food and making it all the more mysterious and desirable. Try just stating that you're going to serve chocolate cake or gourmet ice cream for dessert, and then enjoy it in a casual way. Or make it a routine to have something special at your weekly TGIF celebration or with Sunday dinner. Just enjoy the occasional treat without guilt and you will probably feel a lot less deprived.

Someone Is Sick

How do you keep kids eating well when someone in the family is sick, especially when it is the adult who usually cooks? Most often, you probably don't!

Of course, check with your healthcare provider for specific instructions because diet recommendations will vary depending on the type of illness.

Then, remember that you need to just get through the illness! There is nothing wrong with ordering pizza when you are too sick to cook or serving white crackers and soda to a sick child if that is all she can eat without vomiting.

You have all the skills you need to get back on track with healthy foods when everyone feels better.

Empties Left Over from Parties or Holidays

Most people feel obligated to eat leftovers, even high-calorie holiday treats, chips, whipped cream or cakes. Some people can put leftovers in the freezer and use them for a later party. For other people like me, that doesn't work; I know the food is in there, and I can easily gnaw through anything frozen. Some people give the leftover food away, but remember that then someone else is stuck eating a bunch of Empties.

The best thing to do with major supplies of Empties is to throw them out. As discussed in "Week 6: Escaping from Empties," this is hard to do, but it solves the problem of overeating for the next few days or weeks. You are not really wasting food if you think about the greater cost of weight gained or poor nutrition—or even crabby kids after too much sugar.

Busy, Busy Schedule with NO Time to Think or Cook

Life is already busy, and then a holiday arrives or the kids start soccer season. Or maybe you have out-of-town visitors. These super-busy times call for drastic help.

Some tricks for desperately busy times include:

- Order veggie pizza. Serve a bag of baby carrots and dip before the pizza arrives.
- Have three or four emergency meals on hand at all times. My favorites are:
  - In-Between frozen chicken strips and frozen low-fat olive oil French fries (brand names listed at www.feedingthekids.com). Serve with frozen vegetables.

- Baked corn chips dipped into warmed nonfat refried beans mixed with salsa and topped with a sprinkle of 2% cheddar cheese. This meal doesn't even require plates or forks!
- Whole-grain crackers and milk served with enhanced canned soup (see the recipe section).
- Whole-grain pasta topped with tomato sauce and parmesan cheese. Serve edamame in the pod while the pasta cooks.

- Run into the grocery store and grab a veggie tray from the deli or a prewashed bag of lettuce, then get a rotisserie chicken (pull the skin off before serving), some whole-grain bakery bread and some easy-to-serve fruit, such as apples or bananas.

- Cook once, eat three times. Cook on nights you are home or on the weekend, but cook huge amounts. You can freeze the extra or serve it again by adding a few extra ingredients to make it taste different. My favorite is soup; the next day I add something new such as whole-wheat noodles, beans or extra vegetables.

- Crock-Pot meals. You can make almost anything in a Crock-Pot from chicken to stew. To make life easier, I usually make something that includes at least one serving of vegetables and the protein, such as beef stew or chicken and vegetables. A Crock-Pot cookbook really helps with lots of good ideas.

Your Family Starts Complaining or Begging for Junk Food

If you get complaints about what you're serving, don't argue. Put the complainers to work fixing the problem in a way that makes everyone happy!

- Set out healthy options, then let each person make his own: pizza, salad, stuffed baked potato, sandwich, pasta salad, etc. If someone skips all the vegetable options, just be glad you used whole grains!

- Once a week, eat dinner while watching a movie or even playing cards. Food tastes better accompanied by "fun," and the distraction might limit whining.

- Show complainers the daily eating pattern itinerary from this book and let them request anything they want—as long as it fits in the chart and doesn't involve too much work. My kids are always smugly satisfied with their selections, especially if they aren't my favorites. (Sardines on whole-wheat pasta, anyone?)

- See if the complainers are missing particular items. Remember, everyone should love the Empties they eat. Maybe some members of your family would rather have different Empties or In-Betweens than others.

- Take the kids on a treasure hunt at the store. Teach them the field test for a type of food—whole-grain cereal, for example—and let them select any item they want if they can prove it qualifies as a Smart or In-Between food.

- Or, if the begging is happening at the store, go shopping without the kids for a while. They may not miss the food as much if they don't have to hear it calling to them from the store shelves.

You Want Something New

Eating well can become a very interesting and creative part of your life. Still, there are times when even the most creative, enthusiastic cook just can't think of anything interesting to fix for a meal.

At a school in Denver, each class gets to pick a theme for their own garden plot each year. One creative class picked "Vegetables We Hate to Eat." Once they grew all the vegetables, the director of the program (who, I admit, was a professional chef) talked the kids into trying several eggplant recipes, which they loved! Soon, shocked parents started calling for recipes because their children were requesting eggplant at home. ✗

There are amazing foods that your family might like if you're willing to give them a taste test. If you are ready to expand your repertoire, here are some ways to do it:

- Look hard at *all* the vegetables available. Pick a new one and check out recipes on the Internet. Or, ask a fellow shopper how he uses the vegetable he just put in the cart. I've gotten some great ideas doing this.

- Watch a cooking show on TV or rent one on DVD.

- Take a healthy or natural cooking class.

- Ask an experienced cook for a lesson or ideas.

- Shop at a new grocery store that features healthier options. Check out the recipe cards most stores offer. You can even ask store employees for ideas on how to cook a new type of fish or what to do with an unusual fruit.

- Buy a cookbook or a magazine on lighter eating. Some of my favorites are listed at www.feedingthekids.com.

- Get some ideas from a friend who is from a different country or ethnic background. A Japanese friend recently taught me to make "family-friendly" sushi. It is now one of our favorite meals—fairly easy, healthy and a total change of pace.

- Ask your kids to look for ideas in the store or in cookbooks and magazines. Kids often come up with great creative and fun ideas.

Your Family Enjoys Eating Out Frequently

If your family eats in restaurants once a week or less, you might decide to let everyone order whatever sounds good. However, eating out more than once a week makes it necessary to look for healthy options.

I've talked about traps and survival tips for eating in restaurants throughout the book, but we can all use more ideas. A few of my favorites for avoiding Empties and finding healthy foods in restaurants include:

- Pick a restaurant that will support your healthy eating values. It is much easier to make good choices if you are not at a location that has all your very favorite Empty foods and not much else. Some types of restaurants tend to serve more vegetables, including Chinese, Japanese, burrito places or pasta restaurants that have good salads.

- Collect menus from your favorite restaurants. Ask if they have ingredients or nutrition information available for any of their foods.

- Talk to the family before going into the restaurant and make the rules clear. Decide what each person will order ahead of time. Many people go into a burger place vaguely imagining ordering a grilled chicken sandwich with no mayo and a salad, but leave with a burger and fries! Here are some examples of helpful eating-out rules:
  - Nobody orders fried foods.
  - Everyone gets a salad, vegetable soup or a vegetable side dish brought out first.
  - Whole grains are chosen when available.
  - Water only to drink if they don't offer nonfat or low-fat milk.

- Have dessert at home after the meal—serve fruit, nonfat yogurt or homemade pudding.
- Add a salad or a side vegetable to your usual order.
- Snack on baby carrots or an apple in the car on the way to the restaurant.
- If you do want an Empty, split an order among the family.
- Ask to have the bread or chips served *with* the meal—not before—so you don't pig out on Empties or In-Betweens before the meal.
- Ask to substitute a menu item, such as a baked potato for the fries.
- Remember that most children's menus offer only Empties followed by a cookie or ice cream, served with a soda. When this is the case, order from the adult menu for your kids. If the meal is too big, they can either split the order with a sibling or take leftovers home for lunch. However, most kids' meals actually contain just as many calories as a healthy adult entrée.

Another choice, of course, would be to break the Empties habit by eating at home more often, where you can control your eating environment. Eating quick and easy Smart foods at home might make everyone feel less deprived than trying to enforce rules when you eat out.

Your Child Gets Empties for Snack at Preschool or Childcare

A lot of children end up having snacks and meals at childcare or preschool. If you're sending the snacks, always include some Smart choices, such as fruit, vegetable sticks, whole-grain crackers and so on. If the snacks are parent contributions or supplied by the school, consider suggesting a "picked or plucked" policy for snacks so that each snack will contain at least one plain fruit or vegetable.

You might also let the school know about the American Academy of Pediatrics limited-juice guidelines. Most teachers will be more than happy to give up sticky, messy juice once they know that water or nonfat milk is so much healthier for the kids.

If you can't get the school to change its snack policy or you don't feel like making a fuss, just relax and feed your kids healthy snacks whenever they are with you.

Each year, Sue taught her preschool students a nutrition unit, then watched in frustration as the kids hopped up and went to the snack table. She had a policy of assigning the snack basket to a different family each week. Each child looked forward to his turn. Sometimes the contributions weren't too bad, but too often they were cupcakes (sometimes called "muffins"), bags of corn puffs, cookies, "granola" bars and sugary "juice" drinks. Obviously, these foods didn't fit in with the nutrition message Sue was trying to teach. So the next year, she changed the snack policy. The school provides healthy crackers and water, and the parents contribute fruits or vegetables. The kids still get to enjoy bringing in the snack basket on their week, and the parents actually have an easier time knowing what to buy. Best of all, these little kids are getting a wonderful introduction to lots of types of fruits and vegetables. Plus, Sue knows she is giving a consistent message when she teaches the nutrition unit!

Your Child's School Lunches Aren't Following Healthy Guidelines

More schools are serving healthier foods thanks to new local and federal laws. Unfortunately, some school cafeterias still offer unhealthy options or do not have to follow the new wellness food laws because they meet exemptions. That's too bad, since schools lunches could be a "hands-on" opportunity to teach children about the pleasures of a varied and healthy diet.

Schools that change their menus to offer healthier choices such as whole grains and vegetables are surprised to find that children eat them. Encourage your child's school to continue expanding healthier choices and to eliminate Empty offerings.

My son's kindergarten teacher figured out a meaningful and healthy way to get into the holiday spirit with her students. The children brought in donations of scarves, mittens and hats to decorate a "Giving Tree." They also decorated the tree with handmade paper ornaments and paper chains. By the time school let out for the holidays, the tree was covered with their handmade crafts and gifts for those in need. The children felt a real sense of pride and accomplishment—and they didn't seem to notice the lack of the usual holiday junk-food party

Meanwhile, you may have to call on your own survival skills by sending a healthy packed lunch with your kids. If packing a lunch or snack is just not an option for you, be sure you serve only healthy foods at other meals and snacks on school days.

Kids Are Getting Lots of Empty "Treats" at School

This is a tricky and difficult issue! Many teachers, parents and administrators see junk food as an important way to make children feel happy and loved. They may view any concern about providing healthier choices for the children as restrictive or uptight. This is partly because Empties are so common in our everyday lives that people now consider them part of normal eating.

If this is a problem that concerns you, your first step is to have a conversation with your child's teacher or the school principal. If done calmly and logically (you might share this book with them), you may inspire some positive action. Specific suggestions and alternatives, such as the following, can help:

- Cakes, candies and other sugary foods do not need to be served at every school event or for every minor holiday. Children might enjoy non-food celebrations, such as extra recess, yelling as loud as possible or creating artwork.
- Children shouldn't be given food treats to reward academic progress or for good behavior. There are plenty of positive non-food rewards such as stickers, notes or just high-fives.
- Holiday celebrations should be limited to just a few holidays. Even then, the kids can be offered a variety of food, some of which is healthy.

There Are Tons of Empties at Every Activity

Churches, school groups, scout meetings, sports teams and other large groups often turn to bulk Empties because they are so easy and cheap when feeding a big crowd. Again, if this is an occasional situation, don't worry about it! If your children attend an event involving lots of Empties once a week or more, however, you'll need to figure out a solution. Some of the following might help:

- Use this book to help your group develop a list of Smarter snack ideas. Talk to the organizers about changing the menu or food policies.

- Feed your kids a large snack, or even an entire meal, before they go.

- Offer to take charge of the food and make healthy changes yourself.

- Pack a cool and healthy alternative for your child.

- If it's all right with your kids, arrive after (or leave before) the meal or snack. (Many kids don't mind this since, as my oldest explained to me, the food is often "weird.")

Facing Down Wild Empties:
Holidays and Other Special Occasions

Easter egg hunts, holiday parties, birthday parties, weddings, bar mitz-vahs, carnivals, pizza parties, potlucks, group picnics, school parties, church dinners, trick-or-treating . . . the list goes on and on! These events are important, fun and meaningful parts of life. And they usually involve copious amounts of junk food. That's fine as long as your family is able to find their way back to Smart foods after it is all over!

Holidays

Most holidays involve eating Empties. Before this thought makes you duck and run for cover, remember that it is perfectly possible for your whole family to really enjoy celebrating holidays with food without getting too far off-track nutritionally. That's because you now eat very well most of the time, so doing a little pigging out on junk foods for holidays really won't hurt you or your kids. In general, it is easier and more fun to limit the number of events you attend rather than what you eat at each event. So try to only attend events you'll actually enjoy (or are obligated to attend!). The other tricks offered here for facing down these Empty monsters might help as well.

> ### A Closer Look at Holiday Overeating
> The average adult American gains one or more pounds between Christmas or Hanukkah and New Year's Day. Why? Since holiday foods are often high in fats and sugar, many people end up eating more calories than their body needs. And for every 3,500 calories eaten but not needed by the body for energy, the scale shows a one-pound gain in body fat. To put that number of calories in perspective, you could get around 3,500 calories just from eating four or five holiday treats such as a piece of cheesecake, a slice of frosted carrot cake, a handful of cookies, several chocolates, some cheese and crackers, a couple of pastries or a slice of pie with whipped cream. The best strategy is to reduce exposure to high-calorie Empties and add in extra Smart foods, especially fruits and vegetables.

Halloween

I think most parents are somewhat conflicted about Halloween. It's one of the kids' favorite holidays, but they end up with *so* much candy. Here are a few ideas for finding a balance:

- Let the children pick only one trick-or-treating session. There is no reason for kids to trick-or-treat at the mall, at church, downtown, at the parent's workplace, at school, around your neighborhood and then around a best friend's neighborhood. Young children, especially, are overwhelmed and exhausted, rather than delighted, by all this trick-or-treating.

- Feed your kids their favorite, healthy foods before and after they go trick-or-treating. Also, give your children a glass of nonfat milk to enjoy along with their candy. At least they will get some nutrition— and they might even eat less candy.

- Have the children walk—don't drive them from house to house. This gets them some exercise and limits the distance they can cover. If you are still worried about your kids getting too much candy, limit them to visiting only houses of people you know—which is not a bad idea for safety reasons, anyway.

- Consider being a good role model at your house by handing out pennies, trinkets or gum to the children who ring your doorbell. This will also prevent your family from eating candy beforehand and finishing up leftovers later.

- When kids get home from a party or trick-or-treating, they will inevitably start sorting and trading their haul. Provide a trash can to encourage them to throw away any stuff they dislike. This is when I also like to limit my kids' intake by begging for some candy for myself!

- Consider letting your kids eat their candy whenever and however they want. They most likely will overeat, feel sick and possibly have trouble sleeping. But when you dole out the candy over time, they will end up eating just as much and enjoying it less, all the while learning that candy is such a big deal that they can't have control over it. Also, it is healthy for children to learn to enjoy Empties and to find out how they feel when they overeat them! Since they eat well most of the time, there really is no need to create a fight by attempting to police their Halloween candy eating.

Valentine's Day

Isn't it ironic that we celebrate loving each other with tons of junk food for gifts? A few Empty treats are fine on Valentine's Day, but here are a few ideas to keep it from getting out of hand:

- Volunteer to provide refreshments for class parties so that you can bring an In-Between or Smart treat such as strawberries, homemade muffins or bubbly water.

- If you feel comfortable, ask the teacher if she would make a rule that only non-food valentines be traded among classmates.

- Give your kids a non-food gift: tickets to a play or ballet, passes to the museum, coupons to get out of chores, new clothes or new sporting equipment.

- Serve fun (preferably pink or red) Smart or In-Between foods: heart-shaped pancakes, strawberries, homemade pudding, cherries, etc.

- However, don't get carried away with the healthy stuff. A man should *always* give his wife some expensive chocolate on Valentine's Day . . . at least that's my rule!

The Holiday Season (Thanksgiving, Christmas, Hanukkah, Kwanza, New Year's)

This is the big one—so many Empties packed into one month! A few survival tips:

- Consider limiting your baking to two or three favorite Empties, especially if you or your children get enormous amounts of junk food from somewhere else.

- Experiment with changing some old recipes to healthier versions. In many cases, you can swap ingredients or add healthy stuff to breads, sauces, main dishes, dips and drinks without anyone noticing.

- Try new recipes that feature healthier ingredients. Check out ideas in holiday issues of light-cooking magazines available in mid-October.

- Give your family and friends non-edible gifts.

- At big dinners, serve or offer to bring a healthy appetizer or first course, such as a large veggie tray or a vegetable-based soup. This will make certain that kids get their vegetables first, and it will cut hunger so that your family eats less at the meal.

- Instead of putting out traditional Empty sweets after meals or during gatherings, use trays of veggies and fruits. It is amazing how kids and adults will casually snack on baby carrots, pepper slices or olives instead of cookies or candy—and never notice.

- Serve the kids nonfat milk or water with holiday treats.

- Unless you really enjoy them, consider boycotting cookie exchanges. These events often lead to bringing home a big box of Empties. Even if you don't really love all the selections, if you are like me, you will probably end up eating them when holidays get stressful.

- Remember to keep holidays in perspective! If your family eats well most of the time, they can handle extra junk food for a few weeks.

Birthdays

The cake! The ice cream! The lemonade and soda! The piñatas full of lollipops! Birthdays are lots of fun, but they certainly involve lots of Empties.

Friends' Birthday Parties

If your child attends a birthday party only once in a while, just don't worry about the Empties. But if birthday parties seem to happen several times a month, try these ideas:

- Check in with your child. Does she really enjoy these celebrations, or would she prefer to politely decline some of the invitations from people she doesn't know as well?

- Feed your child a large Smart snack prior to heading to the party so she won't eat Empties out of hunger. Also, be sure she isn't thirsty when she arrives so she won't drink as much soda or lemonade.

- Have a conversation with your child about which Empties she really loves. (She may love them all, and that is fine!) If she doesn't actually like some of the food served at the party or realizes she dislikes it after tasting it, teach her how to graciously say, "No, thank you."

- Make the rest of the foods your child eats that day Smart.

A Family Birthday

Personally, I let my kids eat pretty much all the cake and ice cream they want on their own birthday. They eat well most of the time, and they enjoy pigging out on their special day. But there are other ways to keep birthdays under control:

- Limit the celebration to just one party! If you end up needing another celebration (if the child's "real" birthday isn't on the same day as the birthday party, for example), have either leftover cake or a favorite In-Between for the family celebration.

- If Grandma or someone else wants to throw a second party, suggest candles in a Smart fruit such as watermelon, or an In-Between treat such as muffins or pudding. Better yet, ask Grandma to take the child on a special outing instead.

- Ask your child what she would like to eat for dinner on her birthday, and let her help make a complete meal by picking out the vegetables or fruits, too.

Birthday Parties at School

Many schools allow children to bring treats to celebrate their birthdays. Almost everyone thinks "cupcakes!" A big problem with this practice is that the typical frosted cupcake is about 250 calories. That one cupcake contains the same number of calories in all of these combined: a glass of nonfat milk, three apple slices, two broccoli spears, four whole-wheat crackers and two slices of deli turkey! In other words—lunch. Most young children are so excellent at self-regulation that they will eat the cupcakes and then skip lunch because they know they're full.

At the very least, celebrate your own child's birthday with a healthier treat, such as whole-wheat cookies or muffins, a favorite fruit or juice popsicles. Young children, especially, may not even notice, but the teachers will probably be very happy. Alternatively, you could celebrate your child's birthday with a non-food treat: Pass out bubble solution, pencils or stickers.

Then, if you feel comfortable doing so, talk to the school about creating a healthier way for handling treats in the classroom. But be prepared: As we've talked about earlier, people are often very attached to feeding children treats. One of my child's teachers totally rejected the idea of healthier birthday celebrations. But if enough parents ask, these policies will eventually change.

Eating with Others

Of course your family will end up eating with others who do not share your nutritional values—or even your tastes in food! Being flexible is the general rule, but some specific adaptive behaviors can help you survive.

Kids Eating at Friends' Houses

Ideally, I want my children to be polite about food at other people's houses and learn that different people eat different types of food. So I encourage my children to eat what they are served or politely say, "No, thank you." Since they eat well most of the time, occasionally eating some Empties at a friend's house shouldn't hurt.

But if your kids are getting lots of Empties on a regular basis at friends' homes, you may decide to take action. Here are some options:

 After Kevin and Sarah had their second child, a friend brought a food gift—a beautiful store-bought carrot cake. Another friend brought cookies. Stress from sleepless nights and a demanding older sibling made the cake and cookies look like the perfect snacks, so Sarah started eating them. After feeling sick and overly full, Sarah took a deep breath and threw them into the garbage can. She knew that the last thing she needed for her recovery and for the family's "mood" was too much junk food lurking around the house. Of course, she almost pulled some of it back out of the trash later that day, but she managed to stop herself by opening a can of peaches and a bag of frozen strawberries to make a quick fruit salad instead. After that experience, Sarah also made a point of taking a large bowl of fresh, cut-up fruit to sick or postpartum friends. ✗

- Insist that your kids come home for meals most of the time.
- Invite the friends to your house and supply healthier meals and snacks.
- Offer to pack your child's favorite healthier snacks to share with his friends.
- Make sure he has a snack and something to drink at home or in the car before he heads to the friend's house.

Empties from People Who Love Your Kids

Babysitters, grandparents, neighbors, family friends—they all love to feed the kids treats. If your kids are frequent recipients of Empty food treats, you may have to have an awkward conversation with the generous person. Actually, sometimes a subtle hint will help a lot. Just tell them all about the healthy changes your family is working on. If that doesn't work, parents are completely within their rights to politely request that the children not be given junk food.

You may also have friends or relatives who think it's funny (or nice for the children) to feed your kids lots of junk food as a meal because they know about your interest in a healthy diet. If you run into this, just limit the number of times they get to feed your kids, and the rest of the time, let your kids enjoy the Empties if they want to. I personally don't think these situations are really worth an uncomfortable conversation.

In general, if unhealthy food is brought to you to be eaten later, say thank you when you take the food, and either enjoy eating it in combination with a bunch of healthier foods or throw it away. If the food is an Empty, you are under no obligation to eat it, especially if it isn't an Empty you love.

Picnics, Parties and Dinners with Friends

Again, these events can be a lot of fun, but they are often centered around Empties. Still, they can be fairly effectively managed in advance, leaving you free to just enjoy. Here are some ways to make these times a bit healthier:

- Fill up on Smart foods before you go. Serve raw vegetables or fruit either before you go or in the car on the way. That way, the kids start out with some nutrition, and if they aren't as hungry when they arrive, they'll eat less.

- To cut back on soda consumption, give your family some water before they go, too. My kids love drinking

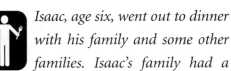 *Isaac, age six, went out to dinner with his family and some other families. Isaac's family had a water-only rule at restaurants, but his dad didn't mind lifting the rule when all the other kids got to have lemonade. Unfortunately, the lemonade came out before the meal, and there were unlimited refills. The kids each had several cups while waiting for their meals. By the time the food did arrive, they were all way too full of lemonade to eat! While taking his son to the bathroom for the third time, Isaac's dad pondered the wisdom of having his kid guzzle lemonade before a meal. The next time they went out to eat with friends, Isaac's dad simply asked the other parents if they could all request that drinks be brought out with the rest of the food. Then, he asked the waiter to bring out water and a side order of vegetables to entertain the kids before the meal. This worked out much better. Besides the fact that the kids ate a few vegetables and most of their meal, Isaac's dad was pleased that he only had to take his son to the restroom once.* 🍴

a can of bubble water in the car. Just be sure there is a bathroom at your destination!

- Always offer to bring food, and then bring something Smart that your family enjoys. Watermelon, strawberries or vegetables and dip are good choices. For potlucks, think about whole-wheat rolls, healthy peanut butter sandwiches, or salads.

- Ask if your child can have some of the healthier "adult" food, if there is enough. Hosts might assume your kids won't eat salad or fish even if they do.

- Don't be shy about serving good-tasting Smart foods to your guests. Many people won't even notice leaner burgers, part whole-wheat rolls or a salad served as a first course.

Be Prepared for Anything

Even with all the survival tips you've learned, expect days when coping with the wild, wonderful (and sometimes frightening) world of food seems, more than anything, like a huge pain. On these days, you will be really glad if you have prepared in advance to help your family weather the storm.

Prepare for Problem Days

To maintain your Smart diet over the long haul, you need to prepare for those days when:

- You are exhausted and can't face the kitchen.
- You don't have time to get to the grocery store even though you need to.
- Your family has back-to-back activities scheduled from dawn to way past dusk.
- You just feel like eating junk food.
- You have to work and don't have time to deal with food.

I know I have one of these days at least once a week! For those days when healthy foods threaten to become an endangered species at your house, use these tips now so you'll be ready.

Find at Least Three Nearby Restaurants That Serve Smart Foods

Ask friends, look online (some of my favorites are listed at www.feedingthe kids.com) or spend a few minutes calling places from the phone book. Ask if they serve any whole grains and if they have vegetables or fruit on the menu. You might also ask if they have nonfat or low-fat milk available.

Write Down Three or Four Super-Quick Smart Dinners

Choose ones that you usually have the ingredients for in your house, such as sandwiches, soup or scrambled eggs and toast. You might get some ideas from the menu section that follows the recipes at the end of this book. Post the list on the refrigerator or tape it to the back of a cupboard door. That way, when you can't think at the end of a long day, you can just open the cupboard and read a few ideas. If you pack lunches for your kids, write down two or three ideas for complete lunches, too.

Buy a Stash of Healthy Quick Foods That Keep Well

There are days when I simply *can't* get to the grocery store no matter how low on provisions I am. Some foods to keep around (just in case) are boxes of whole-grain crackers, canned soup, a few bags of frozen vegetables, whole-wheat pasta and canned sauce, canned or dried fruit and a few cans of tuna. Or, keep a few healthy frozen microwavable meals in the freezer at all times. You can use these supplies when you can't make it to the grocery store—or just need to make a meal fast.

A Closer Look at How Change Happens: By Never Giving Up

Much of what we do every day is done without our effort or even full awareness. Why? It involves routines that we have practiced over and over again. Our brain becomes familiar with these routine behaviors, and we do them easily without stress or even conscious thinking. An example: When people first learn to drive, it takes more energy and thought for each driving task. But eventually, driving becomes more relaxing and automatic.

New eating routines can feel the same way: hard at first, but easier with practice. Changing ingrained food choices can feel thorny at times, and it's easy to fall back into what is familiar and comfortable. For many people, falling back feels like failure, and this leads to quitting. It is important to remember that slipping back into old eating habits is normal. The important thing is getting back on track as soon as possible. Whatever you do, don't give up!

Tips for Getting Back on Track

Many aspects of life go through cycles of being easier and harder. Changing your family's eating patterns is no different: It may change with the seasons, holidays, vacations, your schedules and the needs of your growing family. So take a few minutes to make a mental plan of attack—right now—for getting back on track if (for most of us, this means "when"!) you find your family's diet is no longer as Smart as it should be. Here are a few ideas:

Go Back to Fruits and Vegetables

Repeat Week 1 and add in three fruits a day to your daily schedule. Just adding in fruits, and then the vegetables as in Week 2, will help you refocus and provide your family with a lot of the nutrients and fiber they need.

Double-Check Your Routine

Make sure that you still remember when to eat what. If you haven't done it already, post your family's routine on the fridge to help you remember—then stick to it!

Do a Week of Just Smart and In-Between Foods without Any Empties

First, jump-start this All-Smart-Foods week by getting rid of junk foods that have snuck back into your kitchen, then restock your house with healthy foods. Try to eat almost entirely Smart foods for every meal or snack. I often do a Smart week with my family following a vacation or major holiday. The trick to sticking with an All-Smart-Foods week is serving all your *favorite* Smart foods so you don't feel deprived.

Eat Only at Home for A While

If eating out often seems to be part of the reason for getting off-track, set a goal to eat only at home for three or four days. If you eat a meal away from home, remember to bring Smart food with you to eat on the way.

Keeping Your Enthusiasm

Keeping a family eating well does take work. Sometimes nothing really happens to cause your family to stop eating well—you just lose focus. That is when you'll need a few strategies for keeping your enthusiasm.

Look for Friends Who Are Also Interested in Healthy Eating.

There are other people who want to feed their family well, and it really helps to find them! You might know them already, or you might want to take a healthy cooking class. You could even start a group by posting a notice at your kids' school or a local health-food store.

Once you find a few like-minded people, enjoy a meal together, cook together or just exchange ideas and recipes. I have one friend who always calls me when she finds a new healthy product or cookbook and another friend who is an endless source of recipes. They have really helped me stick with Smart foods over the years.

Remind Yourself That Eating Well Is Also a Safety Issue

Eating healthy foods is just as important as wearing seat belts, staying off busy streets, wearing a bike helmet, getting immunizations, washing hands and staying away from vicious dogs. By insisting on healthy food choices most of the time, you are helping protect your family from long-term health issues.

Bon (Smart) Appétit!

Finally, there are two other ideas that keep me on track. The first is that feeding the kids healthy food (at least most of the time) is a wonderful way to show children how much they are loved. The other idea is that when you make eating healthy a fun, relaxed and delicious experience, it will put your kids on track for enjoying a lifetime of healthy eating, even when they grow up and are feeding their own kids!

I hope this adventure has made feeding *your* kids not only healthier and less stressful . . . but more fun, too. Take a moment to congratulate yourself, and your family, for all your successes in conquering the wild, wonderful and sometimes frightening world of food.

PART **4** FOUR

Mini-Recipes

There are probably millions of cookbooks out there—and some of them contain healthy recipes. However, most busy parents don't need recipes. What they really need is dinner, breakfast, lunch or a decent snack on the table without any hassles like hours of chopping or millions of dishes.

With that in mind, the following section contains *mini*-recipes that require few ingredients, are easy to change based on family tastes and can be made quickly. In other words, these are practical day-in-day-out ideas for getting food on the table.

If you want to add in a particular type of food, these icons can help you locate the right recipe:

 fruit

 whole grain

 vegetable

 lean protein

 low-fat dairy

Breakfast

Breakfast is such a rushed meal—prepared when many of us would rather still be in bed. However, breakfast is important for good health. So, if you are going to be awake, you might as well start the day off right with some Smart foods.

Super Smoothie  SMART

Serves 4

Smoothies are a great way to start the day. I always make a double batch and freeze the leftovers in short, screw-top plastic bottles for packing in lunches. Include a spoon, since the smoothie won't be thawed by lunchtime . . . but that is the whole point. Kids love to have a frozen dessert at school.

NOTE: *The quantities in this recipe are very flexible—you do not need to measure the ingredients.*

> 1 12-ounce can pineapple chunks, canned in fruit juice
> 2 cups still-frozen strawberries (a 12-ounce bag)
> 1 cup plain nonfat yogurt

Pour pineapple, juice and all, into blender. Add other ingredients. Blend all until smooth. Add some nonfat milk or orange juice if you prefer a thinner consistency.

Variations:

- Use flavored nonfat yogurt instead of plain yogurt. However, this adds extra sugar, which makes the Smoothie an In-Between.
- Use frozen unsweetened peaches, blueberries, raspberries, mangos or mixed fruits in place of strawberries.
- Use 1½ cups unsweetened orange juice and a banana instead of pineapple.
- Make extra to pack in lunch boxes along with a spoon. Freeze in plastic, screw-top containers. (If your child has an early lunchtime, move the smoothie to the fridge the night before or run it under hot water before you pack it.)
- Add ½ of a 12-ounce block of "silken" tofu for extra protein, or to replace the yogurt.
- Freeze leftovers in a plastic popsicle mold (available at grocery stores in early summer) for snacks or even for a crazy, fun breakfast the next morning.

Freezer-Fruit Cup ⬛ SMART

Serves 1

To make the morning easier, put the fruit cup in bowls the night before and refrigerate. After eating the fruit, avoid extra dishes by using the same bowl for your cold cereal with milk. Fruit cup also makes a great dessert or snack.

¼ cup fresh or unsweetened frozen strawberries
¼ cup fresh or unsweetened frozen blueberries
¼ cup sliced peaches or pears—fresh, frozen or canned in juice

In the evening, place fruits in a mug or bowl. Cover and refrigerate. The berries will thaw overnight. Or, if you forgot, microwave the frozen fruit for 1 to 2 minutes.

Variations:
- Just use frozen, unsweetened, mixed berries in place of all the fruit.
- Use frozen cherries, raspberries or mangos in place of blueberries.
- Warm the fruit in the microwave for cold mornings.
- Add any fresh fruit like mango, cantaloupe, honeydew melon, grapes, apple or bananas.
- Label containers with names for kids to "go find" while parents are busy (lounging in bed, perhaps?).
- Top with flavored nonfat yogurt and whole-grain cereal for a complete breakfast. However, this adds extra sugar which makes the Fruit Cup an In-Between.

Warm Fruit Sundae ⬛ ⬛ IN-BETWEEN

Serves 1

An easy and warm way to enjoy fruit on a cold day. Serve with whole-wheat toast and almond butter for a complete breakfast. This also makes a great dessert or snack.

1 cup frozen unsweetened blueberries, cherries, peaches and/or strawberries
1 carton flavored nonfat yogurt
A few walnuts, slivered almonds or pecans (optional)

Put the fruit in a microwave-safe cereal bowl and microwave for 1 minute, or until heated to taste (some kids prefer fruits still slightly frozen in the middle). Serve warm, topped with yogurt and/or nuts, if desired.

Variations:
- Use fresh, sliced apples or pears and 1 tablespoon of water in place of frozen fruit.
- Use unsweetened applesauce alone or mixed with other fruits.
- Sprinkle with nutmeg, cinnamon or apple pie spice.
- Sprinkle with your favorite healthy breakfast cereal.

Tropical Yogurt   SMART

Serves 2

Try serving this with 100% whole-wheat graham crackers, for dipping.

> 1 cup plain nonfat yogurt
> ½ sliced banana
> ½ cup crushed pineapple, canned in 100% juice
> 1 ounce (about ¼ cup or a small handful) walnuts

Mix all ingredients and serve.

Variations:
- Replace bananas and/or pineapple with one or more of the following: diced peaches, diced mangos, raisins, berries or any other fruit.
- Replace walnuts with any other nuts or your favorite whole-grain breakfast cereal.

Breakfast in a Bag   IN-BETWEEN

Serves 1

This recipe makes a quick, portable breakfast or a fun snack. Serve it with a glass of nonfat milk, if possible.

NOTE: *This recipe is an In-Between because most cold breakfast cereals are In-Betweens.*

> Handful of favorite whole-grain cereal
> Handful of another favorite whole-grain cereal
> Small handful of nuts
> Small handful of dried fruit (raisins, apricots, apples, etc.)

Put all ingredients into a plastic bag. Seal and shake.

Hot Flavored Milk ⬛ SMART

Serves 1

A Smart change from hot chocolate for cold mornings . . . and this also makes a soothing bedtime snack.

> 1 mug skim milk
> A sprinkle or drop of (choose one or more): cinnamon, nutmeg, vanilla extract or almond extract

Microwave milk until warm but not hot, about 30 seconds to 1 minute (depending on your microwave). Stir in flavoring.

Variations:
- Stir in about 2 tablespoons dry nonfat milk for extra creaminess.
- Add a cinnamon stick for flavor and stirring.
- Use a small amount of honey, if desired (but then count the hot milk as that meal's In-Between).

Healthier Hot Chocolate Mix ⬛ IN-BETWEEN

Serves 24 (but not all at once)

Using dry milk in hot chocolate does several things: It adds extra milk for calcium and protein, sweetens it without as much sugar and makes the skim milk seem more creamy. Make sure you show your kids how to make it! You have to stir a bit of water into the mix before adding milk or you get lumps!

> 1 cup unsweetened cocoa powder (in the baking section of the store)
> 1 cup dry nonfat milk
> ½ cup sugar
> Small pinch salt

Place all ingredients in a lidded jar or container. Shake well. Store in refrigerator.

Using the mix for hot chocolate:
> 1 heaping tablespoon of Healthier Hot Chocolate Mix (above)
> 1 tablespoon or more water
> 1 cup nonfat milk
> Vanilla, to taste (optional)

Put a heaping spoonful of mix into a mug. Add a spoonful or two of water and stir until creamy. Fill the mug with milk. Stir. Microwave 30 seconds to 1 minute on high until warm, but not hot. Add vanilla, if you like.

Variation:

- Create a milkshake by combining 1 cup nonfat milk, 1 heaping table-spoon mix and 4 ice cubes in a blender.

Instant Oatmeal 🍎 🥛 🍞 SMART

Serves 16 (but not all at once)

The bad news is that packs of flavored oatmeal are usually packed with sweet-eners. The good news is that you can make your own instant oatmeal that is inexpensive, healthy and quick. Mix up a big batch over the weekend, store it in the refrigerator and serve the kids healthy oatmeal before school.

NOTE: *This mix does not contain added sweetener. So, Instant Oatmeal is a Smart food even if you top each bowl with a spoonful of sugar or honey.*

8 cups old-fashioned oats (not quick oats)
Pinch of salt
2 cups nonfat dry milk
2 teaspoons cinnamon (optional)
1 cup raisins (optional)

Pour oats and salt into food processor fitted with a steel blade or blender. Pulse until most of the oats are broken up. Pour into storage container, along with nonfat dry milk, raisins and optional cinnamon. Stir to combine.

To prepare for breakfast: Put ½ cup mix into a cereal bowl. Add 1 cup boil-ing water. Stir. Cover with a plate; wait about 3 minutes. Stir again. Add nonfat milk and a little brown sugar or other sweetener, if desired.

Variations:

- Add diced dried apples or other unsweetened dried fruit to the mix.
- Add nuts either to dried mix or individual bowls.
- Stir 1 cup sugar into the dry mix, but then don't add extra sugar or honey on top (unless you want to count this as an In-Between).
- Top oats with nuts or fresh, diced fruit like berries, banana or peach.
- Put individual servings into small, sealable baggies. This is helpful if each member of the family wants to "personalize" with their favorite choices of dried fruits, nuts and cinnamon.

Fruit and Oats ⬤⬤⬤ SMART

Serves 2

Cooking oats in milk is a great way to add some extra dairy.
Note: *Even with a spoonful or two of sugar or honey, Fruit and Oats is still a Smart food.*

> 1 apple, chopped into small cubes (skin on for more nutrition)
> 1 cup regular (not quick) oats
> ½ teaspoon cinnamon
> 2 cups nonfat milk

Bring all ingredients to a very gentle boil, then simmer on low for about 5 minutes—stirring occasionally so it doesn't stick. Scoop into bowls—add extra nonfat milk and some sugar or honey, if desired.

Variations:
- In place of or in addition to apples, try: raisins, blueberries (fresh or frozen), peaches, pears or cranberries.
- Top with: walnuts, almonds or flaxseeds.

Breakfast Bars ⬤⬤⬤ IN-BETWEEN

Serves 12

These breakfast bars are easy to make and store well in the freezer. If you prepackage them in small baggies, they make a great on-the-go breakfast.

> 2 cups oats
> 1 cup whole-wheat flour
> ½ cup canola oil
> ½ cup brown sugar
> 1 cup walnuts
> 1 cup diced apples (or ½ cup dried)
> ½ cup nonfat dry milk
> 1 teaspoon vanilla
> 1 teaspoon cinnamon
> ¼ teaspoon salt
> 2 eggs

Mix all ingredients in a large bowl using a spoon or electric mixer. Pat into oiled or nonstick 9 x 12 baking dish. Bake at 350 degrees for ½ hour. Slice into squares or bars.

Variations:
- Use pecans, peanuts or almonds in place of walnuts.
- Use ½ cup raisins or diced apricots in place of apples.
- Use blueberries instead of apples.

English Muffins 🍎 🍞 🐔 SMART

Serves 1

Whole-grain breads are often much healthier than typical cold cereals. They are just as quick, too. By topping English muffins (or bread or bagels) with peanut butter and fruit, you increase nutrition and make the meal more satisfying.

> 1 whole-grain English muffin (or whole-grain toast or bagel)
> Natural peanut butter (or almond butter)
> Raisins (or banana or apple slices)

Split and toast English muffin halves. Cover with peanut butter and sprinkle with raisins. Serve with milk.

Variation:
- Use low-fat cream cheese, and add walnuts or pecans along with raisins.

Banana Bread Muffins

IN-BETWEEN

Serves 18

These muffins taste extra-sweet because of the bananas. Try them—even the most selective eater I know loved them and ate three as fast as he could! I usually serve fruit with these muffins because each muffin only contains part of a banana.

3 ripe or overripe bananas
⅓ cup applesauce or canola oil
¼ cup brown sugar
3 eggs
¼ teaspoon salt
2 teaspoons baking powder
1½ cups white whole-wheat flour**
½ cup oats
½ cup chopped walnuts or pecans

In a mixer, beat peeled bananas until they are mush. Add applesauce, sugar and eggs. Beat until well combined. Add other ingredients except nuts and oats. Mix until just combined. Add nuts and oats. Mix gently just until combined. Spray muffin cups with canola cooking spray or use cupcake papers. Fill each muffin cup ¾ full of batter. Bake at 350 degrees for 20 minutes, or until a toothpick poked into the middle of a muffin comes out clean.

**If your store doesn't carry white whole-wheat flour, substitute with half whole-wheat and half unbleached flour.*

Variations:
- Add ½ cup raisins, blueberries or diced fresh apple (skin on is fine).
- Add a nutritional boost by using ⅓ cup canned pumpkin in place of the applesauce.
- Use grated zucchini in place of the bananas, but use ½ cup brown sugar.
- This recipe can also be baked as a loaf. Pour the batter into two oiled loaf pans and bake for 50 minutes at 350 degrees, or until a knife inserted into the center of the loaf comes out clean.

Pancakes **SMART**

Serves 6

This incredibly healthy version of the classic pancake has passed taste testing by several selective children. The key is to just serve them—don't mention that these are new, different or healthier . . . until after they enjoy them. If you think your kids will notice the new recipe, top the pancakes with a little squirt of light whipped cream (an Empty, but it isn't worse than syrup and it thrills children of all ages).

> 2 cups skim milk
> 2 eggs
> 2 cups white whole-wheat flour**
> 2 teaspoons baking powder
> ½ teaspoon salt

Heat up a nonstick griddle or pan, or lightly oil a regular pan. Whisk the milk and eggs together. Add everything else and whisk until it isn't too lumpy. Pour about ¼ cup per pancake onto nonstick frying pan over medium-high heat. Flip over when a slight crust forms along the outside. Serve hot.

You can store leftovers in the freezer between sheets of wax paper or parchment paper, then reheat in the microwave or toaster.

***If your store doesn't carry white whole-wheat flour, substitute with a mixture of half whole-wheat and half unbleached flour.*

Topping ideas:
- Spread with a small amount of butter or healthy margarine, and then dust with powdered sugar (place in a small sieve and stir with spoon).
- Cover with unsweetened applesauce.
- Sprinkle with cinnamon and sugar.
- Warm frozen cherries or peaches in the microwave, then add walnuts and a dusting of powdered sugar.
- Or, just use maple syrup and call it an In-Between!

Variations:
- If you have a waffle-maker, add an extra egg to the batter and cook according to the waffle-maker's instructions.
- Add ½ cup pureed pumpkin for extra nutrition (most kids won't even notice).
- Add chopped walnuts or pecans.
- Add blueberries (frozen or fresh).

Lunch

Lunch can be a difficult meal because it is often eaten away from home. Unfortunately, many cafeterias and restaurants don't have nearly enough appealing healthy choices. The answer is to pack your own family lunch, which is why most of these recipes are designed for portability.

Veggie Roll-up or Sandwich

 **SMART**

Serves 1

Roll-up sandwiches are quick to make and easy to pack.

> Whole-grain flour tortillas or whole-wheat bread
> Nonfat or reduced-fat cream cheese or light ranch dressing
> Sprinkle of lemon pepper, garlic salt, seasoned salt or your favorite spice mixture
> Nuts or seeds (sunflower seeds, pumpkin seeds, walnuts, sliced almonds, pecans)
> Thinly sliced tomato and/or thinly sliced pepper (red, yellow, orange or green)
> Grated carrots and/or thinly sliced cucumber
> Baby spinach or shredded lettuce

Spread a thin layer of cream cheese or salad dressing on entire tortilla or bread. Sprinkle with nuts or seeds, plus seasonings. Add other ingredients in rows, and then roll up. If you are packing it in a lunch box, roll the sandwich in foil or plastic wrap to keep it from falling apart.

Variations:
- Replace nuts with lean deli meat (roast turkey, lean ham, roast beef).
- Add hummus.
- If you cannot find a good-tasting whole-wheat tortilla, use your favorite refined-grain type and make this your In-Between.

Pasta and Vegetable Salad SMART

Serves 4

This healthy version of pasta salad is great for lunch or dinner. It also packs well if you keep it cold by packing it next to a frozen smoothie.

½ pound whole-wheat pasta shapes (like spirals)
1 cup frozen peas
½ cup Italian salad dressing made with olive or canola oil
1 cup grated carrots or diced red pepper
½ cup garbanzo beans or leftover diced chicken, turkey or ham
½ cup parmesan cheese

Cook pasta according to package directions. Drain well. Add other ingredients and stir.

Variations:
- Use other vegetables, such as steamed broccoli, green beans or shredded spinach, in place of peas.
- Add herbs, fresh or dried, like basil, parsley or oregano.

Black Bean Salad SMART

Serves 4

This salad makes a quick lunch that is easy to pack. It also makes a healthy contribution to a potluck. To complete the meal, my kids like popcorn cakes and Super Smoothies.

1 cup frozen corn kernels
2 cans black beans, rinsed and drained
½ onion, chopped (or 1 tsp onion powder)
3 carrots, grated
2 teaspoons oregano
3 tablespoons vinegar
2 tablespoons olive oil or canola oil
Salt to taste

Thaw the corn (in microwave). (If you are packing the salad, leave the corn frozen to keep everything cold.) Then, just add all ingredients and stir.

Variations:
- Use 3 or 4 green onions in place of regular onions.
- Replace carrots with finely diced red or orange peppers.
- Use other beans: garbanzos, white beans or pinto beans.
- Serve with fresh lime wedges to squeeze on top.
- Serve with crushed red pepper for your hot and spicy family members.

Orange Juice Hummus 🐔 SMART
Serves 4

This is a kid-friendly version of hummus. Our testers really liked it—once they actually tried it. Hummus is easy to make once you find the tahini, which is just sesame seed butter, in your grocery store. It is often with the organic peanut butter and cashew butter. Tahini is a bit pricy, but if you get into making hummus, it's worth it. Also, it lasts a long time stored in the refrigerator. However, hummus can be made without tahini; just add some extra juice for moisture.

    1 clove garlic, peeled, or one teaspoon minced from a jar
    1 can garbanzo beans, drained and rinsed
    ¼ teaspoon salt
    2 tablespoons tahini paste (optional)
    ¼ cup orange juice

Place the garlic clove in the food processor alone. Pulse the food processor until the garlic clove is chopped up. Add other ingredients. Process for 3 to 5 minutes, until the hummus is smooth and creamy. Serve as a dip with raw vegetables or in a piece of pita bread with spinach, grated carrots, sliced cucumbers and/or diced tomatoes.

Variations:
- Use lemon juice instead of orange juice for a more traditional hummus.
- Add ½ teaspoon cumin powder.

Chunky Salsa Dip and Chips

 **SMART**

Serves 2

For a fun lunch alternative, pack this wonderful salsa dip and chips. Add a peach or some watermelon chunks, plus a piece of part-skim string cheese—and it makes a complete lunch!

> ¼ cup salsa
> ¼ cup nonfat sour cream
> ¼ cup black or pinto beans
> ¼ cup corn kernels
> A few handfuls baked corn chips

Mix all ingredients except chips. Serve chips for dipping.

Variations:
- Use baby carrots, pepper slices or jicama slices for dipping.
- Stir in ¼ mashed avocado.

Warm Bean Dip and Chips **SMART**

Serves 4

More instant, healthy food! I serve this with apple slices and a glass of milk as lunch on weekends—no plates needed!

> 1 can nonfat refried beans (regular or black bean)
> 1 cup salsa
> ¼ cup low-fat grated cheese
> Baked corn chips

Mix the refried beans and salsa. Top with cheese. Heat in the microwave for 4 minutes, or until cheese melts. Dip chips in bean mixture.

Variations:
- Skip heating the dip and serve it cold. Try packing the cold dip in a small container for lunch. But send the chips in a separate bag.
- Mix in ½ cup thawed frozen corn.
- After cooking, top dip with ½ cup nonfat sour cream and/or 1 diced avocado.
- Serve the dip with carrot sticks, pepper sticks or jicama slices, instead of or with the corn chips.
- Use whole-wheat crackers, rice or popcorn cakes instead of corn chips.

Salmon Salad SMART
Serves 2

Don't be afraid to try this on your kids—mine really like it and they aren't exactly fans of canned salmon. This quick salad makes a wonderful lunch with a few crackers. Pack it next to a frozen smoothie to keep it cold.

> 1 8-ounce can salmon
> 1 tablespoon canola-oil mayonnaise
> 1 tablespoon nonfat sour cream or plain yogurt
> 1 grated carrot
> 1 stalk finely diced celery
> 1 teaspoon lemon-pepper or seasoned salt
> Pinch of salt or to taste (canned salmon varies in saltiness!)

Drain juice out of salmon and place the fish in a large bowl. With a fork, mash any bones (they are edible). Mix in all remaining ingredients.

Variations:
- Use canned tuna or diced leftover chicken instead of salmon.
- Add minced fresh herbs: basil, parsley or cilantro.
- Use salad as a sandwich or pita filling.

Pack-n-Go Berry Dessert 🍎 🥛 IN-BETWEEN

Serves 1

This is a very quick and easy way to pack a serving of dairy and fruit in a lunch box. The frozen fruit keeps the yogurt cold. Plus, making your own individual servings of yogurt from a large tub is much cheaper than buying those little cups, and yours will contain real fruit. This also makes a great dessert or snack.

> 1 cup frozen berries, cherries, pineapple, peaches or a mixture
> 1 cup vanilla, lemon or maple flavored nonfat yogurt

For packing: Place still-frozen fruit in plastic lidded container and spoon yogurt on top. Pack with a spoon.
For serving right away: Microwave the fruit until almost thawed. Stir in yogurt.

Variations:
- Add nuts, such as almonds or pecans.
- Try unsweetened yogurt for a Smart version—if you don't mind the tart flavor. Or, use half plain and half flavored yogurt.

Milk Cubes 🥛 SMART

Serves 4

If your kids cannot buy nonfat milk at school, you may want to pack milk. You could send it in a thermos or use a cold pack . . . but the milk stays colder if you use "milk cubes." My kids also use Milk Cubes at home to make their milk extra cold.

> 1 cup nonfat milk

Pour milk into an ice cube tray and freeze. To pack, place 4 milk cubes into a plastic lidded container or small thermos. Add liquid nonfat milk on top. Pack with a straw!

Variations:
- Add 1 teaspoon vanilla to the milk before freezing.

Dinner

Serving a healthy family dinner night after night is one of the very greatest gifts you can possibly give to your children. It is also a huge pain sometimes! All of us end up grabbing fast food once in a while, but if you have a few quick ideas up your sleeve, you will be able to avoid some of those desperate Empty meals and serve your own cheaper and Smarter homemade fast food more often.

Veggies and Dip SMART

Serves 4

Vegetables and dip are a fantastic way to get your kids to eat their vegetables before dinner even starts—and to stop the "I'm starving! When's dinner ready?" routine. You might also try giving kids vegetables with dip when they arrive home from school or while they work on homework, watch TV or play video games.

And don't be overwhelmed by the thought of making a dip—most plain salad dressings work perfectly as a dip!

Choices of vegetables to use with dips:

- Carrots, peppers (various colors), tomatoes, cucumbers, radishes, celery, broccoli, cauliflower, sliced jicama or even lettuce leaves. If you are in a hurry, use baby carrots, cherry tomatoes, sugar snap peas or other vegetables that don't require slicing.

Dip choices:

- Bottled salad dressing made with healthy oils.
- Bottled salad dressing mixed with nonfat sour cream.
- Mix 1 cup nonfat yogurt with ½ cup salsa. Try adding in ½ teaspoon of any or all of the following: oregano, basil, onion flakes, garlic powder.
- Low-fat or nonfat sour cream and a powdered dip mix, such as French onion or ranch.
- Hummus (recipe in the lunch section).
- Canned nonfat refried beans, microwaved in a bowl until heated, about 3 minutes. Top with salsa and/or low-fat grated cheese, if desired.
- A mashed avocado mixed with either ½ cup of salsa or a splash of lemon juice and a sprinkle of garlic salt. Stir in nonfat sour cream, too, if desired.

To make serving easier, place a small bowl of dip in the middle of a plate. Put the vegetables around the dip, on the plate.

Mandarin Orange Salad 🍎 🥕 SMART

Serves 4

This is another raw veggie idea. This salad looks great, and kids love the mandarin oranges.

The salad:

½ bag pre-washed baby spinach or bite-size lettuce

1 can of juice-packed mandarin oranges

1 avocado, diced (optional)

Handful of walnuts, almonds or pine nuts (also optional)

Drain the oranges, reserving the juice to make the dressing. Arrange all ingredients on salad plates or in bowls.

The dressing:

Juice from the mandarin oranges

2 tablespoons olive oil or canola oil

2 tablespoons balsamic vinegar, or your favorite vinegar

Pinch of salt or more, to taste

Mix dressing ingredients and pour over salad.

Variations:

• Use sliced canned pears or pineapple in place of mandarin oranges.

• Add diced cooked chicken breast for a light main course.

One-Vegetable Salad  SMART

Serves 4

Here is another raw vegetable first-course idea. My daughter, who dislikes most salads (at the moment), will eat this because it is just one type of vegetable, so it is OK if the pieces touch each other.

> 2 cucumbers, tomatoes or bell peppers, diced
> 4 tablespoons apple cider vinegar or your favorite vinegar
> 2 tablespoons canola, olive or other oil
> A few dashes of salt
> A few dashes of pepper

Mix all ingredients together.

Variations:
- Use bottled salad dressing.
- Use grated carrots for the vegetable.
- Use three different vegetables and call it a 3-vegetable salad.
- Use three different colors of bell peppers—very pretty.

Stir-Fried Garlic Broccoli  SMART

Serves 4

I like the old standby of steamed broccoli as much as the next guy, but cooking it this way makes broccoli even better.

> 1 tablespoon roasted sesame oil or olive oil
> 2 cloves sliced, fresh garlic or 1 teaspoon garlic powder
> 1 head broccoli, washed and cut into chunks
> 1 tablespoon soy sauce

Heat the oil on medium-high in a large pan or wok. Add garlic and stir. (If using powdered garlic, add it at the same time as the broccoli.) Add broccoli and stir to distribute oil. Then, turn heat to medium and cover. Cook for 5 minutes. Turn off heat. Uncover and stir in soy sauce.

Variations:
- Substitute cabbage, carrots, zucchini, kale or your favorite vegetable for all or part of the broccoli.
- Add leftover pieces of cooked chicken just before covering, and increase soy sauce and garlic to taste. Serve over brown rice for a complete, quick meal.
- Try "Ume Plum Vinegar," available near the soy sauce at health food stores, instead of soy sauce for an interesting new flavor.

Veggies from the Freezer  SMART

Serves 4

This is the easiest way to get vegetables on the table in a hurry. And they taste pretty good—as long as you don't overcook them.

> 1 cup frozen petite (also called baby) green peas
> ½ teaspoon salt, or salt to taste (optional)
> 2 tablespoons water

Place frozen vegetables in microwave-safe bowl. Sprinkle with salt and add water. Microwave on high for about 2 minutes, or until very hot. Drain and serve.

Variations:
- Substitute all or part of the peas with frozen green beans, corn, broccoli, cauliflower or mixed plain vegetables.
- Sprinkle finished vegetables with a small amount of seasoned salt.
- Try serving peas or corn still frozen to little kids for a silly snack.

Grilled (or Baked) Sweet Potato Pouches  SMART

Serves 4

This is an easy way to cook sweet potatoes—and many other types of vegetables. Best of all, there is no cleanup afterwards. You can either grill these pouches outdoors or bake them in the oven. Your children might enjoy making customized pouches for themselves.

> 2 large sweet potatoes, peeled and sliced into 1/4-inch-thick rounds
> Salt, seasoned salt, curry powder or your favorite herb mixture
> 1 tablespoon olive oil or other oil (optional)

Lay out 4 squares of aluminum foil. Divide the sweet potato slices among them. Sprinkle with salt and/or herbs. Drizzle with a bit of olive oil, if desired. Fold up the pouches, folding the edges over carefully to seal in juices. Bake at 350 degrees for 30 minutes, or place on cooler spot on grill while cooking other foods.

Variations:
- Use new potatoes, baby carrots, slices of regular potatoes or diced winter squash in place of or in addition to the sweet potatoes.
- Use broccoli or zucchini in place of potatoes. Reduce cooking time to 15 minutes.
- Add onion slices, mushrooms or whole cloves of garlic into pouches for those who would enjoy them.

Enhanced Canned Soup   SMART

Serves 4

I know homemade soup is wonderful, but canned soup sure is convenient and quick. Plus, it is much healthier than most fast food. Make your canned soup smarter by selecting a low-fat, lower-sodium version and then adding extra vegetables.

> ½ cup frozen corn
> ½ cup frozen peas
> 1 can favorite soup, like chicken rice or turkey noodle

Heat up soup in the usual way, but add in the vegetables.

Variations:
- Replace peas and corn with other fresh, frozen or leftover vegetables. Try: green beans, diced celery, broccoli, spinach, diced carrots.
- Add a handful of leftover whole-wheat pasta shapes or instant brown rice.

Enhanced Spaghetti Sauce   SMART

Serves 4

Tomato-based pasta sauce is already very healthy, especially if you select a brand lower in sodium. Adding some vegetables and meat makes it a meal. Please note: Vegetarian variations are listed below the recipe! I like to serve a salad or vegetables and dip as a first course before the pasta.

> One bottle pasta sauce
> ½ bag frozen spinach or ½ bag fresh baby spinach
> 1 grated carrot (optional)
> 1 pound extra-lean ground turkey or beef (optional)
> 1 pound whole-wheat pasta, cooked according to the package directions
> Parmesan cheese (optional)

Thoroughly brown the ground meat in a large saucepan or small pot. Meanwhile, finely chop the spinach. Then, put all ingredients, except pasta, in the saucepan and stir. Heat over medium heat until the sauce is bubbly. Serve over whole-wheat pasta with a sprinkle of parmesan cheese.

Variations:
- Use soy veggie crumbles or sausage crumbles in place of the meat. These are available in the frozen health food section of most stores.
- Instead of beef, add about ¼ cup low-fat cottage cheese to each serving of pasta. Pour sauce on top.
- Replace spinach with grated zucchini.

Quinoa and Tomato Soup  SMART

Serves 4

Quinoa is a type of grain but is also an excellent source of lean protein. Look for quinoa at your grocery store either in the natural foods section or near the rice and couscous. It usually comes in small boxes. I like to serve this as a simple main course, along with a salad and whole-wheat bread topped with melted 2% cheese.

> 1 can favorite tomato soup
> ½ cup quinoa
> ½ cup extra water

Place all ingredients in a saucepan and cook for 10 minutes.

Variations:
- Add vegetables: peas, sliced carrots, spinach or corn.
- Add quinoa to your favorite homemade soups in place of either rice or pasta.

Carrot Cake Whole-Wheat Pancakes

 SMART

Serves 6

Here is a fun way to add some vegetables to a breakfast-for-dinner meal. To complete the menu, add some vegetarian breakfast links, and serve some fruit in place of the other vegetable.

> 2 cups skim milk
> 2 eggs
> 2 cups white whole-wheat flour **
> 2 teaspoons baking powder
> ½ teaspoon salt
> 2 carrots, grated
> ½ cup walnuts or pecans, chopped
> ½ cup raisins (optional)
> 1 teaspoon cinnamon

Heat up a nonstick griddle or pan. Oil it just a bit even though it is nonstick. Whisk the milk and eggs together. Add everything else and whisk until it isn't too lumpy. Pour into what your family considers to be regular-size pancakes.

Top with a dusting of powdered sugar, applesauce and/or canned crushed pineapple.

**If your store doesn't carry white whole-wheat flour, substitute with half whole-wheat/half unbleached flour.

Variations

- Top these pancakes with a little maple syrup, but then count them as your In-Between.
- If you can find whole-wheat pancake mix (that doesn't contain trans fat), follow package directions, then add in carrots, nuts, raisins and pecans.

Instant Mini Pizza   IN-BETWEEN

Serves 1

Look for whole-grain English muffins, whole-wheat tortilla shells or whole-wheat pita bread to use for pizza crust. For a complete dinner, add plenty of veggies to the pizza, and also serve a green salad topped with leftover salmon or chicken.

> Whole-grain English muffin halves
> Tomato sauce
> Part-skim grated mozzarella cheese (or cheddar)
> Chopped onions, mushrooms, peppers or olives (optional)
> Parmesan cheese
> Italian seasoning (optional)

Place English muffin, pita or other "crust" on cookie sheet. Top with a tablespoon of spaghetti sauce. Sprinkle toppings and 2 tablespoons of part-skim mozzarella cheese. Top off with a shake of parmesan cheese and Italian seasoning and pop under broiler. Watch carefully for burning!

Variations:

- Use 100% whole-wheat bagels, pita bread or tortilla shells for "crust."
- For a big pizza, use a whole-grain prepared crust, available in the bread section at most grocery stores.
- Add diced leftover chicken, Canadian bacon or sliced "vegetarian" sausages.
- Let each person prepare his or her own pizza. Kids might like to make a face or their initials with the toppings.
- Make your own pizza crust from scratch—it is not that hard. Follow the recipe for Great, Great Bread (in this section), but roll the dough out flat, add toppings and bake for about 15 minutes at 425 degrees.

Chicken Nuggets SMART
Serves 4

Honestly, this recipe involves more work than I usually put into dinner. It takes about 45 minutes from start to finish, though 20 minutes of that is baking time. I only make it because the kids love chicken nuggets so much—and most of the commercial ones are extremely high in fat. These nuggets go well with either Sweet Potato Pouches (see recipe in this section) or oven-baked olive oil fries found in the natural foods freezer section of the store.

1 pound boneless, skinless chicken (still a bit frozen is easiest to slice)
2 cups nonfat milk
6 slices dried-out whole-wheat bread **
3 tablespoons canola or olive oil
Dash of powdered garlic (more for garlicky families)
1 teaspoon salt

Preheat oven to 425 degrees. To make cleanup easy, line a cookie sheet with parchment paper, or use foil sprayed with canola cooking spray. Slice chicken into nugget-size chunks. Place the chicken in a bowl with the milk; set aside. Use a food processor to pulverize the dried bread until it looks like playground sand. Add garlic, salt and oil. Pulse several times to mix well. Dump this crumb mixture into a plastic freezer bag. Drain all the milk off the chicken, discarding the milk (of course)! Add the nuggets to the bag and shake well to coat. Place nuggets on cookie sheet without letting them touch. Bake for 20 minutes or until the largest nugget is no longer pink inside.

*** Dry out bread by placing it in a pan on top of the refrigerator or in the turned-off oven for a couple days. If you haven't done this step, you can also dry the bread by placing it in the preheating oven while you slice the chicken.*

Variations:
- Use pre-sliced boneless-skinless chicken, available at some stores, and make the pieces into chicken fingers.
- Use a mild fish, like trout or perch, to make fish nuggets.
- Use crushed cheese-flavored whole-wheat crackers in place of bread and oil. (Place crackers in a closed baggie and let your kids whack the crackers with a spoon or small pan, then add spices and shake.)

Easy Orange Chicken SMART

Serves 4

I love this recipe because it takes no time at all and you barely have to touch the raw chicken. Plus, you only have one dish to clean. If you have leftovers, this chicken tastes great made into chicken salad. (See variation of Salmon Salad in Lunch recipe section).

> 1 cup orange juice
> 1 tablespoon soy sauce
> ½ teaspoon powdered ginger (optional)
> 1 pack boneless skinless chicken breasts, about 1 pound
> 1 16-ounce bag baby carrots or 3 sliced carrots (optional)
> 2 cups instant brown rice

Place chicken, carrots, juice, soy sauce and optional ginger in large, lidded sauté pan. Cook, covered, on medium-high for 15 minutes, or until chicken is no longer pink in the middle, flipping once in the middle of cooking time. Meanwhile, prepare instant rice according to package directions. Remove chicken to a plate. Let sauce cook, uncovered, about 1 minute or until slightly thickened. Serve sauce over chicken on brown rice or (for the kids, especially) as a dip for the chicken.

Variations:

- Replace orange juice with the juice from a can of sliced pineapple. Serve the pineapple slices with the chicken.
- If your family loves garlic, slice 4 cloves in half lengthwise and add them with the chicken.

Beef Stew  SMART

Serves 8

This beef stew is a delicious way to serve vegetables and meat together. Plus, the meat stretches much further than when eaten on its own. The recipe is not hard, but it takes quite a few ingredients and a bit of thyme (pun intended). The recipe makes enough for two meals for a typical family. On the first night, if you want your family to go crazy with happiness, serve it with Great, Great Bread (see recipe in this section). On the second night, you might want to serve the stew on top of some instant brown rice.

1 pound of 1-inch cubes of lean beef
  (ask the butcher to chop up a lean sirloin)
2 teaspoons olive or canola oil
2 tablespoons flour
2 carrots, sliced
1 large onion, sliced
2 large potatoes, scrubbed, then diced with skin on
1 28-ounce (large) can diced tomatoes
1½ cups water
2 bouillon cubes (any flavor)**
2 cloves garlic, minced or crushed
1 bay leaf
1 cup red wine
1 teaspoon thyme

In a large pot, brown the beef over medium heat. Sprinkle with flour; stir. Then, stir in the carrots and onions. Add other ingredients. Simmer gently for 1 hour.

**If using salt-free bouillon, add salt to taste.*

Variations:
- Add any of the following: green beans, peas and/or mushrooms.
- Cook the stew in your slow cooker. Brown the meat, flour, carrots and onions in a sauté pan. Then place the sauté plus everything else in your slow cooker on low for 8 or 9 hours.

Beans and Rice   SMART

Serves 4

One of my all-time favorite one-dish dinners! This is quick and easy to make—and quick and easy to clean up.

> 3 cups brown rice (leftover or make some instant)
> 1 16-ounce jar salsa (mild, medium or hot—it's up to you!)
> 1 can black or pinto beans, drained and rinsed
> 1 cup frozen corn kernels
> 1 cup sour cream
> 1 cup reduced-fat shredded cheddar cheese
> 1 avocado, diced (optional)

Mix rice, salsa, beans and corn together in microwavable dish. Cover and heat about 6 minutes, or until hot. Sprinkle with cheese and microwave 1 or 2 minutes more to melt the cheese. Spread with sour cream and sprinkle with diced avocado, if desired.

Edamame   SMART

Serves 4

Edamame are whole soybeans, and they are both a vegetable and a protein! Kids tend to like them (once they try them) because the beans are sweet and salty. In fact, my daughter's preschool teacher told me that she has never met a kid who didn't like them.

You can buy Edamame at most grocery stores in the natural food freezer section. Edamame is a great way to add extra protein to the classic pasta-with-tomato-sauce meal.

> 1 bag Edamame (in the pods)
> Water
> Salt

Follow the easy directions on the package. They usually only need to cook for a few minutes—just make sure the beans are hot all the way through. Drain, sprinkle with salt and serve. To eat, stick the entire pod in your mouth and bite down gently on the end closest to your fingers. Pull the pod through your teeth to release the Edamame into your mouth. Throw the pods away.

Variations:
- Buy shelled Edamame, cooked according the package directions, for added protein in salads or stir-fries.

Tuna-Cheese Burgers SMART

Serves 4

With Veggies and Dip before and Garlic Broccoli alongside, this makes a very fast, healthy meal. (Actually, I use it as a quick lunch, too.)

> 1 can water-packed tuna
> 1 teaspoon seasoned salt
> 1 cup grated 2% cheddar cheese
> 4 whole-wheat hamburger buns

Divide tuna among the bottom halves of the buns. Sprinkle with seasoned salt, then cheese. Place on cookie sheet along with tops (to toast the tops). Broil until the cheese is bubbly.

Variations:
- Use canned salmon instead of tuna.
- Use whole-wheat English muffins, pita bread or bagels instead of buns.

Plain Fish SMART

Serves 2

Fish can be tricky! A lot of kids won't touch it. Or they prefer it as the often-unhealthy fish "sticks." To make plain fish more appealing, buy a very fresh, mild fish like farm-raised trout. (For information on which fish are safest for children, see "A Closer Look at Which Types of Fish are Safe for Kids," page 122.) Then flavor it with a familiar spice your children like and serve it with ketchup. It's not gourmet, but it sure is healthy!

> ¼ pound (or more) boneless, farm-raised trout fillet per person **
> Olive or canola oil
> Seasoning mix (lemon pepper, garlic salt, seasoned salt, etc.)
>   that your family is already familiar with and likes
> Ketchup

Cover a cookie sheet or baking dish with foil. (Covering it with foil makes cleanup much easier.) Place fish skin side down. Drizzle about 1 teaspoon of olive oil on each piece. Sprinkle with seasoning mix. Broil fish for about 10 minutes per ½-inch thickness. To see if it is done, dig into one piece with a knife. It should look white and not be at all rubbery, but it should be flaky. Serve the fish with ketchup for dipping!

**Be sure to ask the person at the fish counter if the fish you are buying contains any bones. If it does, use tweezers to remove the bones before serving it to your kids. (Or just buy a different type of fish that doesn't have bones.)*

Variations:
- Try other types of fish. Ask the person at the fish counter to recommend some mild, boneless types to try.
- If you have a countertop two-sided grill, grill the fish for about 5 minutes per ½-inch thickness of fish.

Salsa Bean Soup   SMART
Serves 4

This is healthy fast food—it's ready in less than 10 minutes. This soup tastes great with baked corn chips or rice cakes spread with avocado.

> 1 16-ounce can diced or crushed tomatoes
> 1 can pinto, black or adzuki beans, rinsed and drained
> ½ bean can full of water
> 1 8-ounce bottle of salsa (mild, medium or hot)
> ¼ cup chopped onions, any type (optional)
> 1 cup frozen corn (optional)
> 1 cup nonfat sour cream

Put all ingredients except sour cream in a large pot. Cook on medium-high heat until just boiling. Top each bowl with nonfat sour cream.

Healthy Hamburgers SMART

Serves 4

Turn ever-popular burgers from an Empty into a Smart food with just a few changes. The zucchini helps moisten the lean beef and, of course, helps get in some extra vegetables. I like to serve these on whole-wheat buns with lettuce, tomatoes and onions, ketchup, mustard and a little mayonnaise. They go well with Veggies from the Freezer (this section).

> 1 pound extra-lean ground beef (95% lean or higher)
> 1 zucchini squash, grated
> 2 tablespoons steak sauce

Combine all ingredients, but don't squash the mixture too much. Form patties and grill or pan fry until no longer pink. Do not overcook. Serve on whole-wheat buns or toasted bread with lettuce, tomatoes, ketchup and mustard.

Many stores do not sell whole-wheat hamburger buns. Instead, they sell "wheat" buns with only a small amount of whole grain. If you use these for your burgers, count the burgers as your In-Between.

Twice-Baked Potatoes ⬜ ⬜ SMART

Serves 2

Though technically a starchy vegetable, baked potatoes make a great replacement for whole grains at dinner. This recipe also takes care of a dairy serving.

> 2 potatoes, baked (cold is fine)
> ½ cup nonfat or low-fat cottage cheese
> ½ cup nonfat milk
> ¼ cup parmesan cheese or extra-sharp grated cheddar cheese
> ¼ teaspoon salt or more, to taste

Slice potatoes in half lengthwise. With a spoon, scoop insides out, leaving a shell of skin and some potato. Mix and mash other ingredients with potato insides until combined. Bake at 350 degrees until warmed through, about ½ hour.

Variations:
- Add diced cooked ham or sunflower seeds.
- Add cooked broccoli, green onions or olives.

Salmon Patties  SMART

Serves 4

Kids seem to either love these or totally reject them. If your kids love them, you are seriously in luck. Salmon patties are quick, inexpensive, easy and healthy. Serve with ketchup, if that's what it takes.

> 1 15-ounce can wild-caught Alaskan salmon, drained
> 3 slices whole-wheat bread, torn into tiny bits
>   (great job for a preschooler!)
> 2 egg whites
> 1 teaspoon soy sauce**
> 1 tablespoon canola oil

Pour the canned salmon into a bowl. Use a fork to mash it, thereby crushing any bones and skin. (Gross, but the bones add calcium and the skin contains healthy oils.) Add torn-up bread, egg whites and soy sauce. Stir, then form into small, hamburger-sized patties. Cook over medium-high heat in a non-stick pan lightly coated with the canola oil. Flip after about 4 minutes to cook the other side. Serve hot.

***Canned salmon varies in saltiness. Change the amount of soy sauce to suit your brand.*

Variations:

- Add finely chopped onions, chopped parsley or snipped green onions for color and flavor.
- Add ½ cup finely diced bell peppers.
- Use ½ cup crushed whole-grain crackers or cornmeal instead of bread.
- Add an extra egg white if the mixture is too dry to form patties.

Great, Great Bread ▣ SMART
(or Rolls or Pizza Crust or Pretzels...)

Serves 6

Think your family will never go for whole wheat? Try this bread. I'd estimate there are less than six children in the entire United States who will turn down a warm, freshly baked roll that they helped make. In fact, I brought these rolls to my son's kindergarten class (at his request, not mine!) instead of cupcakes for his birthday. I was expecting a serious protest—but the kids loved them.

Even if you have been frustrated making your own bread in the past, try this. This recipe is very easy—and forgiving if you get something wrong.

> 1 cup warm water
> 1 package yeast (2¼ teaspoons)
> 1 tablespoon honey (or white sugar or brown sugar)
> 3 cups white whole-wheat flour**
> 1 teaspoon salt
> 2 tablespoons olive or canola oil

Mix together yeast and water. Let it get foamy. Add in other ingredients and mix well. Add a bit of extra flour, and knead the dough about 20 times. Cover it and let it rise for between 30 minutes and 2 hours. Punch it down (literally punch it!). Shape it into a round loaf, about 18 little buns or into whatever other shape you prefer. Let it rest for between 10 minutes and overnight (in the fridge). Bake at 375 degrees, 40 minutes for a loaf and 20 minutes for rolls. Test for doneness by tapping with a spoon. The bread will sound hollow when it is done.

**If your store doesn't carry white whole-wheat flour, substitute with half whole-wheat/half unbleached flour.

Variations:
- Shape it like pizza dough and make a pizza using bottled spaghetti sauce, grated 2% cheese and toppings of your choice.
- Roll into snakes, and shape it like pretzels. Then quickly dip each pretzel in water and sprinkle with coarse salt. Bake about 10 minutes, depending on the size of the pretzels. This is a fun activity for kids.
- For delicious apple bread, add ½ cup walnuts or pecans, ½ cup dried apple pieces (chopped) and cinnamon.
- Add up to ½ cup flaxseeds, sunflower seeds or oatmeal.

Snacks, Desserts and Beverages

Snacks and desserts are a great opportunity to fit in some extra nutrition for your family. The following section lists a number of Smart and In-Between possibilities that are great for everyday.

Of course, snacks and desserts are also a time when many people like to have treats. If you are picking an Empty for a special treat—find the healthiest version your family loves—then enjoy.

Beverages deserve a special mention here, though you can read more about them throughout this book. Basically, growing kids need milk and water! Remember that vitamin drinks, sports drinks, lemonade and soda are all Empties.

Tip: *If you delay dessert until an hour or so after dinner, the fruit dessert might also replace an evening snack.*

Sorbet   IN-BETWEEN
Serves 4

This is extremely easy to make and very popular with kids . . . creamy, smooth and icy cold. Plus, the ingredients are easy to keep on hand for a last-minute dessert.

> 1 16-ounce (1-pound) bag frozen strawberries
> 1 6- or 8-ounce container strawberry-flavored yogurt

Place both ingredients in a food processor fitted with a steel blade. Process until all the berries are pulverized and the mixture looks smooth and fluffy. Serve immediately.

Variations:
- Replace strawberries with frozen blueberries, raspberries, cherries or peaches.
- Use any flavored yogurt, including lemon or vanilla.
- Use plain yogurt, and add honey or a tablespoon of frozen fruit juice concentrate.
- Add a squeeze of fresh lemon, lime or orange juice.

Popsicles 🍎 IN-BETWEEN

Serves 4

I am always amazed that kids (and my husband) are so thrilled with juice and fruit when it is served frozen on a stick. Healthy homemade popsicles are easy to make with the molds available at grocery stores during the summer months. Alternatively, you can make popsicles in small paper cups with a plastic spoon for a stick.

> 1 cup orange juice
> 1 sliced banana

Place several banana slices in each section of the popsicle molds. Add juice. Freeze overnight.

Variations:

- Replace bananas with sliced strawberries, raspberries or pineapple "tidbits."
- Use other 100% fruit juices: pineapple, blueberry, or juice mixture.
- Use leftover smoothie to fill popsicle molds (see recipe in Breakfast section).

Almost Instant Pudding 🥛 IN-BETWEEN

Serves 4

Pudding is such a comfort food! Unfortunately, store-bought pudding cups and instant pudding mixes are packed with sweeteners, chemicals and just the tiniest amount of milk. Not this pudding! Because of the dry milk, each 1/2-cup serving contains about the equivalent of a full cup of milk, but with much less added sugar. Plus, it is super easy to make. The texture is creamiest if you stir it well after chilling.

> 2 cups skim milk
> 3 tablespoons sugar
> Pinch of salt
> 2 tablespoons cornstarch
> 1 cup nonfat dry milk
> 1 teaspoon vanilla or lemon flavoring

Measure milk into a large, microwavable measuring cup or bowl. Whisk in all other ingredients except flavoring. Microwave on high for 3 minutes. Whisk the pudding, then return it to the microwave on high for 3 minutes more, stopping occasionally to whisk. If the pudding hasn't thickened at this point, continue microwaving and whisking at 1-minute intervals. Once thickened, remove the pudding from the microwave and whisk in vanilla or lemon flavoring. Lay plastic wrap on the surface to prevent skin from forming on top of the pudding. Cool in the refrigerator. Stir well before serving.

Variations:

- For chocolate pudding, add ¼ cup cocoa powder along with sugar and cornstarch.
- If you want to eat the pudding without waiting for it to cool, mix frozen fruit, such as cherries, blueberries or raspberries, into the warm pudding.
- For banana pudding, stir sliced or mashed bananas into warm vanilla pudding before cooling.
- Serve the pudding on top of raspberries, strawberries, blueberries, sliced peaches or other fruit.
- If you pack this in the lunch box, tell the kids to stir the pudding well if they want to make it smoother.

Banana Milkshakes SMART
Serves 4

This is the ideal after-school snack. It tastes wonderfully sweet and creamy—and is a totally Smart food! Also, it is a great use for bananas that are getting too ripe. To prepare for this recipe, place very ripe, peeled bananas into a resealable plastic bag and freeze them.

Tip: *Some kids steal the frozen bananas and eat them like popsicles, so you might need extra.*

> 2 frozen bananas (peel before freezing)
> 3 cups skim milk
> 1 teaspoon vanilla

Place all ingredients in a blender and blend until creamy. Serve immediately, with a straw if you have one.

Variations:
- Add 1 tablespoon cocoa.
- Add 3 tablespoons peanut butter.
- Add a few strawberries to make it pink, or blueberries to make it purple.
- Add up to ½ cup nonfat dry milk for an extra shot of calcium.

Fruity Yogurt SMART
Serves 4

Fruit-flavored yogurts are convenient, but they are loaded with sugar and contain almost no fruit. By using super-sweet fruits, you can mix up a Smart yogurt and get a fruit serving at the same time.

> 2 cups plain nonfat yogurt
> 2 cups frozen or canned unsweetened cherries, microwaved or thawed

Stir fruit and yogurt together until the yogurt is a purplish pink. Serve immediately.

Variations:
- Use other extra-sweet fruits like frozen peaches or a can of mandarin oranges (drained, but add a few tablespoons of juice into the yogurt).
- Use mashed banana instead of cherries.
- Top with your favorite nuts.
- Sprinkle each serving lightly with chocolate powder.

Oatmeal Raisin Cookies  IN-BETWEEN
Serves 12

All cookies are not created equal. Some are much healthier than others—but most kids will eat all cookies happily. This cookie uses nonfat dry milk to give a calcium and protein boost and to replace some of the sugar.

½ cup canola, soy or safflower oil
½ cup brown sugar, packed
1 single-serving cup applesauce (or ½ cup)
2 large eggs
1 cup nonfat dry milk
2 teaspoons vanilla
¼ teaspoon salt
1 teaspoon baking powder
1 cup white whole-wheat flour**
1 cup oats
1 cup raisins (optional)

Line a baking dish with parchment paper (or use a nonstick pan). With electric mixer, beat together oil and sugar. Beat in applesauce, eggs and nonfat dry milk. Mix in vanilla and salt, then flour and baking soda, followed by oats and raisins plus any additions (see variations, below). Bake at 350 degrees for about 12 minutes.

***If your store doesn't carry white whole-wheat flour, substitute with half whole-wheat/half unbleached flour.*

Variations:
- Add 1 cup walnuts and/or ½ cup chocolate chips.
- Add ½ teaspoon cinnamon.

Cold Herbal Tea SMART
Serves 6
Here is an easy change from water.

> 3 herbal tea bags—try lemon or fruit flavors
> 3 cups boiling water
> 3 cups cool water

Pour boiling water over tea bags in a pitcher or other beverage container. Steep for 5 to 10 minutes. Then remove tea bags and add cool water. Serve over ice or place in the refrigerator to cool.

Bubble Juice IN-BETWEEN
Serves 1
My kids love this. You don't have to measure the ingredients, of course.

> ¾ cup bubble water (unsweetened)
> ¼ cup 100% fruit juice (try a canned juice blend)
> Ice

Pour ingredients in a glass. Serve immediately, preferably with a straw.

Variations:
- Use a squeeze of lemon or lime with, or instead of, the juice.
- Use frozen fruit, like cherries or raspberries, instead of ice.

Sample Menus

Breakfast

At my house, breakfast is rushed every single weekday. So it has to be quick and healthy—and not use many dishes.

- Super Smoothie, Breakfast Bars
- Freezer-Fruit Cup, whole-grain cereal, nonfat milk
- Warm Fruit Sundae, whole-grain bagel topped with low-fat cream cheese, warm or cold herbal tea
- Tropical Yogurt, whole-grain graham crackers, warm or cold herbal tea
- Healthier Hot Chocolate, English Muffins
- Homemade Instant Oatmeal, Hot Flavored Milk, orange slices
- Banana Bread Muffins, nonfat milk, unsweetened applesauce
- Fruit and Oats, orange juice
- Super Smoothie, Breakfast Bars
- English Muffin Pizzas, orange juice
- Leftover pizza made with Great, Great Bread, pineapple chunks, nonfat milk
- Super Smoothie popsicle, whole-grain toast

To eat in the car or at the bus stop (because that happens to all of us some mornings . . .)

- Whole-grain crackers and peanut butter "sandwiches," nonfat milk in disposable cup, fruit-only fruit leather
- Breakfast in a Bag, nonfat milk in disposable cup, apple or banana
- Yogurt tube, handful of whole-grain crackers, box of raisins
- String cheese, whole-grain crackers, grapes
- Oatmeal Raisin Cookies

Weekend brunches

- Pancakes topped with powdered sugar, melon slices, milk
- Scrambled eggs, veggie sausage links, whole-wheat toast, fruit salad topped with yogurt, herbal tea
- Freshly baked Banana Bread Muffins, grapefruit, warm milk with cinnamon
- Great, Great Bread, Super Smoothie (freeze leftovers for lunches!)

Lunches to Pack

If you hate packing lunches, you are not alone! It is hard to think of things to pack and painful to create lunch at 7 a.m. Here are a few ideas to help. (Most of these ideas include something frozen to keep the other foods cold until lunchtime.)

- Turkey, ham or roast beef sandwich, cherry tomatoes, grapes, nonfat milk with Milk Cubes
- PB&J on whole-wheat bread, Pack-n-Go Berry Dessert, pepper slices, water
- Deli chicken slices, low-fat cheese cubes, crackers, cucumber slices, peach, water with ice
- Leftover vegetable chicken soup in a thermos, whole-wheat crackers, part-skim string cheese, grapes
- Leftover Beef Stew in thermos, baked potato chips, easy-to-peel orange, nonfat milk with Milk Cubes
- Black Bean Salad, Almost Instant Pudding, baked corn chips, apple slices, water
- Baby carrots, deli meat, crackers, frozen Super Smoothie
- Whole-grain cereal, thermos of skim milk, blueberries, celery topped with peanut butter
- Beef jerky, vegetable sticks with container of dip, apple, string cheese, Oatmeal Raisin Cookies
- Orange Juice Hummus, mini pita bread, cucumber slices, dried apricots, Almost Instant Pudding, water
- Chunky Salsa Dip and Chips, part-skim string cheese, mini can pineapple chunks, water
- Salmon Salad, Smoothie (frozen, packed with spoon), whole-grain crackers, water
- Whole-wheat pasta topped with cheese, dried apricots, celery sticks with peanut butter to dip, water
- Cottage cheese mixed with drained canned peaches and walnuts, baby carrots, baked potato chips, water with ice cubes

Dinners

- Veggies and Dip, Enhanced Spaghetti Sauce with whole-wheat pasta
- One-Vegetable Salad, Enhanced Canned Soup, whole-grain crackers, reduced-fat sliced cheese
- Green Salad, Quinoa and Tomato Soup, whole-grain rice cakes topped with avocado
- Carrot Cake Whole-Wheat Pancakes, strawberries, nonfat milk
- Mandarin Orange Salad, Instant Mini Pizza, Veggies from the Freezer
- Celery sticks and dip, Chicken Nuggets, low-fat olive-oil French fries (from natural foods freezer section)
- One-Vegetable Salad, Easy Orange Chicken with carrots, served on brown rice
- Veggies and Dip, Beef Stew, Great Great Bread
- Baby carrots and dip, Healthy Hamburgers on whole-wheat buns, Sweet Potato Pouches
- Edamame, brown rice, Stir-Fried Garlic Broccoli with added chicken
- Veggies and Dip, Beans and Rice
- Tomato slices, Tuna-Cheese Burgers, Veggies from the Freezer
- Low-sodium canned (or leftover) vegetable soup, Healthy Hamburgers on whole-wheat buns with lettuce and tomatoes, corn on the cob
- One-Vegetable Salad, Salmon Patties, Twice-Baked Potatoes, steamed zucchini
- Tomato slices, Plain Fish with ketchup, whole-wheat garlic toast, steamed kale
- Veggies and Dip, Salsa Bean Soup, baked corn chips

Snacks

Because most kids are "starving" at snack time, it is a great time to feed them something Smart.

- Banana Milkshake with whole-wheat graham crackers
- Fruit Sorbet, pecans
- Veggies and Dip, baked potato chips
- Tropical Yogurt and whole-grain cereal
- Vegetables and whole-grain crackers with Orange Juice Hummus
- Salsa and baked whole-grain corn chips, low-fat cheese cubes
- Super Smoothie
- Fruity Yogurt
- Almost Instant Pudding mixed with black cherries
- Milk, whole-grain graham crackers, a peach
- Popsicles

If your kids eat their snacks on the run, here are a few options.

- Apple slices and nonfat, flavored yogurt
- Banana, thermos of nonfat milk
- Popcorn, celery with peanut butter
- Breakfast in a Bag, nonfat milk with Milk Cubes
- Part-skim string cheese and a pear
- Healthy granola bar, cubes of 2% cheddar
- Baked chips, baby carrots
- Unsweetened fruit chew, cashews
- Raisins, low-fat cheese
- Clementine and fruit-flavored yogurt
- Banana Bread Muffin
- Oatmeal Raisin Cookies

Be sure to visit www.feedingthekids.com for lists of my favorite brand names, new recipes and even more ideas.

Appendix: Reading Labels

Contrary to popular belief, reading labels is not a mysterious or difficult-to-master skill! If you can read and do a little basic math (or use a calculator), you can use labels to select healthier food for your family.

The first step in reading a label is to identify whether the food is a fruit, vegetable, dairy food, grain product or protein food. In most cases, it's pretty obvious. But when the food is a combination, use the first word on the Ingredients list as your guide. (Of course, if the first word is sugar, corn syrup or other sweetener, a field test isn't necessary because the food is an Empty!) Once you have identified what type of food you are looking at, use the appropriate field test to figure out if the food is an Empty, an In-Between or a Smart food.

On the following pages you will see examples of how the field tests are used to read labels on real foods.

Fruit Labels

Be sure to read "Week 1: Starting the Adventure with Fruit," starting on page 27.

Field Test for Fruit

1. Look for fresh, plain fruit and unsweetened frozen, canned or dried fruit.
   - If the fruit **has nothing added to it,** it is a **Smart fruit.**

2. Read the Ingredients list. Check for added sweeteners. For drinks, skip to step 3.
   - If the fruit contains **fruit plus fruit juice,** but **no added sweetener,** it is S**mart.**
   - If **fruit is first on the Ingredients list,** but the fruit contains **added sweetener,** it is an **In-Between fruit.**
   - However, if **fruit is not first on the Ingredients list and it contains sweetener,** it is an **Empty.**

3. For a drink, read the Ingredients list.
   - If the drink is **100% fruit juice,** without added sweeteners, it is an **In-Between fruit.**
   - If a drink's Ingredients list includes added **sweetener,** it is an **Empty.**

A Smart Fruit
Dark Sweet Pitted Cherries

Plain fresh or frozen fruits are always Smart.

1. Look on front of package. This one says "dark sweet pitted cherries." It may be unsweetened, but do step 2 to be sure.

2. Check the Ingredients list for added sweeteners. This one has none and contains just cherries. It is a Smart fruit.

NOTE: The Nutrition Facts label shows that these cherries contain 18 grams of sugar. This is from the naturally occurring fructose in the fruit itself.

An In-Between Fruit
Orange Juice

Fruit juice lacks the fiber and other nutrients found naturally in fruit. That is why even unsweetened 100% juice is always an In-Between.

1. This is a juice; so skip to step 3 of the field test.

2. Skip this step.

3. Check the Ingredients list for added sweeteners. This one has none. It contains just orange juice. Since it is 100% fruit juice and has no added sweetener—it is an In-Between.

Vegetable Labels

Be sure to read "Week 2: Exploring Vegetables," starting on page 43.

Field Test for Vegetables

1. Read the Ingredients list. Look for added fats and oils.
   - If a vegetable has **no added fat,** it is a **Smart vegetable.** All fresh, plain, unpackaged vegetables are Smart.

2. Check the Nutrition Facts label for trans fat and/or check the Ingredients list for "partially hydrogenated" oil (which contains trans fat).
   - If the vegetable **contains trans fat,** it is an **Empty.**

3. Double the calories from fat** listed on the Nutrition Facts label. Compare that number to total calories per serving.
   - If the **total calories are MORE than two times the fat calories,** it is **at least an In-Between vegetable.** But, it could be Smart … so, do step 4.
   - If the **total calories are LESS than two times the fat calories,** it is an **Empty.**

4. Multiply the number of calories from fat by 3. ** Compare the number to the total calories.
   - If the **total calories are MORE than three times the fat calories,** it is a **Smart vegetable.**

**If you prefer, round all numbers to the nearest 10 for easier math.

A Smart Vegetable
Fresh or Frozen Plain Vegetable

All plain, fresh vegetables are Smart. So are all frozen vegetables that only contain the vegetable itself.

1. Read the Ingredients list for added fats. Since this bag contains only peas and nothing else, this food is Smart. No need to do the rest of the steps in the field test.

A Smart Vegetable
Tomato Pasta Sauce

Most tomato-based sauces have a bit of olive oil, but not too much. They are usually Smart.

1. Read the Ingredients list for fats. Olive oil is listed, so this vegetable does contain added fat.

2. Read the Nutrition Facts label for trans fat. It says "0." Also, the Ingredients list does not include any "partially hydrogenated" oils.

3. Find the Calories from Fat (20) and double them: 20+20=40. Compare the total Calories (70) to the double fat (40). Total calories are higher, so this sauce is at least an In-Between. But it might be Smart, so do step 4.

4. Now triple the Calories from Fat: 20+20+20=60. Compare the total Calories (70) to the triple fat (60). Total calories are still higher, so this pasta sauce is Smart.

An In-Between Vegetable
Salad with Chicken Strips, Wonton Strips and Sesame-Ginger Dressing

Many pre-packed and restaurant salads are good In-Between choices. But, if you have time, a homemade salad would be an even better choice because you could select healthier toppings. Make it even healthier by replacing the pale-colored iceberg lettuce with a deep green lettuce, such as romaine or spinach.

Nutrition Facts

Serving Size: 1 container (227g)
Servings Per Container: 1

Amount Per Serving

Calories 230   Calories from Fat 100

	% Daily Value
Total Fat 11g	**17%**
Saturated Fat 2.5g	**11%**
Trans Fat 0g	**0%**
Cholesterol 30mg	**10%**
Sodium 820mg	**34%**
Total Carbohydrate 19g	**6%**
Dietary Fiber 2g	**7%**
Sugars 10g	
Protein 13g	

Vitamin A 25%	•	Vitamin C 15%
Calcium 4%	•	Iron 10%

INGREDIENTS: Lettuce Mix (Iceberg & Romaine, red cabbage, carrots), **Chicken Breast with Rib Meat** (chicken breast with rib meat, water, seasoning [salt, sugar, chicken flavor {with hydodrolyzed corn soy wheat gluten protein, autolyzed yeast extract, dehydrated chicken broth, chicken fat, thiamine hydrochloride, corn syrup solids}, dextrose, natural flavorings], modified potato starch, dextrose, sodium phosphates), **Sesame Ginger and Orange Dressing** (water, sugar, sesame oil, rice wine vinegar, vegetable oil [soybean oil, canola oil], ginger, salt, modified food starch, soy sauce [water, soybeans, wheat, salt], spices, dextrose, natural flavors, hydrolyzed soy protein, sesame seeds, xanthan gum, lemon juice concentrate, citric acid, phosphoric acid, dehydrated orange peel, dehydrated lemon peel, sodium benzoate and potassium sorbate [as preservatives], calcium disodium edta added to protect flavor), **Celery Wonton Strips** (wheat flour {niacin, thiamine mononitrate, riboflavin, reduced iron, folic acid}, vegetable oil {soybean and/or cottonseed}, eggs, salt, water). **Contains: soy, wheat, eggs.**

1. Read the Ingredients list for fats. Vegetable oil is listed twice, so this vegetable does contain added fats.

2. Read the Nutrition Facts label for trans fat. It says "0." Also, the Ingredients list does not include any "partially hydrogenated" oils.

3. Find the Calories from Fat (100) and double them: 100+100=200. Compare the total Calories (230) to the double fat (200). Total Calories are higher, so this salad is at least an In-Between. But it might be Smart, so do step 4.

4. Now triple the Calories from Fat: 100+100+100=300. Compare the total Calories (230) to the triple fat (300). Total calories are not higher, so this salad is not Smart—it is an In-Between (from step 3).

Dairy Labels

Be sure to read "Week 3: Navigating Dairy Foods," starting on page 69.

Field Test for Dairy

1. Find a product labeled "nonfat," "fat-free" or "low-fat." For cheese, skip to step 4.

2. Read the Ingredients list.
   - If there is **no sweetener** listed* on a low-fat dairy food, it is a **Smart dairy.**

3. Compare the total number of grams of sugar** on the Nutrition Facts label to the Percent Daily Value (%DV) for calcium.
   - If the **sugar is LESS than the calcium,** it is an **In-Between dairy.**
   - If the **sugar is MORE than the calcium,** it is an **Empty dairy.**

4. For cheeses, find lower-fat products labeled as "part-skim" or "2%," or with nonfat or 2% milk in the Ingredients list.
   - **Lower-fat cheeses are In-Betweens.**
   - **Regular cheeses are Empty.**

Dairy products often contain an artificial sweetener, such as Splenda or NutraSweet. Many parents choose to avoid feeding their children artificial sweeteners.
**Remember, grams of sugar on Nutrition Facts labels include both the added sweeteners and the naturally occurring "milk sugar" called lactose.*

A Smart Dairy
Carton of Nonfat Milk

All plain, unflavored nonfat milk and yogurts are Smart.

1. The front of the carton says "nonfat."

2. Read the Ingredients list. It has no sweetener words, so this is Smart milk. No need to do step 3 on the field test.

NOTE: The Nutrition Facts label shows Sugars 12g. However, all this sugar is from the lactose, which occurs naturally in milk.

Nutrition Facts	
Serving Size: 1 cup (240mL)	
Servings Per Container: about 8	

Amount Per Serving	
Calories 80	Calories from Fat 0

	% Daily Value
Total Fat 0g	**0%**
Saturated Fat 0g	**0%**
Trans Fat 0g	**0%**
Cholesterol 5mg	**1%**
Sodium 125mg	**5%**
Potassium 125mg	**4%**
Total Carbohydrate 12g	**4%**
Dietary Fiber 0g	**0%**
Sugars 12g	
Protein 9g	

Vitamin A 10%	•	Vitamin C 4%
Calcium 30% • Iron 0%	•	Vitamin D 25%

*Percent Daily Values are based on a 2,000 calories diet. Your daily values may be higher or lower depending on your calorie needs:

		Calories:	2,000	2,500
Total Fat	Less than		65g	80g
Sat Fat	Less than		20g	25g
Cholesterol	Less than		300mg	300mg
Sodium	Less than		2,400mg	2,400mg
Potassium			3,500mg	3,500mg
Total Carbohydrate			300g	375g
Dietary Fiber			25g	30g

INGREDIENTS: Organic Grade A Fat Free Skim Milk, Vitamin A Palmitate and Vitamin D3

An In-Between Dairy

Parmesan Cheese

More and more part-skim and 2% cheeses are becoming available. But the ever-popular parmesan cheese has always been lower in fat than most cheese.

1. This product is cheese; so skip to step 4 on the field test.

2. and 3. Skip these steps.

4. The package does not claim part-skim or 2%, but the Ingredients list shows that the cheese is made of "part-skim milk." This cheese is an In-Between.

An Empty Dairy

Reduced-Fat Ice Cream Bar

Although reduced-fat ice cream is usually a better choice than premium ice cream, many brands still contain a huge dose of saturated or trans fats, plus plenty of sweetener.

1. The front of the carton says "reduced fat." That just means it contains less fat than another ice cream bar. It really tells you nothing.

2. Read the Ingredients list. It says, "milk," "buttermilk," "cream" and "partially hydrogenated soybean oil" (a trans fat even though the label says "trans fat 0 grams.") So this food is an Empty.

3. Look at the Nutrition Facts label. Notice that the "% Daily Value" for calcium (6%) is a lower number than the grams of sugar (11g). The sugar is higher, so this ice cream bar is even more Empty!

Nutrition Facts

Serving Size: 2 tsp (5g)
Servings Per Container: about 45

Amount Per Serving

Calories 20   Calories from Fat 15

	% Daily Value
Total Fat 1.5g	**2%**
Saturated Fat 1g	**5%**
Trans Fat 0g	**0%**
Cholesterol <5mg	**2%**
Sodium 85mg	**4%**
Total Carbohydrate 0g	**0%**
Dietary Fiber 0g	**0%**
Sugars 0g	
Protein 2g	

Vitamin A 0%	•	Vitamin C 0%
Calcium 6%	•	Iron 0%

*Percent Daily Value are based on a 2,000 calories diet. Your daily values may be higher or lower depending on your calorie needs:

		Calories:	2,000	2,500
Total Fat		Less than	65g	80g
Sat Fat		Less than	20g	25g
Cholesterol		Less than	300mg	300mg
Sodium		Less than	2,400mg	2,400mg
Potassium			3,500mg	3,500mg
Total Carbohydrate			300g	375g
Dietary Fiber			25g	30g

INGREDIENTS: Parmesan cheese (pasteurized part-skim milk, salt, less than 2% of enzymes, cheese cultures, cellulose powder to prevent caking, potassium sorbate to protect flavor), aged 6 months.

Nutrition Facts

Serving Size: 1 bar (49g)
Servings Per Container: 12

Amount Per Serving

Calories 130   Calories from Fat 70

	% Daily Value
Total Fat 8g	**12%**
Saturated Fat 6g	**31%**
Trans Fat 0g	**0%**
Cholesterol <5mg	**2%**
Sodium 35mg	**1%**
Total Carbohydrate 14g	**5%**
Dietary Fiber 0g	**0%**
Sugars 11g	
Protein 2g	

Vitamin A 4%	•	Vitamin C 0%
Calcium 6%	•	Iron 2%

*Percent Daily Value are based on a 2,000 calories diet. Your daily values may be higher or lower depending on your calorie needs:

		Calories:	2,000	2,500
Total Fat		Less than	65g	80g
Sat Fat		Less than	20g	25g
Cholesterol		Less than	300mg	300mg
Sodium		Less than	2,400mg	2,400mg
Potassium			3,500mg	3,500mg
Total Carbohydrate			300g	375g
Dietary Fiber			25g	30g

INGREDIENTS: Ice Cream: milk, sugar, syrup, corn syrup, buttermilk, high fructose corn syrup, whey, cream, guar gum, mono- and diglycerides, locust bean gum, polysorbate 80, carrageenan, artificial flavor, annatto (for color), vitamin A palmitate. **Chocolate coating:** coconut oil, sugar, cocoa processed with alkali, partially hydrogenated soybean oil, soy lecithin, salt, and natural flavor. **Contains: milk, soy**

A Somewhat Better Empty Dairy

Low-Fat Ice Cream

This is one of my family's favorite treats. Even though it is an Empty, it is a much healthier option than many frozen dairy treats because it is low-fat, does not contain trans fat and contains a little calcium and protein, too.

1. This ice cream carton says "low fat," so this ice cream must contain low-fat milk.

2. Read the Ingredients list. It says "skim milk" and does *not* list "partially hydrogenated" oil. But, it does contain corn syrup and sugar.

3. Look at the Nutrition Facts label. Notice that the "% Daily Value" for calcium (10%) is a lower number than the grams of sugar (13g). The sugar is higher, so this ice cream is an Empty!

Nutrition Facts

Serving Size: 1/2 cup (67g)
Servings Per Container: 14

Amount Per Serving

Calories 90   Calories from Fat 0

	% Daily Value
Total Fat 0g	**0%**
Saturated Fat 0g	**0%**
Trans Fat 0g	**0%**
Cholesterol 0mg	**0%**
Sodium 40mg	**2%**
Total Carbohydrate 19g	**6%**
Dietary Fiber 0g	**0%**
Sugars 13g	
Protein 3g	

Vitamin A 0%	•	Vitamin C 0%
Calcium 10%	•	Iron 0%

Percent Daily Value are based on a 2,000 calories diet. Your daily values may be higher or lower depending on your calorie needs:

		Calories:	2,000	2,500
Total Fat	Less than		65g	80g
Sat Fat	Less than		20g	25g
Cholesterol	Less than		300mg	300mg
Sodium	Less than		2,400mg	2,400mg
Potassium			3,500mg	3,500mg
Total Carbohydrate			300g	375g
Dietary Fiber			25g	30g

INGREDIENTS: cultured skim milk, corn syrup, sugar, modified corn starch, cocoa processed with alkali, whey protein, calcium carbonate, cellulose gel, cellulose gum, mono and diglycerides, tara gum, natural flavor, carrageenan, dextrose, annatto color.

Grain Labels

Be sure to read "Week 4: Tracking Down Whole Grains," starting on page 87.

Field Test for Whole Grains

1. Find a package that reads:"whole grain wheat" on the front of the package OR one that lists a whole grain first on the Ingredients list. If neither is true, skip to step 3.

2. Look at the Nutrition Facts label. Compare the number of grams of fiber to the number of grams of sugar and fat.
   - If a whole-grain food has **MORE fiber than sugar and fat,** it is a **Smart grain.**

3. If the Ingredients list starts with a refined grain, or if it is whole grain with too much sugar or fat to be Smart (from step 2), double the grams of fiber and compare that number to the grams of sugar and fat.
   - If **the sugar or fat is LESS than double the fiber,** it is an **In-Between grain.**
   - If **the sugar or fat is MORE than double the fiber,** the food is an **Empty.**

A Smart Grain

100% Whole-Wheat English Muffins

Smart English muffins are easy to find in most grocery stores and they taste great.

1. This package says "100% Whole Wheat" on the package front and the Ingredients list has "whole-wheat flour" listed first.

2. Look at the Nutrition Facts label. Notice that the number of grams of fiber (3) is higher than the grams of sugar (2) and grams of fat (1). Since there is more fiber than both sugar and fat, these English muffins are Smart. Since they are Smart, there is no need to do step 3 in the field test.

Nutrition Facts

Serving Size: 1 muffin (62g)
Servings Per Container: 6

Amount Per Serving

Calories 130   Calories from Fat 10

	% Daily Value
Total Fat 1g	**2%**
Saturated Fat 0g	**0%**
Trans Fat 0g	**0%**
Polyunsaturated Fat 0g	**0%**
Monounsaturated Fat 0g	**0%**
Cholesterol 0mg	**0%**
Sodium 270mg	**11%**
Total Carbohydrate 25g	**8%**
Dietary Fiber 3g	**12%**
Sugars 2g	
Protein 5g	

Vitamin A 0%	•	Vitamin C 0%
Calcium 10%	•	Iron 6%

*Percent Daily Value are based on a 2,000 calories diet. Your daily values may be higher or lower depending on your calorie needs:

		Calories:	2,000	2,500
Total Fat	Less than		65g	80g
Sat Fat	Less than		20g	25g
Cholesterol	Less than		300mg	300mg
Sodium	Less than		2,400mg	2,400mg
Potassium			3,500mg	3,500mg
Total Carbohydrate			300g	375g
Dietary Fiber			25g	30g

INGREDIENTS Whole wheat flour, water, wheat starch, high fructose corn syrup, farina, wheat gluten, yeast, salt, preservative (calcium propionate, sorbic acid), honey, natural flavor, grain vinegar, soybean oil, ethoxylated mono- and diglycerides, monocalcium phosphate, guar gum, **nonfat milk,** sodium stearoyl lactylate, xanthan gum, agar, **soy flour,** soy lecithin, **whey,** sucralose, natamycin (a natural mold inhibitor).

An Empty Grain
Corn Chips

All corn chips are not the same. Be certain to read the label and find a Smart version.

Nutrition Facts
Serving Size: 1oz. (28g) about 32 chips
Servings Per Container: 3

Amount Per Serving **Cereal**	
Calories 160 Calories from Fat 90	
	% Daily Value
Total Fat 10g	16%
Saturated Fat 1.5g	7%
Trans Fat 0g	0%
Cholesterol 0mg	0%
Sodium 170mg	7%
Total Carbohydrate 15g	5%
Dietary Fiber 1g	4%
Sugars < 1g	
Other Carbohydrates 1g	
Protein 2g	

Vitamin A 0%	•	Vitamin C 0%
Calcium 2%	•	Iron 0%
Vitamin E 6%	•	VitaminB6 2%
Phosphorus 4%		

INGREDIENTS corn, corn oil, and salt. No preservatives

1. The front of the package says "corn chips" and the first ingredient is "corn." So, these chips are probably not a whole-grain food. However, they do not contain any trans fat.

2. Look at the Nutrition Facts label. Notice that the number of grams of fiber (1) is higher than the grams of sugar (less than one), but it is much lower than the grams of fat (10). Since there is more fat than fiber, this is not a Smart grain.

3. Double the fiber: 1+1=2. Compare double fiber (2) to fat (10). It is not even close—there is way too much fat. These corn chips are an Empty.

A Really Empty Grain

Cereal Bar

Never trust the healthy claims on the fronts of boxes—especially for any type of "bars." Though some are In-Betweens, Empty bars are often labeled with healthy-sounding words, such as "protein," "cereal," "oatmeal," "milk," "granola," "fruit" or "energy." Always read the labels carefully.

1. The front of the package says only "Cereal Bar," and the Ingredients list has "whole-grain oats" listed, but not first. So this is a refined grain, which means it is either In-Between or Empty. So you can skip step 2 in the field test.

2. Skip this step.

3. Double the grams of fiber: 1+1=2. Compare double fiber (2) to fat (4) and sugar (14). It's easy to see that these cereal bars are an Empty.

NOTE: Although the Nutrition Facts label says "Trans Fat 0g," partially hydrogenated soybean oil occurs twice in the Ingredients list. This food must contain some trans fat, but less than 0.5 gram. When each serving has less than 0.5 gram, the manufacturer rounds down to zero. However, foods containing this very unhealthy fat are always Empties.

Nutrition Facts

Serving Size: 1 bar (40g)
Servings Per Container: 6

Amount Per Serving **Cereal**

Calories 160   Calories from Fat 40

	% Daily Value
Total Fat 4g	6%
Saturated Fat 2g	10%
Trans Fat 0g	0%
Cholesterol 0mg	0%
Sodium 120mg	5%
Potassium 115mg	3%
Total Carbohydrate 28g	9%
Dietary Fiber 1g	4%
Sugars 14g	
Other Carbohydrates 13g	
Protein 63g	

Vitamin A 15%	•	Vitamin C 15%
Calcium 25%	•	Iron 30%
Vitamin D 25%	•	Thiamin 30%
Riboflavin 35%	•	Niacin 30%
Vitamin B6 30%	•	Folic Acid 50%
Vitamin B12 35%	•	Phosphorus 15%
Magnesium 4%	•	Zinc 30%

INGREDIENTS: Cereal: crisp rice [rice flour, sugar, malt extract, salt], distilled monoglycerides, rice extract, whole grain oats, textured soy flour, sugar, corn meal, honey, brown sugar syrup, salt, calcium carbonate, trisodium phosphte, distilled monoglycerides, dextrose, iron and zinc [mineral nutrients], a B vitamin (niacinamide), vitamin B6 (pyridoxine hydrochloride), vitamin B2 (riboflavin), a B vitamin (folic acid), almond flour, wheat flour, vitamin E (mixed tocopherols), added to preserves freshness; **Milk filling:** sugar, palm kernel oil, lactose, nonfat milk, dried sweetened condensed milk [sugar, milk] partially hydrogenated soybean oil, monglycerides, soy lecithin, salt, natural and artificial flavor, TBHQ and citric acid added to preserve freshness; corn syrup, high fructose corn syrup, fructose, maltodextrin, isolated soy protein, glycerin, tricalcium phosphate, rice bran oil, canola or partially hydrogenated soybean oil, sbitol, almonds, caramel and annatto extract color, sugar, gelatin, vitamin C (sodium ascorbate), iron and zinc (mineral nutrients), honey, calcium carbonate, mon and diglycerides, salt, vitamin A (palmitate), a B vitamin (niacinamide), natural and artificial flavor, vitamin D, vitamin B2, (riboflavin), Vitamin B6 (pyridoxine hydrochloride), vitamin B1 (thiamin mononitrate), a B vitamin (folic acid), vitamin b12, peanut flour, sunflower meal, freshness preserved by BHT. **Contains milk, almonds, wheat and sunflower ingredients.**

Protein Labels

Be sure to read "Week 5: Hunting for Smart Proteins," starting on page 113.

Field Test for Meats, Beans and Soy Foods*

1. Find the number of calories from fat on the Nutrition Facts label. Double that number. **

2. Find total calories on the Nutrition Facts label. Compare double the fat calories to total calories.
   - If the **total calories are LOWER than the fat calories doubled,** the food is an Empty (because over half the calories in the food come from fat).

   - If the **total calories are HIGHER than the fat calories doubled,** it is **at least an In-Between.** But, it could be Smart . . . so, do step 3.

3. Next, triple the fat calories and compare it to the total calories in one serving.
   - If **the total calories are HIGHER than the fat calories tripled,** the food is **Smart** (because less than 33 percent of the calories come from fat).

*For other protein foods, such as nuts and eggs, see the protein identification chart on pages 124-125.

**If you prefer, round all numbers to the nearest 10 for easier math.

A Smart Protein

Pork Sirloin Chops

Many lean loin cuts of meat (especially sirloin) are Smart. Be sure to check the label when available.

1. Find the calories from fat on the Nutrition Facts label: 35. Double them: 35+35=70.

2. Find the total Calories: 135 for one (4-ounce) serving. Total calories (135) are higher than double the calories from fat (70), so these pork chops are at least an In-Between.

3. Now triple the calories from fat by adding another 35: 70+35=105. The total calories (135) are still more than triple the fat calories (105), so these pork chops are a Smart protein.

Nutrition Facts
Serving Size: 4oz. (112g)
Servings Per Container: varied

Amount Per Serving Cereal

Calories 135	Calories from Fat 35
	% Daily Value
Total Fat 4g	**6%**
Saturated Fat 1g	**6%**
Trans Fat 0g	**0%**
Cholesterol 20mg	**7%**
Sodium 240mg	**10%**
Total Carbohydrate 0g	**0%**
Dietary Fiber 0g	**0%**
Sugars 0g	
Protein 22g	**44%**

Vitamin A 0%	•	Vitamin C 0%
Calcium 2%	•	Iron 4%

INGREDIENTS: pork loin sirloin chops boneless

An In-Between Protein

Plain Fast-Food Hamburger

(No cheese, mayo, bacon or other added fat)

Combination foods are trickier to analyze. This food combines a refined white flour bun with meat. The bun is an In-Between grain, so the whole burger is either an In-Between or an Empty. Use the protein field test to decide if the hamburger contains too much fat to be an In-Between.

1. Find the calories from fat on the Nutrition Facts label: 80. Double them: 80+80=160.

2. Find the total calories: 260 for one hamburger. The total calories (260) are higher than double the calories from fat (160), so this hamburger is an In-Between. Since this hamburger has an In-Between refined-grain bun, it cannot be Smart. So, no need to do step 3 of the field test.

Nutrition Facts
Serving Size: 1 hamburger
Servings Per Container: 1

Amount Per Serving

Calories 260	Calories from Fat 80
	% Daily Value
Total Fat 9g	**14%**
Saturated Fat 3.5g	**17%**
Trans Fat 0.5g	
Cholesterol 30mg	**9%**
Sodium 530mg	**22%**
Total Carbohydrate 33g	**11%**
Dietary Fiber 1g	**5%**
Sugars 7g	
Protein 13g	

Vitamin A 2%	•	Vitamin C 2%
Calcium 15%	•	Iron 15%

An Empty Protein

Ground Turkey

Contrary to popular belief, most ground turkey and chicken are not lean because globs of poultry fat and greasy skin are ground in with the meat. This means you'll want to look for "extra-lean" ground meats or use the field test.

Nutrition Facts
Serving Size: 4 oz (112g)
Servings Per Container: varied

Amount Per Serving	
Calories 180 Calories from Fat 100	

	% Daily Value
Total Fat 11g	**17%**
Saturated Fat 6g	**31%**
Cholesterol 130mg	**31%**
Sodium 130mg	**5%**
Total Carbohydrate 1g	**0%**
Dietary Fiber 0g	**0%**
Sugars 0g	
Protein 19g	

Vitamin A 0%	•	Vitamin C 0%
Calcium 10%	•	Iron 15%

INGREDIENTS: ground turkey

1. Find calories from fat on the Nutrition Facts label: 100. Double them: 100+100=200.

2. Find the total calories: 180 for one serving.

   The total calories (180) are lower than double the calories from fat (200), so this ground turkey gets over half its calories from fat. It is an Empty, so no need to do step 3 of the field test.

Subject Index

Recipe Index